# The Privatee

Frederick Marryat

**Alpha Editions**

This edition published in 2024

ISBN 9789362519108

Design and Setting By
**Alpha Editions**
www.alphaedis.com
Email - info@alphaedis.com

# Contents

# Chapter One.

**We cruise off Hispaniola—Capture of a French Ship—Continue our Cruise—Make a Nocturnal Attack upon a Rich Planter's Dwelling—Are repulsed with Loss.**

*To Mistress ——.*

*Respected Madam,*

In compliance with your request I shall now transcribe from the journal of my younger days some portions of my adventurous life. When I wrote, I painted the feelings of my heart without reserve, and I shall not alter one word, as I know you wish to learn what my feelings were then, and not what my thoughts may be now. They say that in every man's life, however obscure his position may be, there would be a moral found, were it truly told. I think, Madam, when you have perused what I am about to write, you will agree with me, that from my history both old and young may gather profit, and I trust, if ever it should be made public, that, by Divine permission, such may be the result. Without further preface I shall commence with a narrative of my cruise off Hispaniola, in the Revenge privateer.

The Revenge mounted fourteen guns, and was commanded by Captain Weatherall, a very noted privateer's-man. One morning at daybreak we discovered a vessel from the masthead, and immediately made all sail in chase, crowding every stitch of canvass. As we neared, we made her out to be a large ship, deeply laden, and we imagined that she would be an easy prize; but as we saw her hull more out of the water, she proved to be well armed, having a full tier of guns fore and aft. As it afterwards proved, she was a vessel of 600 tons burden, and mounted twenty-four guns, having sailed from Saint Domingo, and being bound to France.

She had been chartered by a French gentleman (and a most gallant fellow we found him), who had acquired a large fortune in the West Indies, and was then going home, having embarked on board his whole property, as well as his wife and his only son, a youth of about seventeen. As soon as he discovered what we were, and the impossibility of escape from so fast a sailing vessel as the Revenge, he resolved to fight us to the last. Indeed he had everything to fight for; his whole property, his wife and his only child, his own liberty, and perhaps life, were all at stake, and he had every motive that could stimulate a man. As we subsequently learnt, he had great difficulty in inspiring the crew with an equal resolution, and it was not until he had engaged to pay them the value of half the cargo, provided they succeeded in beating us off and forcing their way in safety to France, that he could rouse them to their duty.

Won by his example, for he told them that he did not desire any man to do more than he would do himself, and perhaps more induced by his generous offer, the French crew declared they would support him to the last, went cheerfully to their guns, and prepared for action. When we were pretty near to him, he shortened sail ready for the combat, having tenderly forced his wife down below to await in agony the issue of a battle on which depended everything so dear to her. The resolute bearing of the vessel, and the cool intrepidity with which they had hove-to to await us, made us also prepare on our side for a combat which we knew would be severe. Although she was superior to us in guns, yet, the Revenge being wholly fitted for war, we had many advantages, independent of our being very superior in men. Some few chase-guns were fired during our approach, when, having ranged up within a cable's length of her, we exchanged broadsides for half an hour, after which our captain determined upon boarding. We ran our vessel alongside, and attempted to throw our men on board, but met with a stout resistance. The French gentleman, who was at the head of his men, with his own hand killed two of our stoutest seamen, and mortally wounded a third, and, encouraged by his example, his people fought with such resolution that after a severe struggle we were obliged to retreat precipitately into our own vessel, leaving eight or ten of our shipmates weltering in their blood.

Our captain, who had not boarded with us, was much enraged at our defeat, stigmatising us as cowards for allowing ourselves to be driven from a deck upon which we had obtained a footing; he called upon us to renew the combat, and leading the way he was the first on board of the vessel, and was engaged hand to hand with the brave French gentleman who had already made such slaughter among our men. Brave and expert with his weapon as Captain Weatherall undoubtedly was, he for once found rather more than a match in his antagonist; he was slightly wounded, and would, I suspect, have had the worst of this hand-to-hand conflict, had not the whole of our crew, who had now gained the deck, and were rushing forward, separated him from his opponent. Out-numbered and over-matched, the French crew fought most resolutely, but notwithstanding their exertions, and the gallant conduct of their leader, we succeeded in driving them back to the quarter-deck of the vessel. Here the combat was renewed with the greatest obstinacy, they striving to maintain this their last hold, and we exerting ourselves to complete our conquest. The Frenchmen could retreat no further, and our foremost men were impelled against them by those behind them crowding on to share in the combat. Retreat being cut off, the French struggled with all the animosity and rage of mingled hate and despair; while we, infuriated at the obstinate resistance, were filled with vengeance and a thirst for blood. Wedged into one mass, we grappled together, for there was no room for fair fighting, seeking each other's hearts with shortened weapons, struggling and falling together on the deck, rolling among the dead and the dying, or trodden underfoot by the others who still maintained the combat with unabated fury.

Numbers at last prevailed; we had gained a dear-bought victory—we were masters of the deck, we had struck the colours, and were recovering our lost breaths after this very severe contest, and thought ourselves in full possession of the ship; but it proved otherwise. The first-lieutenant of the privateer and six of us had dashed down the companion, and were entering the cabin in search of plunder, when we found opposed to our entrance the gallant French gentleman, supported by his son, the captain of the vessel, and five of the French sailors; behind them was the French gentleman's wife, to whose protection they had devoted themselves. The lieutenant, who headed us, offered them quarter, but, stung to madness at the prospect of the ruin and of the captivity which awaited him, the gentleman treated the offer with contempt, and rushing forward attacked our lieutenant, beating down his guard, and was just about to pierce him with the lunge which he made, when I fired my pistol at him to save the life of my officer. The ball entered his heart, and thus died one of the bravest men I ever encountered. His son at the same time was felled to the deck with a pole-axe, when the remainder threw themselves down on the deck and cried for quarter. So enraged were our men at this renewal of the combat that it required all the efforts and authority of the lieutenant to prevent them from completing the massacre by taking the lives of those who no longer resisted. But who could paint the condition of that unhappy lady who had stood a witness of the horrid scene—her eyes blasted with the sight of her husband slain before her face, her only son groaning on the deck and weltering in his blood; and she left alone, bereft of all that was dear to her; stripped of the wealth she was that morning mistress of, now a widow, perhaps childless, a prisoner, a beggar, and in the hands of lawless ruffians, whose hands were reeking with her husband's and offspring's blood, at their mercy, and exposed to every evil which must befall a beautiful and unprotected female from those who were devoid of all principle, all pity, and all fear! Well might the frantic creature rush as she did upon our weapons, and seek that death which would have been a mercy and a blessing. With difficulty we prevented her from injuring herself, and, after a violent struggle, nature yielded, and she sank down in a swoon on the body of her husband, dabbling her clothes and hair in the gore which floated on the cabin-deck. This scene of misery shocked even the actors in it. Our sailors, accustomed as they were to blood and rapine, remained silent and immoveable, resting upon their weapons, their eyes fixed upon the unconscious form of that unhappy lady.

The rage of battle was now over, our passions had subsided, and we felt ashamed of a conquest purchased with such unutterable anguish. The noise of this renewed combat had brought down the captain; he ordered the lady to be taken away from this scene of horror, and to be carefully tended in his own cabin; the wound of the son, who was found still alive, was immediately dressed, and the prisoners were secured. I returned on deck, still oppressed with the scene I had witnessed, and when I looked round me, and beheld the deck strewed with the dead and dying—victors and vanquished indiscriminately mixed up together—the blood of both nations meeting on the deck and joining their streams, I could not help putting the question to myself, "Can this be right and lawful—all this carnage to obtain the property of others, and made legal by the quarrels of kings?" Reason, religion, and humanity answered, "No."

I remained uneasy and dissatisfied, and felt as if I were a murderer; and then I reflected how this property, thus wrested from its former possessor, who might, if he had retained it, have done much good with it, would now be squandered away in riot and dissipation, in purchasing crime and administering to debauchery. I was young then, and felt so disgusted and so angry with myself and everybody else, that if I had been in England I probably should never again have put my foot on board of a privateer.

But employment prevented my thinking; the decks had to be cleaned, the bodies thrown overboard, the blood washed from the white planks, the wounded to be removed and their hurts dressed, the rigging and other damages to be repaired, and when all this had been done we made sail for Jamaica with our prize. Our captain, who was as kind and gentle to the vanquished as he was brave and resolute in action, endeavoured by all the means he could think of to soften the captivity and sufferings of the lady. Her clothes, jewels, and everything belonging to her, were preserved untouched; he would not even allow her trunks to be searched, and would have secured for her even all her husband's personal effects, but the crew had seized upon them as plunder, and refused to deliver them up. I am almost ashamed to say that the sword and watch of her husband fell to my lot, and, whether from my wearing the sword, or from having seen me fire the pistol which had killed him, the lady always expressed her abhorrence of me whenever I entered her presence. Her son recovered slowly from his wound, and on our arrival at Port Royal was permitted by the admiral to be sent to the King's Hospital, and the lady, who was most tenderly attached to him, went on shore and remained at the Hospital to attend upon him. I was glad when she was gone, for I knew how much cause she had for her hatred of me, and I could not see her without remorse. As soon, as we had completed our repairs, filled up our provisions and water, we sailed upon another cruise, which was not so successful, as you will presently perceive.

For five or six weeks we cruised without success, and our people began to grumble, when one morning our boats in shore off Hispaniola surprised a small schooner. A negro who was among the prisoners offered to conduct us through the woods by night to the house of a very rich planter, which was situated about three miles from a small bay, and at some distance from the other plantations. He asserted that we might there get very valuable plunder, and, moreover, obtain a large ransom for the planter and his family, besides bringing away as many of the negro slaves as we pleased.

Our captain, who was tired of his ill-success, and who hoped also to procure provisions, which we very much wanted, consented to the negro's proposal, and standing down abreast of the bay, which was in the Bight of Lugan, he ran in at dark, and anchoring close to the shore we landed with forty men, and, guided by the negro, we proceeded through the woods to the house. The negro was tied fast to one of our stoutest and best men, for fear he should give us the slip. It was a bright moonlight; we soon arrived, and surrounding the house forced our way in without opposition. Having secured the negroes in the out-houses, and placed guards over them, and videttes on the look-out to give timely notice of any surprise, we proceeded to our work of plunder. The family, consisting of the old planter and his wife and his three daughters, two of them very beautiful, was secured in one room. No words can express their terror at thus finding themselves so suddenly in the power of a set of ruffians, from whose brutality they anticipated every evil. Indeed, the horrid excesses committed by the privateersmen when they landed on the coast fully justified their fears; for as this system of marauding is considered the basest of all modern warfare, no quarter is ever given to those who are taken in the attempt. In return, the privateersmen hesitate at no barbarity when engaged in such enterprises.

Dumb with astonishment and terror, the old couple sat in silent agony, while the poor girls, who had more evils than death to fear, drowned in their tears fell at the captain's feet and embraced his knees, conjuring him to spare and protect them from his men.

Captain Weatherall, who was, as I have before stated, a generous and humane man, raised them up, assuring them, on his word, that they should receive no insult; and as his presence was necessary to direct the motions of his people, he selected me, as younger and less brutal than most of his crew, as a guard over them, menacing me with death if I allowed any man to enter the room until he returned, and ordering me to defend them with my life from all insults. I was then young and full of enthusiasm; my heart was kind, and I was pure in comparison with the major portion of those with whom I was associated.

I was delighted with the office confided to me, and my heart leaped at having so honourable an employment. I endeavoured by every means in my power to dissipate their terrors and soothe their anxious minds; but while I was thus employed, an Irish seaman, distinguished even amongst our crew for his atrocities, came to the door, and would have forced his entrance. I instantly opposed him, urging the captain's most positive commands; but, having obtained a sight of the young females, he swore with a vile oath that he would soon find out whether a boy like me was able to oppose him, and finding that I would not give way he attacked me fiercely. Fortunately I had the advantage of position, and, supported by the justice of my cause, I repelled him with success. But he renewed the attack, while the poor young women awaited the issue of the combat with trembling anxiety—a combat on which depended, in all probability, their honour and their lives. At last I found myself very hard pushed, for I had received a wound on my sword arm, and I drew a pistol from my belt with my left hand, and fired it, wounding him in the shoulder. Thus disabled, and fearing at the same time that the report would bring back the captain, who he well knew would not be trifled with, he retired from the door vowing vengeance. I then turned to the young women, who had witnessed the conflict in breathless suspense, encircled in the arms of the poor old couple, who had rushed towards them at the commencement of the fray, offering them their useless shelter. Privateersman as I was, I could not refrain from tears at the scene. I again attempted to re-assure them, pledged myself in the most solemn manner to forfeit my life if necessary for their protection, and they in some degree regained their confidence. They observed the blood trickling down my fingers from the wound which I had received, and the poor girls stained their handkerchiefs with it in the attempts to staunch the flow.

But this scene was soon interrupted by an alarm. It appeared that a negro had contrived to escape and to rouse the country. They had collected together from the other plantations, and our party being, as is usually the case when plunder is going on, very negligent, the videttes were surprised, and had hardly time to escape and apprise us of our danger. There was not a moment to be lost; our safety depended upon an immediate retreat. The captain collected all hands; and while he was getting them together, that the retreat might be made in good order, the old planter, who, by the report of the fire-arms and the bustle and confusion without, guessed what had taken place, pressed me to remain with them, urging the certainty of our men being overpowered, and the merciless consequences which would ensue. He pledged himself, with his fingers crossed in the form of the crucifix, that he would procure me safe quarter, and that I should ever enjoy his protection and friendship. I refused him kindly but firmly, and he sighed and said no more. The old lady put a ring on my finger, which she took from her own hand, and kissing my forehead told me to look at that ring and continue to do good and act nobly as I had just done.

I waved my hand, for I had no time even to take the proffered hands of the young ones, and hastened to join my shipmates, already on the retreat, and exchanging shots with our pursuers. We were harassed by a multitude, but they were a mixed company of planters, mulattoes, and slaves, and not half of them armed, and we easily repelled their attacks whenever they came to close quarters. Their violent animosity, however, against us and our evil doings induced them to follow close at our heels, keeping up a galling irregular fire, and endeavouring to detain us until we might be overpowered by their numbers, every minute increasing, for the whole country had been raised, and were flocking in. This our captain was well aware of, and therefore made all the haste that he could, without disturbing the regularity of his retreat, to where our boats were lying, as should they be surprised and cut off our escape would have been impossible. Notwithstanding all his care, several of our men were separated from us by the intricacies of the wood, or from wounds which they had received, and which prevented them from keeping up with us. At last, after repelling many attacks, each time more formidable than the preceding, we gained our boats, and embarking with the greatest precipitation we put off for the schooner. The enemy, emboldened by our flight, flocked down in great numbers to the water's edge, and we had the mortification to hear our stragglers who had been captured imploring for mercy; but groans and then silence too plainly informed us that mercy had been denied.

Captain Weatherall was so enraged at the loss of his men that he ordered us to pull back and attack the enemy on the beach, but we continued to pull for the schooner, regardless of his threats and entreaties. A panic had seized us all, as well it might. We even dreaded the ill-aimed and irregular fire which they poured upon us, which under other circumstances would have occasioned only laughter. The schooner had been anchored only two hundred yards from the beach, and we were soon on board. They continued to fire from the shore, and the balls passed over us. We put a spring upon our cable, warped our broadside to the beach, and loading every gun with grape and cannister we poured a whole broadside upon our assailants. From the shrieks and cries, the carnage must have been very great. The men would have reloaded and fired again, but the captain forbade them, saying, "We have done too much already." I thought so too. He then ordered the anchor to be weighed, and with a fresh land breeze we were soon far away from this unlucky spot.

# Chapter Two.

**We are pursued by two Schooner-Privateers, and failing to escape them a terrible Contest ensues—Three Acts of a Murderous Naval Drama—We are worsted—Captain Weatherall is killed—I am plundered and wounded.**

About six weeks after the unlucky affair before described we met with a still greater disaster. We had cruised off the Spanish main, and taken several prizes; shortly after we had manned the last and had parted company, the Revenge being then close in shore, a fresh gale sprung up, which compelled us to make all sail to clear the land. We beat off shore during the whole of the night, when the weather moderated, and at daybreak we found out that we had not gained much offing, in consequence of the current; but, what was more important, the man who went to the look-out at the masthead hailed the deck, saying there were two sails in the offing. The hands were turned up to make sail in chase, but we found that they were resolutely bearing down upon us; and as we neared each other fast we soon made them out to be vessels of force. One we knew well—she was the Esperance, a French schooner-privateer, of sixteen guns and one hundred and twenty men; the other proved to be a Spanish schooner-privateer, cruising in company with her, of eighteen guns, and full manned.

Now our original complement of men had been something more than one hundred; but by deaths, severe wounds in action, and manning our prizes, our actual number on board was reduced to fifty-five effective men. Finding the force so very superior, we made every attempt with sails and sweeps to escape, but the land to leeward of us, and their position to windward, rendered it impossible. Making, therefore, a virtue of necessity, we put a good face upon it, and prepared to combat against such desperate odds.

Captain Weatherall, who was the life and soul of his crew, was not found wanting on such an emergency. With the greatest coolness and intrepidity he gave orders to take in all the small sails, and awaited the coming down of the enemy. When everything was ready for the unequal conflict, he ordered all hands aft, and endeavoured to inspire us with the same ardour which animated himself. He reminded us that we had often fought and triumphed over vessels of much greater force than our own; that we had already beaten off the French privateer on a former occasion; that the Spaniard was not worth talking about, except to swell the merits of the double victory, and that if once we came hand to hand our cutlasses would soon prove our superiority. He reminded us that our only safety depended upon our own manhood; for we had done such mischief on the coast, and our recent descent upon the plantation was considered in such a light, that we must not expect to receive quarter if we were overcome. Exhorting us to behave well and to fight stoutly, he promised us the victory. The men had such confidence in the captain that we returned him three cheers, when, dismissing us to our quarters, he ordered Saint George's ensign to be hoisted at the main-masthead, and hove-to for the enemy.

The French schooner was the first which ranged up alongside; the wind was light and she came slowly down to us. The captain of her hailed, saying that his vessel was the Esperance, and our captain replied that he knew it, and that they also knew that his was the Revenge. The French captain, who had hove-to, replied very courteously that he was well aware what vessel it was, and also of the valour and distinguished reputation of Captain Weatherall, upon which Captain Weatherall, who stood on the gunnel, took off his hat in acknowledgment of the compliment.

Now Captain Weatherall was well-known, and it was also well-known that the two vessels would meet with a severe resistance, which it would be as well to avoid, as even if they gained the victory it would not be without great loss of men. The French captain therefore addressed Captain Weatherall again, and said he hoped, now that he was opposed to so very superior a force, he would not make a useless resistance, but, as it would be no disgrace to him, and would save the lives of many of his brave men, his well-known humanity would induce him to strike his colours.

To this request our commander gave a gallant and positive refusal. The vessels lay now close to each other, so that a biscuit might have been thrown on board of either. A generous expostulation ensued, which continued till the Spanish vessel was a short distance astern of us.

"You now see our force," said the French captain. "Do not fight against impossible odds, but spare your brave and devoted men."

"In return for your kind feeling towards me," replied Captain Weatherall, "I offer you both quarter, and respect to private property, upon hauling down your colours."

"You are mad, Captain Weatherall," said the French captain.

"You allow that I have lived bravely," replied Captain Weatherall; "you shall find that I will conquer you, and if necessary I will also die bravely. We will now fight. In courtesy, I offer you the first broadside."

"Impossible," said the French captain, taking off his hat.

Our captain returned the salute, and then, slipping down from the gunwale, ordered the sails to be filled, and after a minute, to give the Frenchman time to prepare, he fired off in the air the fusee which he held in his hand, as a signal for the action to begin. We instantly commenced the work of death by pouring in a broadside. It was returned with equal spirit, and a furious cannonading ensued for several minutes, when the Spaniard ranged up on our lee quarter with his rigging full of men to board us. Clapping our helm a-weather, and hauling our fore-sheets to windward, we fell off athwart his hawse, and raked him with several broadsides fore and aft; our guns having been loaded with langridge and lead bullets, and his men being crowded together forward, ready to leap on board of us, her deck became a slaughter-house. The officers endeavoured in vain to animate their men, who, instead of gaining our decks, were so intimidated by the carnage that they forsook their own. The Frenchman, perceiving the consternation and distress of his consort, to give her an opportunity of extricating herself from her perilous condition, now put his helm a-weather, ran us on board, and poured in his men; but we were well prepared, and soon cleared our decks of the intruders. In the mean time the Spaniard, by cutting away our rigging, in which his bowsprit was entangled, swung clear of us, and fell away to leeward. The Frenchman perceiving this sheered off, and springing his luff, shot ahead clear of us. Such was the first act of this terrible drama. We had as yet sustained little damage, the enemy's want of skill, and our good fortune combined, having enabled us to take them at such a disadvantage.

But, although inspirited by such a prosperous beginning, our inferiority in men was so great that our captain considered it his duty to make all sail in hopes of being able to avoid such an unequal combat. This our enemies attempted to prevent by a most furious cannonade, which we received and returned without flinching, making a running fight of it, till at last, our fore-yard and foretop-mast being shot away, we had no longer command of the vessel. Finding that, although we were crippled and could not escape, our fire continued unabated, both the vessels again made preparations for boarding us, while we on our part prepared to give them a warm reception.

As we knew that the Frenchman, who was our most serious opponent, must board us on our weather-bow, we traversed over four of our guns, loaded to the muzzle with musket-balls, to receive him, and being all ready with our pateraroes and hand grenades we waited for the attack. As he bore down for our bows, with all his men clinging like bees, ready for the spring, our guns were discharged and the carnage was terrible. The men staggered back, falling down over those who had been killed or wounded, and it required all the bravery and example of the French captain, who was really a noble fellow, to rally the remainder of his men, which at last he succeeded in doing, and about forty of them gained our forecastle, from which they forced our weak crew, and retained possession, not following up the success, but apparently waiting till they were seconded by the Spaniard's boarding us on our lee quarter, which would have placed us between two fires, and compelled us to divide our small force.

By this time the wind, which had been light, left us, and it was nearly a calm, with a swell on the sea which separated the two vessels; the Spaniard, who was ranging up under our lee, having but little way, and not luffing enough, could not fetch us, but fell off and drifted to leeward. The Frenchmen who had been thrown on board, and who retained possession of our forecastle, being thus left without support from their own vessel, which had been separated from us by the swell, or from the Spaniard, which had fallen to leeward, we gave three cheers, and throwing a number of hand grenades in among them we rushed forward with our half-pikes, and killed or drove every soul of them overboard, one only, and he wounded in the thigh, escaped by swimming back to his own vessel. Here, then, was a pause in the conflict, and thus ended, I may say, the second act.

Hitherto the battle had been fought with generous resolution; but after this hand-to-hand conflict, and the massacre with which it ended, both sides appeared to have been roused to ferocity. A most infernal cannonade was now renewed by both our antagonists, and returned by us with equal fury; but it was now a dead calm, and the vessels rolled so much with the swell that the shot were not so effective. By degrees we separated more and more from our enemies, and the firing was now reduced to single guns. During this partial cessation our antagonists had drawn near to each other, although at a considerable distance from us. We perceived that the Spaniard was sending two of his boats full of men to supply the heavy loss sustained by his comrade. Captain Weatherall ordered the sweeps out, and we swept our broadside to them, trying by single guns to sink the boats as they went from one vessel to the other. After two or three attempts, a gun was successful; the shot shattered the first of the boats, which instantly filled and went down. The second boat pulled up and endeavoured to save the men, but we now poured our broadside upon them, and, daunted by the shot flying about them, they sought their own safety by pulling back to the vessel, leaving their sinking companions to their fate. Failing in this attempt, both vessels recommenced their fire upon us, but the distance and the swell of the sea prevented any execution, and at last they ceased firing, waiting till a breeze should spring up, which might enable them to renew the contest with better success.

At this time it was about eleven o'clock in the forenoon, and the combat had lasted about five hours. We refreshed ourselves after the fatigue and exertion which we had undergone, and made every preparation for a renewal of the fight. During the engagement we were so excited that we had no time to think; but now that we were cool again and unoccupied we had time to reflect upon our position, and we began to feel dejected and apprehensive. Fatigued with exertion, we were weak and dispirited. We knew that our best men were slain or groaning under their severe wounds, that the enemy were still numerous, and, as they persevered after so dreadful a slaughter, that they were of unquestionable bravery and resolution. Good fortune, and our captain's superior seamanship, had, up to the present, enabled us to make a good fight, but fortune might desert us, and our numbers were so reduced that if the enemy continued resolute we must be overpowered. Our gallant captain perceived the despondency that prevailed, and endeavoured to remove it by his own example and by persuasion. After praising us for the resolution and courage we had already shown, he pointed out to us that, whatever might be the gallantry of the officers, it was clear that the men on board of the opposing vessels were awed by their heavy loss and want of success, and that if they made one more attempt to take us by the board and failed, which he trusted they would do, no persuasion would ever induce them to try it again, and the captains of the vessels would give over such an unprofitable combat. He solemnly averred that the colours should never be struck while he survived, and demanded who amongst us were base enough to refuse to stand by them. Again we gave him three cheers, but our numbers were few, and the cheers were faint compared with the first which had been given, but still we were resolute, and determined to support our captain and the honour of our flag. Captain Weatherall took care that this feeling should not subside—he distributed the grog plentifully; at our desire he nailed the colours to the mast, and we waited for a renewal of the combat with impatience. At four o'clock in the afternoon a breeze sprang up, and both vessels trimmed their sails and neared us fast—not quite in such gallant trim as in the morning, it is true—but they appeared now to have summoned up a determined resolution. Silently they came up, forcing their way slowly through the water; not a gun was fired, but the gaping mouths of the cannon, and their men motionless at their quarters, portended the severity of the struggle which was now to decide this hitherto well-contested trial for victory. When within half a cable's length, we saluted them with three cheers, they returned our defiance, and running up on each side of us, the combat was renewed with bitterness.

The Frenchman would not this time lay us on board until he was certain that the Spaniard had boarded us to leeward; he continued luffing to windward and plying us with broadsides until we were grappled with the Spaniard, and then he bore down and laid his gunwale on our bow. The Spaniard had already boarded us on the quarter, and we were repelling this attack when the Frenchman laid us on the bow. We fought with desperation, and our pikes gave us such an advantage over the swords and knives of the Spaniards that they gave ground, and, appalled by the desperate resistance they encountered, quitted our decks, strewed with their dead and dying shipmates, and retreated in confusion to their own vessel. But before this repulse had been effected, the French had boarded us on the weather-bow, and driving before them the few men who had been sent forward to resist them, had gained our main deck, and forced their way to the rise of the quarter-deck, where all our remaining men were now collected. The combat was now desperate, but after a time our pikes, and the advantage of our position, appeared to prevail over numbers. We drove them before us—we had regained the main deck, when our brave commander, who was at our head, and who had infused spirit into us all, received a bullet through his right wrist; shifting his sword into his left hand, he still pressed forward encouraging us, when a ball entered his breast and he dropped dead. With his fall fell the courage and fortitude of his crew, so long sustained—and to complete the mischief, the lieutenant and two remaining officers also fell a few seconds after him. Astonished and terrified, the men stopped short in their career of success, and wildly looked round for a leader. The French, who had retreated to the forecastle, perceiving our confusion I renewed the attack, our few remaining men were seized with a panic, and throwing down our arms, we asked for quarter where a moment before victory was in our hands;—such was the finale of our bloody drama.

Out of fifty-five men twenty-two had been killed in this murderous conflict, and almost all the survivors desperately or severely wounded. Most of the remaining crew after we had cried for quarter jumped down the hatchway, to avoid the cutlasses of their enraged victors. I and about eight others, having been driven past the hatchway, threw down our arms and begged for quarter, which we had little reason to expect would be shown to us. At first no quarter was given by our savage enemies, who cut down several of our disarmed men and hacked them to pieces. Perceiving this, I got on the gunwale ready to jump overboard, in the hopes of being taken up after the slaughter had ceased, when a French lieutenant coming up protected us, and saved the poor remains of our crew from the fury of his men. Our lives, however, were all he counted upon preserving—we were instantly stripped and plundered without mercy. I lost everything I possessed; the watch, ring, and sword I had taken from the gallant Frenchman were soon forced from me, and, not stripping off my apparel fast enough to please a Mulatto sailor, I received a blow with the butt-end of a pistol under the left ear, which precipitated me down the hatchway, near which I was standing, and I fell senseless into the hold.

# Chapter Three.

**We are sent in, on board the Revenge, and treated with great cruelty—Are afterwards recaptured by the Hero privateer, and retaliate on the French—I am taken to the hospital at Port Royal, where I meet the French lady—Her savage exultation at my condition—She is punished by one of my comrades.**

On coming to my senses, I found myself stripped naked and suffering acute pain. I found that my right arm was broken, my shoulder severely injured by my fall; and, as I had received three severe cutlass-wounds during the action, I had lost so much blood that I had not strength to rise or do anything for myself. There I lay, groaning and naked, upon the ballast of the vessel, at times ruminating upon the events of the action, upon the death of our gallant commander, upon the loss of our vessel, of so many of our comrades, and of our liberty. After some time, the surgeon, by order of the French commander, came down to dress my wounds. He treated me with the greatest barbarity. As he twisted about my broken limb I could not help crying at the anguish which he caused me. He compelled me to silence by blows and maledictions, wishing I had broken my rascally neck rather than he should have been put to the trouble of coming down to dress me. However, dress me he did, out of fear of his captain, who, he knew well, would send round to see if he had executed his orders, and then he left me, with a kick in the ribs by way of remembrance. Shortly afterwards the vessels separated. Fourteen of us, who were the most severely hurt, were left in the Revenge, which was manned by an officer and twenty Frenchmen, with orders to take her into Port-au-Paix. The rest of our men were put on board of the French privateer, who sailed away in search of a more profitable adventure.

About an hour after they had made sail on the vessel, the officer who had charge of her, looking down the hatchway, and perceiving my naked and forlorn condition, threw me a pair of trousers, which had been rejected by the French seamen as not worth having; and a check shirt, in an equally ragged condition, I picked up in the hold; this, with a piece of old rope to tie round my neck as a sling for my broken arm, was my whole wardrobe. In the evening I gained the deck, that I might be refreshed by the breeze, which cooled my feverish body and somewhat restored me.

We remained in this condition for several days, tortured with pain, but more tortured, perhaps, by the insolence and bragging of the Frenchmen, who set no bounds to their triumph and self-applause. Among those who had charge of the prize were two, one of whom had my watch and the other my ring; the first would hold it to me grinning and asking if Monsieur would like to know what o'clock it was; and the other would display the ring, and tell me that his sweetheart would value it when she knew it was taken from a conquered Englishman. This was their practice every day, and I was compelled to receive their gibes without venturing a retort.

On the eleventh day after our capture, when close to Port-au-Paix, and expecting we should be at anchor before nightfall, we perceived a great hurry and confusion on deck; they were evidently making all the sail that they could upon the vessel; and then, hearing them fire off their stern-chasers, we knew for certain that they were pursued. Overjoyed at the prospect of being released, we gave three cheers. The French from the deck threatened to fire down upon us, but we knew that they dared not, for the Revenge was so crippled in the fight that they could not put sail upon her so as to escape, and their force on board was too small to enable them to resist if overtaken—we therefore continued our exulting clamours. At last we heard guns fired and the shot whizzing over the vessel—a shot or two struck our bull, and soon afterwards, a broadside being poured into us, the Frenchmen struck their colours, and we had the satisfaction of seeing all these Gasconaders driven down into the hold to take our places. It was now their turn to be dejected and downcast, and for us to be merry; and now also the tables had to be turned, and we took the liberty of regaining possession of our clothes and other property which they carried on their backs and in their pockets. I must say we showed them no mercy.

"What o'clock is it, Monsieur?" said I to the fellow who had my watch.

"At your service, Sir," he replied, humbly taking out my watch, and presenting it to me.

"Thank you," said I, taking the watch, and saluting him with a kick in the stomach, which made him double up and turn round from me, upon which I gave him another kick in the rear to straighten him again. "That ring, Monsieur, that your sweetheart will prize."

"Here it is," replied the fellow, abjectly.

"Thank you, Sir," I replied, saluting him with the double kick which I had given to the former. "Tell your sweetheart I sent her those," cried I, "that is, when you get back to her."

"Hark ye, brother," cries one of our men, "I'll trouble you for that jacket which you borrowed of me the other day, and in return here are a pair of iron garters (holding out the shackles), which you must wear for my sake—I think they will fit you well."

"Mounseer," cries another, "that wig of mine don't suit your complexion, I'll trouble you for it. It's a pity such a face as yours should be disfigured in those curls. And while you are about it, I'll thank you to strip altogether, as I think your clothes will fit me, and are much too gay for a prisoner."

"I was left naked through your kindness the other day," said I to another, who was well and smartly dressed, "I'll thank you to strip to your skin, or you shall have no skin left." And I commenced with my knife cutting his ears as if I would skin them.

It was a lucky hit of mine, for in his sash I found about twenty doubloons. He would have saved them, and held them tight, but after my knife had entered his side about half an inch he surrendered the prize. After we had plundered and stripped them of everything, we set to to kick them, and we did it for half an hour so effectually that they were all left groaning in a heap on the ballast, and we then found our way on deck.

The privateer which had recaptured us proved to be the Hero, of New Providence; the Frenchmen were taken out, and some of her own men put in to take us to Port Royal; we, being wounded, and not willing to join her, remained on board. On our arrival at Port Royal, we obtained permission to go to the King's Hospital to be cured. As I went up-stairs to the ward allotted to me, I met the French lady whose husband had been killed, and who was still nursing her son at the hospital, his wounds not having been yet cured. Notwithstanding my altered appearance, she knew me again immediately, and seeing me pale and emaciated, with my arm in a sling, she dropped down on her knees, and thanked God for returning upon our heads a portion of the miseries we had brought upon her. She was delighted when she heard how many of us had been slain in the murderous conflict, and even rejoiced at the death of poor Captain Weatherall, which, considering how very kind and considerate he had been to her, I thought to be very unchristian.

It so happened that I was not only in the same ward, but in the cradle next to her son; and the excitement I had been under when we were recaptured, and my exertion in kicking the Frenchmen, had done me no good. A fever was the consequence, and I suffered dreadfully, and she would look at me, exulting in my agony, and mocking my groans; till at last the surgeon told her it was by extreme favour that her son had been admitted into the hospital instead of being sent to prison, and that if she did not behave herself in a proper manner he would order her to be denied admittance altogether; and that if she dared to torment suffering men in that way, on the first complaint on my part, her son should go to the gaol and finish his cure there. This brought her to her senses, and she begged pardon, and promised to offend no more; but she did not keep her word for more than a day or two, but laughed out loud when the surgeon was dressing my arm, for a piece of bone had to be taken out, and I shrieked with anguish. This exasperated one of my messmates so much that, not choosing to strike her, and knowing how to wound her still worse, he drove his fist into the head of her son as he lay in his cradle, and by so doing reopened the wound that had been nearly healed.

"There's pain for you to laugh at, you French devil," he cried.

And sure enough it cost the poor young man his life.

The surgeon was very angry with the man, but told the French lady, as she kneeled sobbing by the side of her son, that she had brought it upon herself and him by her own folly and cruelty. I know not whether she felt so, or whether she dreaded a repetition, but this is certain, she tormented me no more. On the contrary, I think she suffered very severely, as she perceived that I rapidly mended and that her poor son got on but slowly. At last my hurts were all healed, and I left the hospital, hoping never to see her more.

---

# Chapter Four.

**Sail for Liverpool in the Sally and Kitty—Fall in with a Gale—Boy overboard—Nearly drowned in attempting to save him—See the owners at Liverpool—Embark in the Dalrymple for the Coast of Africa—Arrive off Senegal.**

A great deal of prize-money being due to us, I called upon the agent at Port Royal to obtain an advance. I found him in a puzzle. Owing to the death of Captain Weatherall and so many of the officers, he hardly knew whether those who applied to him were entitled to prize-money or not. Whether he thought I appeared more honest than the others, or from what cause I know not, he requested me, as I knew everything that had passed, to remain with him for a short time: and, finding that I could read and write well, he obtained from me correct lists of the privateer's crew, with those who were killed, and on what occasion. All this information I was able to give him, as well as the ratings of the parties; for on more than one occasion the privateer's-men had come to him representing themselves as petty officers when they were only common seamen on board, and had in consequence received from him a larger advance than they were entitled to. As soon as his accounts were pretty well made up, he asked me whether I intended to go to England, as if so he would send me home with all the papers and documents to the owner at Liverpool, who would require my assistance to arrange the accounts; and, as I had had quite enough of privateering for a time, I consented to go. About two months after leaving the hospital, during which I had passed a very pleasant life, and quite recovered from my wounds and injuries, I sailed for Liverpool in the Sally and Kitty West-Indiaman, commanded by Captain Clarke, a very violent man.

We had not sailed twelve hours before we fell in with a gale, which lasted several days, and we kept under close-reef-topsails and storm-staysails. The gale lasting a week raised a mountainous swell, but it was very long and regular. On the seventh day the wind abated, but the swell continued, and at evening there was very little wind, when a circumstance occurred which had nearly cost me my life, as you will acknowledge, Madam, when I relate the story to you. During the dog-watch, between six and eight, some hands being employed in the foretop, the other watch below at supper, and the captain and all the officers in the cabin, I being at the helm heard a voice, apparently rising out of the sea, calling me by name. Surprised, I ran to the side of the ship, and saw a youth named Richard Pallant in the water going astern. He had fallen out of the forechains, and, knowing that I was at the helm, had shouted to me for help. I immediately called all hands, crying, "A man overboard." The captain hastened on deck with all the others, and ordered the helm a-lee. The ship went about, and then fell round off, driving fast before the swell, till at last we brought her to.

The captain, although a resolute man, was much confused and perplexed at the boy's danger—for his friends were people of property at Ipswich, and had confided the boy to his particular care. He ran backwards and forwards, crying out that the boy must perish, as the swell was so high that he dared not send a boat, for the boat could not live in such a sea, and if the boat were lost with the crew there would not be hands enow left on board to take the vessel home. As the youth was not a hundred yards from the vessel, I stated the possibility of swimming to him with the deep-sea line, which would be strong enough to haul both him and the man who swam to him on board. Captain Clarke, in a great rage, swore that it was impossible, and asked me who the devil would go. Piqued at his answer, and anxious to preserve the life of the youth, I offered to try it myself. I stripped, and, making the line fast round my body, plunged from the ship's side into the sea. It was a new deep-sea line, and stiff in the coil, so that, not drawing close round me, it slipped, and I swam through it, but catching it as it slipped over my feet, I made it secure by putting my head and one arm through the noose. I swam direct for the boy, and found that I swam with ease, owing to the strength and buoyant nature of the water in those latitudes. I had not swum more than half-way before the line got foul on the coil on board, and, checking me suddenly, it pulled me backwards and under water. I recovered myself and struck out again. During this time, to clear the line on board, they had cut some of the entangled parts, and in the confusion and hurry severed the wrong part, so that the end went overboard, and I had half the coil of line hanging to me, and at the same time was adrift from the ship. They immediately hailed me to return, but from the booming of the waves I could not hear what they said, and thought that they were encouraging me to proceed. I shouted in return to show the confidence which I had in myself. I easily mounted the waves as they breasted me, but still I made my way very slowly against such a swell, and saw the boy only at intervals when I was on the top of the wave. He could swim very little, and did not make for the ship, but, with his eyes fixed upon the sky, paddled like a dog to keep himself above water. I now began to feel the weight of the line upon me, and to fear that I should never hold out. I began to repent of my rashness, and thought I had only sacrificed myself without any chance of saving him. I persevered, nevertheless, and having, as I guessed, come to the spot where the boy was, I looked round, and not seeing him was afraid that he had gone down, but on mounting the next wave I saw him in the hollow, struggling hard to keep above water, and almost spent with his long exertion.

I swam down to him, and, hailing him, found he was still sensible, but utterly exhausted. I desired him to hold on by my hand but not to touch my body, as we should both sink. He promised to obey me, and I held out my right hand to him, and made a signal for them to haul in on board, for I had no idea that the line had been cut. I was frightened when I perceived the distance that the ship was from me— at least a quarter of a mile. I knew that the deep-sea line was but a hundred fathoms in length, and therefore that I must be adrift, and my heart sunk within me. All the horrors of my situation came upon me, and I felt that I was lost; but although death appeared inevitable, I still struggled for life—but the rope now weighed me down more and more. While swimming forward it trailed behind, and although it impeded my way, I did not feel half its weight. Now, however, that I was stationary, it sank deep, and pulled me down with it. The waves, too, which, while I breasted them and saw them approach, I easily rose over, being now behind us, broke over our heads, burying us under them, or rolling us over by their force.

I tried to disengage myself from the line, but the noose being jammed, and having the boy in one hand, I could not possibly effect it. But what gave me courage in my difficulties was, that I perceived that the people on board were getting out the boat; for although the captain would not run the risk for one person, now that two were overboard, and one of them risking his life for the other, the men insisted that the boat should be hoisted out. It was an anxious time to me, but at last I had the satisfaction of seeing her clear of the ship, and pulling round her bow. The danger was, however, considered so great, that when they came to man the boat only three men could be found who would go in her, and in the confusion they came away with but two oars and no rudder. Under these disadvantages they of course pulled very slowly against a mountainous sea, as they were obliged to steer with the oars to meet it, that the boat might not be swamped. But the sight of the boat was sufficient to keep me up. My exertions were certainly incredible; but what will not a man do when in fear of death! As it approached—slowly and slowly did my powers decrease. I was now often under water with the boy, and rose again to fresh exertion, when at last a crested wave broke over us, and down we went several feet under the water. The force of the sea drove the boy against me, and he seized me by the loins with my head downwards. I struggled to disengage myself! It was impossible. I gave myself up for lost—and what a crowd of thoughts and memories passed through my brain in a few moments, for it could not have been longer! At last, being head downwards, I dived deeper, although I was bursting from so long holding my breath under water.

This had the desired effect. Finding me sinking instead of rising with him, the boy let go his hold that he might gain the surface. I turned and followed him, and drew breath once more. Another moment had sealed our fates. I no longer thought of saving the boy, but struck out for the boat which was now near me. Perceiving this, the boy cried out to me for pity's sake not to leave him. I felt myself so far recovered from my exhaustion, that I thought I could save him as well as myself, and compassion induced me to turn back. I again gave him my hand, charging him on his life not to attempt to grapple with me, and again resumed the arduous struggle of keeping him as well as myself above water. My strength was nearly gone, the boat approached but slowly, and we now sunk constantly under the water, rising every few seconds to draw breath. Merciful God! How slow appeared the approach of the boat. Struggle after struggle—fainter and fainter still—still I floated. At last my senses almost left me, I took in water in quantities. I felt I was in green fields, when I was seized by the men and thrown into the bottom of the boat, where I lay senseless alongside of the boy. There was great danger and difficulty in getting again to the ship. More than once the boat was half filled by the following seas, and when they gained the ship it was impossible to get us out, as, had they approached the side, the boat would have been dashed to atoms. They lowered the tackles from the yard-arms. The three men clambered up them, leaving us to take our chance of the boat being got in, or her being stove to pieces, in which latter case we should have been lost. They did get us in, with great damage to the boat, but we were saved. The line was still round me, and it was found that I had been supporting the weight of seventy yards. So sore was I with such exertion, that I kept my hammock for many days, during which I reviewed my past life, and vowed amendment.

We arrived at Liverpool without any further adventure worth recording, and I immediately called upon the owner with the papers intrusted to me. I gave him all the information he required, and he asked me whether I should like to return to privateering, or to go as mate of a vessel bound to the coast of Africa. I inquired what her destination was to be, and, as I found that she was to go to Senegal for ivory, wax, gold-dust, and other articles, in exchange for English prints and cutlery, I consented. I mention this, as, had she been employed in the slave-trade, as were most of the vessels from Liverpool to the Coast, I would not have joined her. A few days afterwards I went on board of the Dalrymple, Captain Jones, as mate; we had a very quick passage to Senegal, and brought our vessel to an anchor off the bar.

---

# Chapter Five.

**In crossing the Bar at Senegal the boat is upset by a Tornado—We escape being devoured by Sharks only to be captured by the Natives—Are taken into the interior of the country, and brought before the Negro King, from whose wrath we are saved by the intercession of his female attendants.**

A day or two after we had arrived, the master of another vessel that was at anchor near to us came on board and borrowed our long-boat and some hands that he might go in it to Senegal. The captain, who was an old friend of the party who made the request, agreed to lend it to him, and as accidents are very frequent with boats crossing the bar, on account of the heavy breakers, the best swimmers were selected for the purpose, and the charge of the boat was given to me. We set off, five men rowing and I at the helm. When we approached the bar, a tornado, which had been for some time threatening, came upon us. The impetuosity of these blasts is to be matched in no part of the world, and as it came at once in its full force, we endeavoured, by putting the boat before it, to escape its fury. This compelled us to run to the southward along the coast. We managed to keep the boat up for a long while, and hoped to have weathered it, when, being on the bar, and in broken water, a large wave curled over us, filled the boat, and it went down in an instant.

Our only chance now was to reach the shore by swimming, but it was at a distance, with broken water the whole way; and our great terror was from the sharks, which abound on the coast and are extremely ravenous—nor were we without reason for our alarm. Scarcely had the boat gone down, and we were all stretching out for the shore, when one of our men shrieked, having been seized by the sharks, and instantly torn to pieces. His blood stained the water all around, and this attracting all the sharks proved the means of our escape. Never shall I forget the horrible sensation which I felt as I struggled through the broken water, expecting every minute a limb to be taken off by one of those voracious animals. If one foot touched the other, my heart sunk, thinking it was the nose of a shark, and that its bite would immediately follow. Agonised with these terrors, we struggled on—now a large wave curling over us and burying us under water, or now forced by the waves towards the beach, rolling us over and over. So battered were we by the surf, that we dived under the waves to escape the blows which we received, and then rose and struck out again. At last, worn out with exertion, we gained the shore, but our toil was not over.

The beach was of a sand so light that it crumbled beneath us, and at the return of the wave which threw us on shore we were dragged back again and buried in sand and water. We rose to renew our endeavours, but several times without success, for we could not obtain a firm footing. At last the Negroes, who had witnessed our accident, and who now came down in great numbers on the beach, laid hold of us as the sea threw us up, and dragged us beyond the reach of the waves. Worn out with fatigue we lay on the sand, waiting to ascertain what the savages would do with us; they were not long in letting us know, for they soon began to strip us of every article of clothing on our backs. One of our men attempted to resist, upon which a Negro drove a spear through his thigh.

Having divided our apparel, after some consultation, they tied our hands, and placing us in the midst of a large force, armed with spears and bows and arrows, they went off with us for the inland part of the country. We set off with heavy hearts; taking, as we thought, a last farewell of the ocean, and going forwards in great apprehension of the fate that awaited us. The sand was very deep, and the heat of the sun excessive, for it was then about noon. Without any garments, we were soon scorched and blistered all over, and in intolerable anguish, as well as fatigued; but the Negroes compelled us to move on, goading us with their spears if we slackened our pace, and threatening to run us through if we made a halt. We longed for the night, as it would afford a temporary relief to our sufferings. It came at last, and the Negroes collected wood and lighted a fire to keep off the wild beasts, lying round it in a circle, and placing us in the midst of them. We hoped to have some rest after what we had gone through, but it was impossible—the night proved even worse than the day. The mosquitoes came down upon us in such swarms, and their bites were so intolerable, that we were almost frantic. Our hands being tied, we could not beat them off and we rolled over and over to get rid of them. This made matters worse, for our whole bodies being covered with raised blisters, from the rays of the sun, our rolling over and over broke the blisters, and the sand getting into the wounds, added to the bites of the mosquitoes, made our sufferings intolerable. We had before prayed for night, we now prayed for day. Some prayed for death.

When the sun rose, we set off again, our conductors utterly disregarding our anguish, and goading us on as before. In the forenoon we arrived at a village, where our guards refreshed themselves; a very small quantity of boiled corn was given to each of us, and we continued our journey, passing by several small towns, consisting, as they all do in that country, of huts built of reeds, round in form, and gathered to a point at top. This day was the same as the preceding. We were pricked with spears if we stumbled or lagged, threatened with death if we had not strength to go on. At last the evening arrived, and the fires were lighted. The fires were much larger than before, I presume because the wild beasts were more numerous, for we heard them howling in every direction round us, which we had not done on the night before. The mosquitoes did not annoy us so much, and we obtained some intervals of broken rest. At daylight we resumed our journey, as near as we could judge by the sun, in a more easterly direction.

During the first two days we were badly received by the inhabitants of the towns, whose people had been kidnapped so often for the slave-trade; they hated the sight of our white faces, for they presumed that we had come for that purpose; but as we advanced in the interior, we were better treated, and the natives looked upon us with surprise and wonder, considering us as a new race of beings. Some of the women, seeing how utterly exhausted we were with fatigue and hunger, looked with compassion on us, and brought us plenty of boiled corn and goats' milk to drink. This refreshed us greatly, and we continued our journey in anxious expectation of the fate for which we were reserved.

On crossing a small river, which appeared to be the boundary of two different states, a multitude of Negroes approached, and seemed disposed to take us from our present masters, but after a conference, they agreed among themselves, and a party of them joined with those who had previously conducted us. We soon came to the edge of a desert, and there we halted till the Negroes had filled several calabashes and gourds full of water, and collected a quantity of boiled corn. As soon as this was done, we set off again, and entered the desert. We were astonished and terrified when we looked around us, not a single vestige of herbage, not a blade of grass was to be seen—all was one wide waste of barren sand, so light as to rise in clouds at the least wind, and we sank so deep in walking through it that at last we could hardly drag one foot after the other. But we were repaid for our fatigue, for when we halted at night, no fires were lighted, and to our great delight we found that there were no mosquitoes to annoy us. We fell into a sound sleep, which lasted till morning, and were much refreshed; indeed, so much so as to enable us to pursue our journey with alacrity.

In our passage over the desert we saw numbers of elephants' teeth, but no animals. How the teeth came there, unless it were that the elephants were lost in attempting to cross the desert, I cannot pretend to say. Before we had crossed the desert, our water was expended, and we suffered dreadfully from thirst, walking as we did during the whole day under a vertical sun. The night was equally painful, as we were so tortured with the want of water; but on the following day, when our strength was nearly exhausted, and we were debating whether we should not lie down and allow the spears of our conductors to put an end to our miseries, we came to the banks of a river which the Negroes had evidently been anxiously looking for. Here we drank plentifully, and remained all the day to recruit ourselves, for the Negroes were almost as exhausted as we were. The next morning we crossed the river, and plunged into a deep wood: the ground being high, the mosquitoes did not annoy us so much as they did down on the low marshy land near the sea-coast. During our traverse through the wood we subsisted solely upon the birds and animals which the Negroes killed with their bows and arrows.

When we had forced our way through the forest, we found the country, as before, interspersed with wicker villages or small hamlets at a few miles' distance from each other. Round each village there were small patches of Guinea corn, and we frequently came to clusters of huts which had been deserted. Between the sea-coast and the desert we had traversed we observed that many of the inhabitants had European fire-arms, but now the only weapons to be seen were spears and bows and arrows. As we advanced we were surrounded at every village by the natives, who looked upon us with surprise and astonishment, examining us, and evidently considering us a new species. One morning we arrived at a very large Negro town, and as we approached, our guards began to swell with pride and exultation, and drove us before them among the crowds of inhabitants, singing songs of triumph, and brandishing their weapons. Having been driven through a great part of the town, we arrived at a number of huts separated by a high palisade from the rest, and appropriated, as we afterwards found, to the use of the king of the country, his wives and attendants. Here we waited outside some time, while our guards went in and acquainted this royal personage with the present which they had brought for him.

We had reason to think that our captors were not his subjects, but had been at variance with him, and had brought us as a present, that they might make peace with an enemy too strong for them. We were at last ordered to go inside the enclosure, and found ourselves in a large open building, constructed like the others, of reeds and boughs. In the centre was squatted a ferocious-looking old Negro, attended by four young Negro women. He was raw-boned and lean, and of a very large frame. A diabolical ferocity was imprinted on his grim countenance, and as he moved his arms and legs he showed that under his loose skin there was a muscle of extraordinary power. I never had before seen such a living type of brutal strength and barbarity. On a mat before him were provisions of different kinds. Behind him stood several grim savages who held his weapons, and on each side, at a greater distance, were rows of Negroes, with their heads bent down and their arms crossed, awaiting his orders. The chief or king, as well as the four women, had clothes of the blue cotton cloth of the country, that is, one piece wrapped round the loins and descending to the ankles, and another worn over their shoulders; but, with few exceptions, all the rest, as well as the inhabitants generally, were quite naked. So were we, as the reader may recollect. Round the necks of the women were rows of gold beads, longer by degrees, until the last of the rows hung lower than their bosoms, and both the king and they had large bracelets of gold round their arms, wrists, and legs. The women, who were young and well-looking, stared at us with eager astonishment, while the old king scowled upon us so as to freeze our blood. At last, rising from the ground, he took his sabre from the man who held it behind him, and walked up among us, who with our heads bowed, and breathless with fear, awaited our impending fate. I happened to be standing the foremost, and grasping my arm with a gripe which made my heart sink, with his hand which held the sword he bent down my head still lower than it was. I made sure that he was about to cut off my head, when the women, who had risen from the ground, ran crowding round him, and with mingled entreaties and caresses strove to induce him not to put his intentions, if such he really had, into execution. They prevailed at last; the youngest took away his sword, and then they led him back to his seat, after which the women came to us to gratify their curiosity. They felt our arms and breasts, putting innumerable questions to those who brought us thither. They appeared very much amazed at the length of my hair, for I had worn it tied in a long cue. Taking hold of it, they gave it two or three severe pulls, to ascertain if it really grew to my head, and finding that it did so, they expressed much wonder. When their curiosity was satisfied, they then appeared to consider our condition, and having obtained the old king's permission, they brought us a calabash full of cush-cush, that is, Guinea corn boiled into a thick paste. Our hands being still tied, we could only by shaking our heads express our inability to profit by their kindness. Understanding what we meant, they immediately cut our thongs, and the youngest of the four perceiving that my arms were benumbed from having been confined so many days, and that I could not use them, showed the most lively commiseration for my sufferings. She gently chafed my wrists with her hands, and showed every sign of pity in her countenance, as indeed did all the other three. But I was by far the youngest of the whole party who had been captured, and seemed most to excite their pity and good-will. Shortly afterwards we were all taken into an adjoining tent or hut, and our bodies were rubbed all over with an oil, which after a few days' application left us perfectly healed, and as smooth as silk. So altered was our condition, that those very people who had guarded us with their spears and threatened us with death, were now ordered to wait upon us, and as the king's wives frequently came to see how we were treated, we were served with the utmost humility and attention.

# Chapter Six.

**I am given as a Slave to the old King's Favourite, Whyna—Assist my young Mistress to make her Toilet—Hold frequent Conversations with her, and become strongly attached to her—My Hatred and Dread of the old King increase—He shoots a Man with Bird-arrows.**

One morning, after we had been about three weeks in these comfortable quarters, I was summoned away from my companions into the presence of the king. When I came before him a small manacle was fixed round my left ankle, and another round my left wrist, with a light chain connecting the two. A circle of feathers was put round my head, and a loose cloth wrapped round my loins. I was then led forward to him with my arms crossed over my breast, and my head bowed. By his orders I was then placed behind the youngest of the four women, the one who had chafed my wrists, and I was given to understand that I was her slave, and was to attend upon her, to which, I must say, I gave a joyful assent in my heart, although I did not at that time show any signs of gladness. There I remained, with my arms folded, and bowed as before, until dinner was brought in, and a calabash full of cush-cush was put into my hands to place before the king and his wives. My first attempt at service was not very adroit, for, in my eagerness to do my duty, I tripped over the corner of the mat which served them for a table, and tumbling headlong forward, emptied the calabash of cush-cush which I held in my hand upon the legs of the old king, who sat opposite to where I was advancing. He jumped up roaring out with anger, while I in my fear sprung on my legs, and rushed to the side of the apartment, expecting immediate death. Fortunately the victuals in this country are always served up cool, and my new mistress easily obtained my pardon, laughing heartily at the scene, and at my apprehension.

The repast being over, I was ordered to follow my mistress, who retired to another hut, according to their custom, to sleep during the heat of the day. I was placed before the door to prevent her being disturbed. My only duty now was to attend upon my young mistress. She was the king's favourite wife, and as she was uniformly kind and gentle, I should have almost ceased to lament my loss of liberty had it not been from the fear I had of the old monarch. I knew that my preservation depended entirely upon my mistress's favour, and I endeavoured all I could to conciliate her by the most sedulous attentions to please. Young and generous in disposition, she was easily satisfied by my ready obedience and careful service. I do not think that she was more than seventeen years of age; but they are women at fourteen in that country, and even earlier. She was a Negress as to colour, but not a real Negress; for her hair, although short and very wavy, was not woolly, and her nose was straight. Her mouth was small, and her teeth beautiful. Her figure was perfect, her limbs being very elegantly formed. When she first rose in the morning, I attended her to the brow of a hill just without the palisades, where with devout but mistaken piety she adored the rising sun—at least it appeared to me that she did so. She then went down to the river to bathe, and as soon as her hair was dry she had it dressed. This office, after a short time, devolved upon me, and I became very expert, having to rub her hair with a sweet oil, and then roll it up in its natural curls with a quill, so as to dispose them to the most fanciful advantage as to form.

After her toilet was complete, she went to feed her poultry, and some antelopes and other beasts, and then she practised at a mark with her bow and arrows and javelin till about ten o'clock, when she went to the king's hut, and they all sat down to eat together. After the repast, which lasted some time, if she did not repose with the king, she retired to her own hut, where she usually refreshed herself till about four o'clock, when she returned to the king, or ranged the woods, or otherwise amused herself during the rest of the evening. I will say for the old savage that he did not confine his wives. Such was our general course of life, and wherever she went I attended her. The attachment I showed and really felt for her secured her confidence, and she always treated me in a kind and familiar manner. Their language consists of few words compared to our own, and in a short time, by help of signs, we understood each other tolerably well. She appeared to have a most ardent curiosity to know who we were, and from whence we came, and all the time that we passed alone was employed in putting questions, and my endeavouring to find out her meaning and answer them. This, although very difficult at first, I was eventually enabled to accomplish indifferently well. She was most zealous in her mistaken religion, and one morning when I was following her to her devotions on the hill, she asked me where my God was? I pointed upwards, upon which she told me with great joy and innocency, that hers was there too, and that, therefore, they must be the same God, or if not they must be friends. Convinced that she was right, she made me worship with her, bowing my head down to the sand, and going through the same forms, which of course I did not understand the meaning of; but I prayed to my God, and therefore made no objection, as it was pleasing to her. This apparent conformity in religion recommended me more strongly to her, and we became more intimate, and I was certainly attached to her by every tie of gratitude. I was quite happy in the friendship and kindness she showed towards me; the only drawback was my fear of the proud old king, and the recollection of him often made me check myself, and suddenly assume a more distant and respectful demeanour towards her. I soon found out that she dreaded the old savage as much as I did, and hated him even more. In his presence she treated me very sternly, and ordered me about in a very dictatorial manner; but when we were alone, and had no fear of being seen, she would then be very familiar, sometimes even locking her arm into mine, and laughing as she pointed out the contrast of the colours, and in the full gaiety of her young heart rejoicing that we were alone, and could converse freely together. As she was very intelligent, she soon perceived that I possessed much knowledge that she did not, and that she could not comprehend what I wanted to teach her. This induced her to look upon me with respect as well as kindness.

One day I purposely left her bow behind in the hut where my companions resided; and on her asking me for it, I told her that I had done so, but that I would make my companions send it without my going back. I tore off a piece of the bark of a tree, and with the point of an arrow I wrote to one of them, desiring him to send it by bearer; and calling a young Negro boy, told him in her presence to give that piece of bark to the white man, and come back again to the queen. Whyna, for such was the name of my mistress queen, stood in suspense, waiting the result; in a few minutes the boy returned, bringing the bow. Astonished at this, she made me write again and again for her arrows, her lance, and many other things. Finding by these being immediately sent that we had a method of communicating with each other at a distance, she earnestly insisted upon being taught so surprising an art. Going at a distance from me, she ordered me to talk to her when out of hearing, and finding that I could not, or, as she seemed to suppose, that I would not, she became discontented and out of humour. I could by no means make her comprehend how it was performed, but I made her understand that as soon as I was fully acquainted with her language, I should be able to teach her. She was satisfied with this, but made me promise that I would teach nobody else.

By the canoes in the river, I easily made her comprehend that I came in a vast boat from a distant land, over a great expanse of water, and also how it was that we fell into the Negroes' power. I then found out from her that the Negroes had pretended that we had invaded their land to procure slaves, and that they had vanquished us in battle;

hence their songs of triumph on bringing us to the king. I pointed out the heavenly bodies to her in the evenings, trying to make her comprehend something of their nature and motions, but in vain. This had, however, one good effect; she looked up to me with more respect, hoping that some day, when I could fully explain myself, she might be herself taught all these wonders. With these feelings towards me, added to my sedulous endeavours to please her, and obey her slightest wishes, it is not surprising that she treated me as a companion, and not as a slave, and gave me every innocent proof of her attachment. More I never wished, and almost dreaded that our intimacy would be too great. Happy when alone with her, I ever returned with reluctance to the presence of the old king, whose sight and company I dreaded.

The boundless cruelty of this monster was a continual check to all my happiness. Accustomed to blood from his childhood, he appeared wholly insensible to human feelings, and derided the agonies of the wretches who daily fell by his hands. One day he amused himself by shooting small bird-arrows at a man who was bound to a post before the tent, which was placed there for the punishment of those who were his victims. He continued for hours fixing the arrows in different parts of his body, mimicking and deriding his cries. At last, contrary to his intentions, one of the arrows hit the man in the throat, and his head drooped. As the old savage saw that the poor man was dying, he drew another arrow and sent it through his heart, very much annoyed at his disappointment in not prolonging the poor creature's sufferings. I was witness to this scene with silent horror, and many more of a similar nature. I hardly need say, that I felt what my punishment would be if I had by any means roused the jealousy of this monster; and I knew that, without giving him real cause, a moment of bare suspicion would be sufficient to sacrifice my mistress as well as me.

# Chapter Seven.

I attend the King on a hunting Expedition—Chase of wild Animals—
Whyna and I in great danger from a Tiger—Barbarity of the King to
my young Mistress—I try to soothe her—I and my Companions are
ransomed—Sad parting with Whyna—After an Encounter with a
hostile People, we reach Senegal—Return to England.

I had been about three months in captivity, when the old king, with
his four wives and a large party of Negroes, left the town, and went
into the woods to hunt. My companions were left in the town, but I
was ordered to attend my mistress, and I went with the hopes of
being able by some means to make my escape, for my fear of the old
monarch was much greater than my regard for my mistress. As I had
not become a proficient with the bows and arrows, or in hurling the
javelin, I was equipped with a strong spear. My mistress was skilful to
admiration with the arrow and javelin; she never missed her aim that I
knew, and she certainly never appeared to such advantage as she did
at this hunting-party. Her activity, her symmetry of limb, and her
courage, her skill with her weapons, all won the heart of the old king;
and I believe that his strong attachment to her arose more from her
possession of the above qualities than from any other cause. Certain it
is, that the old savage doted on her—she was the only being who
could bend his stubborn will. As his age prevented him from joining
in the chase, he always appeared to part with her with regret, and to
caution her not to run into useless danger; and when we returned at
night, the old man's eyes sparkled with the rapture of dotage as he
welcomed her return.

The method of our chase was to beat the country, with a number of
men, in a vast circle, until we had gathered all the game into one
thicket; then the strongest warriors with their large spears went in and
drove out the game, which was killed by the hunters who hovered
about within the circle.

The animals which we had to encounter were large fierce black pigs,
leopards, jackals, tigers, mountain cats, and others which I have no
name for;—and in spite of the ferocity of many of these animals when
they bounded out, they were met with such a shower of javelins, or
transfixed by the strong stabbing-spears of the warriors, that few
escaped, and they rarely did any mischief. One day, however, the
beaters having just entered a thicket, Whyna, who was eager for the

sport, and plied within the circle with the other hunters, hearing a rustling in the jungle, went to the verge of it, to be the first to strike the animal which came out. As usual, I was close to her, when a large tiger burst out, and she pierced him with her javelin, but not sufficient to wound the animal so severely as to disable him. The tiger turned, and I drove my spear into his throat. This checked him, as it remained in, but in a spring which he gave the handle broke short off, and although the iron went further in, our danger was imminent. Whyna ran, and so did I, to escape from the beast's fury; for although, after I had wounded it with my spear, we had both retreated, we were not so far, but that in two or three bounds he would have been upon us. My mistress was as fleet as the wind, and soon passed me, but as she passed me she caught me by the hand, and dragged me along at a pace that with difficulty I could keep my legs. The surrounding hunters, alarmed at her danger, and knowing what they had to expect from the mercy of the old king if she was destroyed by the animal, closed in between us and the tiger, and after a fierce combat, in which some were killed and many wounded, they despatched him with their spears. The head of the animal, which was of unusual size, was cut off and carried home to the old king in triumph; and when he heard of the danger that Whyna had been in, he caressed her with tears, and I could not help saying that the old wretch had some heart after all. Whyna told the king that if I had not pierced the animal with my spear, and prevented his taking his first spring, she should have lost her life, and the monster grinned a ghastly smile at me, which I presume he meant for either approbation or gratitude.

At other times the chase would be that of the multitude of birds which were to be found in the woods. The bow and arrow only were used, and all I had to do now was to pick up all my mistress had killed, and return her arrows—she would constantly kill on the wing with her arrow, which not many could do besides her. By degrees I imbibed a strong passion for the sport, attended as it was with considerable danger, and was never so happy as when engaged in it. We remained about two months in the woods, when the king was tired, and we returned to the town, where I continued for some time to pass the same kind of life as I had done before.

I should have been quite happy in my slavery, from my affection to my mistress, had not a fresh instance of the unbounded cruelty of the old monarch occurred a few days after our return from the chase, which filled us all with consternation and horror, for we discovered that not even my mistress, Whyna, could always prevail with the savage monster.

One morning I perceived that one of the king's guards, who had always treated me with great kindness, and with whom I was very intimate, was tied up to the executioner's post before the hut. Aware of the fate which awaited him, I ran to the hut of Whyna, and so great was my distress that I could not speak; all I could do was to clasp her knees and repeat the man's name, pointing to the post to which he was tied. She understood me, and eager to save the man, or to oblige me, she ran to the large hut, and attempted to intercede with the old barbarian for the man's life but he was in an agony of rage and passion; he refused her, lifting up his sabre to despatch the man; Whyna was rash enough to seize the king's arm, and prevent the blow; at this his rage redoubled,—his eyes glowed like live coals, and turning to her with the look of a demon, he caught her by the hair, and dragging her across his feet, lifted up his scimitar in the act to strike off her head. I sickened with horror at the danger she was in, but I thought he would not strike. I had no weapon, but if he had done so, I would have revenged her death, even if I had lost my life. At last the old monster let go her hair, spurning her away with his foot, so that she rolled over on the sand, and then turning to the unhappy man, with an upward slanting blow of his sabre, he ripped him up from the flank to the chest, so that his bowels fell down at his feet; he then looked round at us all with an aspect which froze our blood, and turned away sulkily to his hut, leaving us to recover our spirits how we might.

Poor Whyna, terrified and enraged at the same time, as soon as I had led her to her hut, and we were by ourselves, gave way to the storm of passion which swelled her bosom, execrating her husband with the utmost loathing and abhorrence, and lamenting in the most passionate manner her having ever been connected with him. Trembling alike at the danger to which I had exposed her, and moved by her condition, I could not help mingling my tears with hers, and endeavoured by caresses and condoling with her to reduce her excitement. Had the old king seen me, I know what both our fates would have been, but at that time I cared not. I was very young, very impetuous, and I was resolved that I would not permit either her or myself to die unavenged. At last she sobbed herself to sleep, and I took my usual station outside of the hut. It was well that I did so, for not five minutes afterwards the old wretch, having got over his temper, came out of his tent and bent his steps towards the hut, that he might make friends with her, for she was too necessary to his happiness, he soon treated her with his accustomed kindness, but I perceived that after the scene I have described her aversion for him was doubled.

There were some scores of women in the various huts within the palisade, all of whom I understood were wives to the old monarch, but none but the four we found with him when we were first brought into his presence were ever to be seen in his company. I had, by means of my kind mistress, the opportunity of constantly supplying my companions with fowls and venison, which was left from the king's table, and through her care, they always met with kind and gentle usage.

For another two months did I thus remain happy in the company of Whyna, and miserable when in the presence of the king, whose eye it was impossible to meet without quailing; when one morning we were all ordered out, and were surrounded by a large party armed with spears, javelins, and bird-arrows—I say bird-arrows, as those that they use in war are much larger. We soon discovered that we were to be sent to some other place, but where or why, we could not find out. Shortly afterwards the crowd opened, and Whyna made her appearance. She took the feather circle off my head, and the manacles off my wrist and leg, and went and laid them at the king's feet. She then returned, and told me that I was free as well as my companions, but that I only, if I chose, had permission to remain with her.

I did not at first reply. She then, in the most earnest manner, begged me to remain with her as her slave; and as she did not dare to say what she felt, or use caresses to prevail upon me, she stamped her little feet with eagerness and impatience. The struggle in my own heart was excessive. I presumed that we were about to be made a present to some other king, and I felt that I never could expect so easy and so pleasant a servitude as I then enjoyed. I was sincerely attached, and indeed latterly I was more than attached, to Whyna; I felt that it was dangerous. Had the old king been dead, I would have been content to pass my life with her; and I was still hesitating, notwithstanding the remonstrances of my companions, when the crowd opened a little, and I beheld the old king looking at me, and I felt convinced that his jealousy was at last aroused, and that if I consented to remain, my life would not be worth a day's purchase.

Whyna also turned, and met the look of the old king. Whether she read in his countenance what I did, I know not; but this is certain, she made no more attempts to persuade me, but waving her hand for us to set off on our journey, she slowly retired, and when arrived at the hut turned round towards us. We all prostrated ourselves before her, and then set off on our journey. She retired to the door of her own hut, and two or three times waved her hand to us, at which our guards made us every time again prostrate ourselves. She then walked out to the little hill where she always went up to pray, and for the last time waved her hand, and then I perceived her sink down on the ground, and turn her head in the direction which she always did when she prayed.

We now proceeded on our journey in a north-west direction, our guards treating us with the greatest kindness. We rested every day from ten till four o'clock in the afternoon, and then walked till late at night. Corn was supplied us from the scattered hamlets as we passed along, and our escort procured us flesh and fowl with their bows and arrows; but we were in a state of great anxiety to know where we were going, and nobody appeared able or willing to tell us. I often thought of Whyna, and at times repented that I had not remained with her, as I feared falling into a worse slavery, but the recollection of the old king's diabolical parting look was sufficient to make me think that it was best as it was. Now that I had left my mistress, I thought of her kindness and amiable qualities and her affection for me; and although it may appear strange that I should feel myself in love with a black woman, I will not deny but that I was so. I could not help being so, and that is all the excuse I can offer.

Our guards now informed us that we were about to pass for a few miles through the territory of another king, and that they were not sure what our reception might be; but this was soon made evident, for we observed a party behind us, which moved as we moved, although they did not attack us; and soon afterwards a larger body in front were blocking up our passage, and we found that we were beset. The commander of our party, therefore, gave orders for battle, and he put into our hands strong spears, they being the only weapons we could use, and entreated us to fight. Our party was greatly out-numbered by the enemy, but ours were chosen warriors. As for us white men, we kept together, agreeing among ourselves, that we would defend ourselves if attacked, but would not offend either party by taking an unnecessary part in the fray, as it was immaterial to us to whom we belonged.

The battle, or rather skirmish, soon began. They dispersed, and shot their arrows from behind the trees, and this warfare continued some time without damage to either party, till at last they attacked us closely; then, our commander killing that of the enemy, they gave way, just as another party was coming forward to attack us white men; but finding us resolute in our defence, and our own warriors coming to our assistance, the rout was general. They could not, however, prevent some prisoners from being taken; most of them wounded with the bird-arrows, which, having their barbs twisted in the form of an S, gave great pain in their extraction. I observed that a particular herb chewed, and bound up with the bleeding wound, was their only remedy, and that when the bone was injured, they considered the wound mortal.

We now turned to the eastward to get back into our own territory; we left the prisoners and wounded at a village, and receiving a reinforcement, we took a circuit to avoid this hostile people, and continued our route. On the eighth morning, just as we were stopping to repose, one of the warriors, who had mounted a hill before us, shouted and waved his hand. We ran up to him, and as soon as we gained the summit, were transported with the sight of the British flag flying on Senegal fort, on the other side of the river. We now understood that by some means or another we had been ransomed, and so it proved to be; for the governor hearing that we were prisoners up the country, had sent messengers offering the old king a handsome present for our liberation. I afterwards found out that the price paid in goods amounted to about fifty-six shillings a head. The governor received us kindly, clothed us, and sent us down to the ship, which was with a full cargo in the road, and intending to sail the next day, and we were received and welcomed by our messmates as men risen from the dead.

We sailed two days afterwards, and had a fortunate voyage home to Liverpool.

# Chapter Eight.

**The Liverpool Ladies are very civil to me—I am admitted into good Society—Introduced to Captain Levee—Again sail to Senegal—Overhear a Conspiracy to seize the Ship by the Crew of a Slaver, but am enabled to defeat it—Am thanked and rewarded by the Owner—Take a Trip to London with Captain Levee—Stopped by Highwaymen on the Road—Put up at a Tavern—Dissipated Town Life—Remove to a genteel Boarding-House—Meet with a Government Spy—Return to Liverpool.**

As the captain reported me to be a very attentive and good officer, although I was then but twenty-three years of age, and as I had been previously on good terms and useful to the owner, I was kindly received by him, and paid much more attention to than my situation on board might warrant. My captivity among the Negroes, and the narrative I gave of my adventures, were also a source of much interest. I was at first questioned by the gentlemen of Liverpool, and afterwards one of the merchant's ladies, who had heard something of my adventures, and found out that I was a young and personable man, with better manners than are usually to be found before the mast, invited me one evening to a tea-party, that I might amuse her friends with my adventures. They were most curious about the Negro queen, Whyna, inquiring into every particular as to her personal appearance and dress, and trying to find out, as women always do, if there was anything of an intrigue between us. They shook their little fingers at me, when I solemnly declared that there was not, and one or two of them cajoled me aside to obtain my acknowledgment of what they really believed to be the truth, although I would not confess it.

When they had tired themselves with asking questions about the Negro queen, they then began to ask about myself, and how it happened I was not such a bear, and coarse in my manners and address, as the other seamen. To this I could give no other reply but that I had been educated when a child. They would fain know who were my father and mother, and in what station of life it had pleased God to place them; but I hardly need say, my dear Madam, to you who are so well acquainted with my birth and parentage, that I would not disgrace my family by acknowledging that one of their sons was in a situation so unworthy; not that I thought at that time, nor do I think now, that I was so much to blame in preferring independence in a humble position, to the life that induced me to take the step which I did; but as I could not state who my family were without also stating why I had quitted them, I preserved silence, as I did not think that I had any right to communicate family secrets to strangers. The consequences of my first introduction to genteel society were very agreeable; I received many more invitations from the company assembled, notwithstanding that my sailor's attire but ill corresponded with the powdered wigs and silk waistcoats of the gentlemen, or the hoops and furbelows of satin, which set off the charms of the ladies. At first I did not care so much, but as I grew more at my ease, I felt ashamed of my dress, and the more so as the young foplings would put their glasses to their eyes, and look at me as if I were a monster. But supported as I was by the fair sex, I cared little for them. The ladies vowed that I was charming, and paid me much courtesy; indeed my vanity more than once made me suspect that I was something more than a mere favourite with one or two of them, one especially, a buxom young person, and very coquettish, who told me, as we were looking out of the bay-window of the withdrawing-room, that since I could be so secret with respect to what took place between the Negress queen and myself, I must be sure to command the good-will and favour of the ladies, who always admired discretion in so young and so handsome a man. But I was not to be seduced by this flattery, for somehow or another I had ever before me the French lady, and her conduct to me; and I had almost a dislike, or I should rather say I had imbibed an indifference, for the sex.

This admission into good society did, however, have one effect upon me; it made me more particular in my dress, and all my wages were employed in the decoration of my person. At that time you may recollect, Madam, there were but two styles of dress among the seamen; one was that worn by those who sailed in the northern seas, and the other by those who navigated in the tropical countries, both suitable to the climates. The first was the jacket, woollen frock, breeches, and petticoat of canvass over all, with worsted stockings, shoes, and buckles, and usually a cap of skin upon the head; the other a light short jacket, with hanging buttons, red sash, trowsers, and neat shoes and buckles, with a small embroidered cap with falling crown, or a hat and feather. It was this last which I had always worn, having been continually in warm climates, and my hair was dressed in its natural ringlets instead of a wig, which I was never partial to, although very common among seamen; my ears were pierced, and I wore long gold earrings, as well as gilt buckles in my shoes; and, by degrees, I not only improved my dress so as to make it very handsome in materials, but my manners were also very much altered for the better.

I had been at Liverpool about two months, waiting for the ship to unload and take in cargo for another voyage, when a privateer belonging to the same owner came into port with four prizes of considerable value; and the day afterwards I was invited by the owner to meet the captain who commanded the privateer.

He was a very different looking person from Captain Weatherall, who was a stout, strong-limbed man, with a weather-beaten countenance. He, on the contrary, was a young man of about twenty-six, very slight in person, with a dark complexion, hair and eyes jet black. I should have called him a very handsome Jew—for he bore that cast of countenance, and I afterwards discovered that he was of that origin, although I cannot say that he ever followed the observances of that remarkable people. He was handsomely dressed, wearing his hair slightly powdered, a laced coat and waistcoat, blue sash and trowsers, with silver-mounted pistols and dagger in his belt, and a smart hanger by his side. He had several diamond rings on his finger, and carried a small clouded cane. Altogether, I had never fallen in with so smart and prepossessing a personage, and should have taken him for one of the gentlemen commanding the king's ships, rather than the captain of a Liverpool privateer. He talked well and fluently, and with an air of command and decision, taking the lead in the company, although it might have been considered that he was not by any means the principal person in it. The owner, during the evening, informed me that he was a first-rate officer, of great personal courage, and that he had made a great deal of money, which he had squandered away almost as fast as he received it.

With this person, whose name was Captain Levee, (an alteration, I suspect, from Levi,) I was much pleased; and as I found that he did not appear to despise my acquaintance, I took much pains to please him, and we were becoming very intimate, when my ship was ready to sail. I now found that I was promoted to the office of first mate, which gave me great satisfaction.

We sailed with an assorted cargo, but very light, and nothing of consequence occurred during our passage out. We made good traffic on the coast as we ran down it, receiving ivory, gold-dust, and wax, in exchange for our printed cottons and hardware. After being six weeks on the coast, we put into Senegal to dispose of the remainder of our cargo; which we soon did to the governor, who gave us a fair exchange, although by no means so profitable a barter as what we had made on the coast; but that we did not expect for what might be called the refuse of our cargo. The captain was much pleased, as he knew the owner would be satisfied with him, and, moreover, he had himself a venture in the cargo; and we had just received the remainder of the ivory from the governor's stores, and had only to get on board a sufficiency of provisions and water for our homeward voyage, when a circumstance took place which I must now relate.

Our crew consisted of the captain, and myself, as first mate, the second mate, and twelve seamen, four of which were those who had been taken prisoners with me, and had been released, as I have related, in our previous voyage. These four men were very much attached to me, I believe chiefly from my kindness to them when I was a slave to the queen Whyna, as I always procured for them everything which I could, and, through the exertions of my mistress, had them plentifully supplied with provisions from the king's table. The second mate and other eight men we had shipped at Liverpool. They were fine, stout fellows, but appeared to be loose characters, but that we did not discover till after we had sailed. There was anchored with us at Senegal a low black brig, employed in the slave-trade, which had made the bay at the same time that we did; and to their great surprise—for she was considered a very fast sailer—she was beaten at all points by our ship, which was considered the fastest vessel out of Liverpool. The crew of the slaver were numerous, and as bloodthirsty a set of looking fellows as ever I fell in with. Their boat was continually alongside of our vessel, and I perceived that their visits were made to the eight men whom we had shipped at Liverpool, and that they did not appear inclined to be at all intimate with the rest of the crew. This roused my suspicions, although I said nothing; but I watched them very closely. One forenoon, as I was standing at the foot of the companion-ladder, concealed by the booby-hatch from the sight of those on deck, I heard our men talking over the side, and at last, as I remained concealed, that I might overhear the conversation, one of the slaver's men from the boat said, "To-night, at eight o'clock, we will come to arrange the whole business." The boat then shoved off, and pulled for the brig.

Now, it was the custom of the captain to go on shore every evening to drink sangaree and smoke with the governor, and very often I went with him, leaving the ship in charge of the second mate. It had been my intention, and I had stated as much to the second mate, to go this evening, as it was the last but one that we should remain at Senegal; but from what I overheard I made up my mind that I would not go. About an hour before sunset, I complained of headache and sickness, and sat down under the awning over the after part of the quarter-deck. When the captain came up to go on shore, he asked me if I was ready, but I made no answer, only put my hand to my head.

The captain, supposing that I was about to be attacked by the fever of the country, was much concerned, and desired the second mate to help him to take me down to the state-room, and then went on shore; the boat was, as usual, pulled by the four men who were prisoners with me, and whom the captain found he could trust on shore better than the others belonging to the crew, who would indulge in liquor whenever they had an opportunity. I remained in my bed-place till it was nearly eight o'clock, and then crept softly up the companion-hatch to ascertain who was on deck.

The men were all below in the fore-peak at their suppers, and as I had before observed that their conferences were held on the forecastle, I went forward, and covered myself up with a part of the main-topsail, which the men had been repairing during the day. From this position I could hear all that passed, whether they went down into the fore-peak, or remained to converse on the forecastle. About ten minutes afterwards I heard the boat grate against the ship's side, and the men of the slaver mount on the deck.

"All right?" inquired one of the slavers.

"Yes," replied our second mate; "skipper and his men are on shore, and the first mate taken with the fever."

"All the better," replied another; "one less to handle. And now, my lads, let's to business, and have everything settled to-night, so that we may not be seen together any more till the work is done."

They then commenced a consultation, by which I found it was arranged that our ship was to be boarded and taken possession of as soon as she was a few miles out of the bay, for they dared not attack us while we were at anchor close to the fort; but the second mate and eight men belonging to us were to pretend to make resistance until beaten down below, and when the vessel was in their power, the captain, I, and the other four men who were ashore in the boat, were to be silenced for ever. After which there came on a discussion as to what was to be done with the cargo, which was very valuable, and how the money was to be shared out when the cargo was sold. Then they settled who were to be officers on board of the ship, which there is no doubt they intended to make a pirate vessel. I also discovered that, if they succeeded, it was their intention to kill their own captain and such men of the slaver who would not join them, and scuttle their own vessel, which was a very old one.

The consultation ended by a solemn and most villainous oath being administered to every man as to secrecy and fidelity, after which the men of the slaver went into their boat, and pulled to their own vessel. The second mate and our men remained on deck about a quarter of an hour, and then all descended by the ladder to the fore-peak, and turned into their hammocks.

As soon as I thought I could do so with safety, I came out of my lurking-place, and retreated to the state-room. It was fortunate that I did, for a minute afterwards I heard a man on deck, and the second mate came down the companion-hatch, and inquired whether I wanted anything. I told him no; that I was very ill, and only hoped to be able to go to sleep, and asked him if the captain had returned. He replied that he had not, and then went away. As soon as I was left to myself, I began to consider what would be best to be done. I knew the captain to be a very timorous man, and I was afraid to trust him with the secret, as I thought he would be certain to let the men know by his conduct that they were discovered and their plans known. The four men who were prisoners with me I knew that I could confide in. This was the Tuesday night, and we proposed sailing on the Thursday. Now we had no means of defence on board, except one small gun, which was honey-combed and nearly useless. It did very well to make a signal with, but had it been loaded with ball, I believe it would have burst immediately. It is true that we had muskets and cutlasses, but what use would they have been against such a force as would be opposed, and two-thirds of our men mutineers. Of course we must have been immediately overpowered.

That the slavers intended to take possession of their own vessel before they took ours, I had no doubt. It is true that we outsailed them when we had a breeze, but the bay was usually becalmed, and it was not till a vessel had got well into the offing that she obtained a breeze, and there was no doubt but that they would take the opportunity of boarding us when we were moving slowly through the water, and a boat might easily come up with us. The slaver had stated his intention of sailing immediately to procure her cargo elsewhere, and if she got under weigh at the same time that we did, no suspicion would be created. To apply for protection to the governor would be useless—he could not protect us after we were clear of the bay. Indeed, if it were known that we had so done, it would probably only precipitate the affair, and we should be taken possession of while at anchor, for the shot from the fort would hardly reach us. It was, therefore, only by stratagem that we could escape from the clutches of these miscreants. Again, allowing that we were to get clear of the slavers, we were still in an awkward position, for, supposing the captain to be of any use, we should still only be six men against nine, and we might be overpowered by our own crew, who were determined and powerful men.

All night I lay on my bed reflecting upon what ought to be done, and at last I made up my mind.

The next morning I went on deck, complaining very much, but stating that the fever had left me. The long-boat was sent on shore for more water, and I took care that the second mate and eight men should be those selected for the service. As soon as they had shoved off I called the other four men on the forecastle, and told them what I had overheard. They were very much astonished, for they had had no idea that there was anything of the kind going forward. I imparted to them all my plans, and they agreed to support me in everything—indeed, they were all brave men, and would have, if I had acceded to it, attempted to master and overpower the second mate and the others, and make sail in the night; but this I would not permit, as there was a great risk. They perfectly agreed with me that, it was no use acquainting the captain, and that all we had to do was to get rid of these men, and carry the vessel borne how we could. How that was to be done was the point at issue. One thing was certain, that it was necessary to leave the bay that night, or it would be too late. Fortunately, there was always a light breeze during the night, and the nights were dark, for there was no moon till three o'clock in the morning, by which time we could have gained the offing, and then we might laugh at the slaver, as we were lighter in our heels. The boat came off with the water about noon, and the men went to dinner. The captain had agreed to dine with the governor, and I had been asked to accompany him. It was to be our farewell dinner, as we were to sail the next morning. I had been cogitating a long while to find out how to get rid of these fellows, when at last I determined that I would go on shore with the captain, and propose a plan to the governor. His knowledge of what was about to be attempted could do no harm, and I thought he would help us; so I went into the boat, and when we landed I told the men what I intended to do. As soon as I arrived at the governor's, I took an opportunity, while the captain was reading a book, to request a few moments' conversation, and I then informed the governor of the conspiracy which was afloat, and when I had so done, I pointed out to him the propriety of saying nothing to the captain until all was safe, and proposed my plan to him, which he immediately acceded to. When he returned to where the captain was still reading, he told him that he had a quantity of gold-dust and other valuables, which he wished to send to England by his ship; but that he did not wish to do it openly, as it was supposed that he did not traffic, and that if the captain would send his long-boat on shore after dark, he would send all the articles on board, with instructions to whom they were to be consigned on our arrival. The captain of course consented. We bade the governor farewell about half an hour before dark, and returned on board. After I had been a few minutes on deck, I sent for the second mate, and told him as a secret what the governor proposed to do, and that he would be required to land after dark for the goods, telling him that there was a very large quantity of gold-dust, and that he must be very careful. I knew that this intelligence would please him, as it would add to their plunder when they seized the vessel; and I told him that as we sailed at daylight, he must lose no time, but be on board again as soon as he could, that we might hoist in the long-boat. About eight o'clock in the evening, the boat, with him and the eight men, went on shore. The governor had promised to detain them, and ply them with liquor, till we had time to get safe off. As soon as they were out of sight and hearing, we prepared everything for getting under weigh. The captain had gone to his cabin, but was not in bed. I went down to him, and told him I should remain up till the boat returned, and see that all was right; and that in the mean time I would get everything ready for weighing the next morning, and that he might just as well go to bed now, and I would call him to relieve me at daylight. To this arrangement he consented; and in half an hour I perceived that his candle was out, and that he had retired. Being now so dark that we could not perceive the slaver, which lay about three cables' length from us, it was fairly to be argued that she could not see us; I therefore went forward and slipped the cable without noise, and sent men up aloft to loose the sails. There was a light breeze, sufficient to carry us about two knots through the water, and we knew that it would rather increase than diminish. In half an hour, weak-handed as we were, we were under sail, everything being done without a word being spoken, and with the utmost precaution. You may imagine how rejoiced we all were when we found that we had manoeuvred so well; notwithstanding, we kept a sharp look-out, to see if the slaver had perceived our motions, and had followed us; and the fear of such being the case kept us under alarm till near daylight, when the breeze blew strong, and we felt that we had nothing more to dread. As the day broke, we found that we were four or five leagues from the anchorage, and could not see the lower masts of the slaver, which still remained where we had left her.

Satisfied that we were secure, I then went down to the captain, and, as he lay in bed, made him acquainted with all that had passed. He appeared as if awakened from a dream, rose without making any reply, and hastened on deck. When he found out that we were under weigh, and so far from the land, he exclaimed:

"It must all be true; but how shall we be able to take the ship home with so few hands?"

I replied, that I had no fears on that score, and that I would answer for bringing the vessel safe to Liverpool.

"But," he said at last, "how is it that I was not informed of all this? I might have made some arrangements with the men."

"Yes, Sir," I replied, "but if you had attempted to do so, the vessel would have been taken immediately."

"But why was I not acquainted with it, I want to know?" he said again.

I had by this time made up my mind to the answer I should give him; so I said, "Because it would have placed a serious responsibility on your shoulders, if, as captain of this vessel, you had sailed to England with such a valuable cargo and so few hands. The governor and I, therefore, thought it better that you should not be placed in such an awkward position, and therefore we considered it right not to say a word to you about it. Now, if anything goes wrong, it will be my fault, and not yours, and the owner cannot blame you." When I had said this, the captain was silent for a minute or two, and then said:

"Well, I believe it is all for the best, and I thank you and the governor too."

Having got over this little difficulty, I did not care. We made all sail, and steered homewards; and, after a rapid passage, during which we were on deck day and night, we arrived, very much fatigued, at Liverpool. Of course the captain communicated what had occurred to the owner, who immediately sent for me, and having heard my version of the story, expressed his acknowledgment for the preservation of the vessel; and to prove his sincerity, he presented me with fifty guineas for myself, and ten for each of the men. The cargo was soon landed, and I was again at liberty. I found Captain Levee in port; he had just returned from another cruise, and had taken a rich prize. He met me with the same cordiality as before; and having asked me for a recital of what had occurred at Senegal, of which he had heard something from the owner, as soon as I had finished, he said:

"You are a lad after my own heart, and I wish we were sailing together. I want a first-lieutenant like you, and if you will go with me, say the word, and it will be hard but I will have you."

I replied that I was not very anxious to be in a privateer again; and this brought on a discourse upon what occurred when I was in the Revenge with Captain Weatherall.

"Well," he said at last, "all this makes me more anxious to have you. I like fair fighting, and hate buccaneering like yourself; however, we will talk of it another time. I am about to start for London. What do you say, will you join me, and we will have some sport? With plenty of money, you may do anything in London."

"Yes," I replied, "but I have not plenty of money."

"That shall make no difference; money is of no use but to spend it, that I know of," replied Captain Levee. "I have plenty for both of us, and my purse is at your service; help yourself as you please, without counting, for I shall be your enemy if you offer to return it. That's settled; the horses are all ready, and we will start on Wednesday. How will you dress? I think it might be better to alter your costume, now you are going to London. You'll make a pretty fellow, dress how you will."

"Before I give you an answer to all your kind proposals, I must speak to the owner, Captain Levee."

"Of course you must; shall we go there now?"

"Willingly," I replied. And we accordingly set off. Captain Levee introduced the subject as soon as we arrived at the counting-house, stating that he wanted me to be first-lieutenant of the privateer, and that I was going to London with him, if he had no objection.

"As for going to London with you for five or six weeks, Captain Levee, there can be no objection to that," replied the owner; "but as for being your first-lieutenant, that is another question. I have a vessel now fitting out, and intended to offer the command of it to Mr Elrington. I do so now at once, and he must decide whether he prefers being under your orders to commanding a vessel of his own."

"I will decide that for him," replied Captain Levee. "He must command his own vessel; it would be no friendship on my part to stand in the way of his advancement. I only hope, if she is a privateer, that we may cruise together."

"I cannot reply to that latter question," replied the owner. "Her destination is uncertain; but the command of her is now offered to Mr Elrington, if he will accept of it before his trip to the metropolis."

I replied that I should with pleasure, and returned the owner many thanks for his kindness; and, after a few minutes' more conversation, we took our leave.

"Now I should advise you," said Captain Levee, as we walked towards his lodgings, "to dress as a captain of a vessel of war, much in the style that I do. You are a captain, and have a right so to do. Come with me, and let me fit you out."

I agreed with Captain Levee that I could not do better; so we went and ordered my suits of clothes, and purchased the other articles which I required. Captain Levee would have paid for them, but I had money sufficient, and would not permit him; indeed with my pay and present of fifty guineas I had upwards of seventy guineas in my purse, and did not disburse more than fifty in my accoutrements, although my pistols and hanger were very handsome.

We did not start until three days after the time proposed, when I found at daylight two stout well-bred horses at the door; one for Captain Levee, and the other for me. We were attended by two serving-men belonging to the crew of the privateer commanded by Captain Levee—powerful, fierce-looking, and determined men, armed to the teeth, and mounted upon strong jades. One carried the valise of Captain Levee, which was heavy with gold. The other had charge of mine, which was much lighter, as you may suppose. We travelled for three days without any interruption, making about thirty miles a day, and stopping at the hostelries to sleep every night. On the fourth day we had a slight affair, for as we were mounting a hill towards the evening, we found our passage barred by five fellows with crape masks, who told us to stand and deliver.

"We will," replied Captain Levee, firing his pistol, and reining up his horse at the same time. The ball struck the man, who fell back on the crupper, while the others rushed forward. My pistols were all ready, and I fired at the one who spurred his horse upon me, but the horse rearing up saved his master, the ball passing through the head of the animal, who fell dead, holding his rider a prisoner by the thigh, which was underneath his body. Our two men had come forward and ranged alongside of us at the first attack, but now that two had fallen, the others finding themselves in a minority, after exchanging shots, turned their horses' heads and galloped away. We would have pursued them, but Captain Levee said it was better not, as there might be more of the gang near, and by pursuing them we might separate and be cut off in detail.

"What shall we do with these fellows?" asked our men of Captain Levee.

"Leave them to get off how they can," replied Captain Levee. "I will not be stopped on my journey by such a matter as this. I dare say they don't deserve hanging more than half the people we meet. Let us push on and get into quarters for the night. After all, Mr Elrington," said Captain Levee to me, as we were setting off, "it's only a little land privateering, and we must not be too hard upon them."

I confess, Madam, when I recalled all that I had witnessed on board of the Revenge, that I agreed with Captain Levee, that these highwaymen were not worse than ourselves.

No other adventure occurred during our journey, and when we arrived in London we directed our horses' steps to a fashionable tavern in Saint Paul's, and took possession of apartments, and as Captain Levee was well-known, we were cordially greeted and well attended. The tavern was in great repute, and resorted to by all the wits and gay men of the day, and I soon found myself on intimate terms with a numerous set of dashing blades full of life and jollity, and spending their money like princes; but it was a life of sad intemperance, and my head ached every morning from the excess of the night before, and in our excursions in the evenings we were continually in broils and disturbances, and many a broken head, nay, sometimes a severe wound, was given and received. After the first fortnight, I felt weary of this continual dissipation, and as I was dressing a sword-cut which Captain Levee had received in an affray, I one morning told him so.

"I agree with you," he replied, "that it is all very foolish and discreditable, but if we live with the gay and pretty fellows, we must do as they do. Besides, how could I get rid of my money, which burns in my pocket, if I did not spend as much in one day as would suffice for three weeks?"

"Still I would rather dress a wound gained in an honourable contest with the enemy than one received in a night brawl, and I would rather see you commanding your men in action than reeling with other drunkards in search of a quarrel in the streets."

"I feel that it is beneath me, and I'm sure that it's beneath you. You are a Mentor without a beard," replied Captain Levee. "But still it requires no beard to discover that I have made an ass of myself. Now, what do you say, shall we take lodgings and live more reputably, for while in this tavern we never shall be able to do so?"

"I should prefer it, to tell you the honest truth," I replied, "for I have no pleasure in our present life."

"Be it so, then," he replied. "I will tell them that I take lodgings, that I may be near to a fair lady. That will be a good and sufficient excuse."

The next day we secured lodgings to our satisfaction, and removed into them, leaving our horses and men at the tavern. We boarded with the family, and as there were others who did the same, we had a very pleasant society, especially as there were many of the other sex among the boarders. The first day that we sat down to dinner, I found myself by the side of a young man of pleasing manners, although with much of the coxcomb in his apparel. His dress was very gay and very expensive, and he wore a diamond-hilted sword and diamond buckles—at least so they appeared to me, as I was not sufficient connoisseur to distinguish the brilliant from the paste. He was very affable and talkative, and before dinner was over gave me the history of many of the people present.

"Who is the dame in the blue stomacher?" I inquired.

"You mean the prettiest of the two, I suppose," he replied, "that one with the patches under the eye? She is a widow, having just buried an old man of sixty, to whom she was sacrificed by her mother. But although the old fellow was as rich as a Jew, he found such fault with the lady's conduct that he left all his money away from her. This is not generally known, and she takes care to conceal it, for she is anxious to make another match, and she will succeed if her funds, which are not *very* great, enable her to carry on the game a little longer. I was nearly taken in myself, but an intimacy with her cousin, who hates her, gave me a knowledge of the truth. She still keeps her carriage, and appears to be rolling in wealth, but she has sold her diamonds and wears paste. And that plain young person on the other side of her has money, and knows the value of it. She requires rent-roll for rent-roll, and instead of referring you to her father and mother, the little minx refers you to her lawyer and man of business. Ugly as she is, I would have sacrificed myself; but she treated me in that way, and upon my soul I was not very sorry for it, for she is dear at any price, and I have since rejoiced at my want of success."

"Who is that elderly gentleman with such snow-white hair?" I inquired.

"That," replied my companion, "nobody exactly knows, but I have my idea. I think," said he, lowering his voice to a whisper, "that he is a Catholic priest, or a Jesuit, perhaps, and a partisan of the house of

Stuart. I have my reasons for supposing so, and this I am sure of, which is, that he is closely watched by the emissaries of government."

You may remember, Madam, how at that time the country was disturbed by the landing of the Pretender in the summer of the year before, and the great successes which he had met with, and that the Duke of Cumberland had returned from the army in the Low Countries, and had marched to Scotland.

"Has there been any intelligence from Scotland relative to the movements of the armies?" I inquired.

"We have heard that the Pretender had abandoned the siege of Fort William, but nothing more; and how far the report is true, it is hard to say. You military men must naturally have a war one way or the other," said my companion, in a careless manner.

"As to the fighting part of the question," I replied, "I should feel it a matter of great indifference which side I fought for, as the claim of both parties is a matter of mere opinion."

"Indeed," he said; "and what may be your opinion?"

"I have none. I think the claims of both parties equal. The house of Stuart lost the throne of England on account of its religion—that of Hanover has been called to the throne for the same cause. The adherents of both are numerous at the present moment; and it does not follow, because the house of Hanover has the strongest party, that the house of Stuart should not uphold its cause while there is a chance of success."

"That is true; but if you were to be obliged to take one side or the other, which would it be by preference?"

"Certainly I would support the Protestant religion in preference to the Catholic. I am a Protestant, and that is reason enough."

"I agree with you," replied my companion. "Is your brave friend of the same opinion?"

"I really never put the question to him, but I think I may safely answer that he is."

It was fortunate, Madam, that I replied as I did, for I afterwards discovered that this precious gossiping young man, with his rings and ribbons, was no other than a government spy, on the look-out for malcontents. Certainly his disguise was good, for I never should have imagined it from his foppish exterior and mincing manners.

We passed our time much more to my satisfaction now than we did before, escorting the ladies to the theatre and to Ranelagh, and the freedom with which Captain Levee (and I may say I also) spent his money, soon gave us a passport to good society. About a fortnight afterwards, the news arrived of the battle of Culloden, and great rejoicings were made. My foppish friend remarked to me:—

"Yes, now that the hopes of the Pretender are blasted, and the Hanoverian succession secured, there are plenty who pretend to rejoice, and be excessively loyal, who, if the truth were known, ought to be quartered as traitors."

And I must observe, that the day before the news of the battle, the old gentleman with the snow-white hair was arrested and sent to the Tower, and he afterwards suffered for high treason.

But letters from the owner, saying that the presence of both of us was immediately required, broke off this pleasant London party. Indeed, the bag of gold was running very low, and this, combined with the owner's letter, occasioned our breaking up three days afterwards. We took leave of the company at the lodgings, and there was a tender parting with one or two buxom young women; after which we again mounted our steeds and set off for Liverpool, where we arrived without any adventure worthy of narration.

# Chapter Nine.

**I am put in command of the Sparrow-Hawk—Am directed to take four Jacobite Gentlemen secretly on board—Run with them to Bordeaux—Land them in safety—Dine with the Governor—Meet with the Widow of the French Gentleman I had unfortunately killed—Am insulted by her second Husband—Agree to fight with him—Sail down the River and prepare for Action.**

On our arrival, Captain Levee and I, as soon as we had got rid of the dust of travel, called upon the owner, who informed us that all the alterations in Captain Levee's vessel, which was a large lugger of fourteen guns and a hundred and twenty men, were complete, and that my vessel was also ready for me, and manned; but that I had better go on board and see if anything else was required, or if there was any alteration that I would propose. Captain Levee and I immediately went down to the wharf, alongside of which my vessel lay, that we might examine her now that she was fitted out as a vessel of war.

She had been a schooner in the Spanish trade, and had been captured by Captain Levee, who had taken her out from under a battery as she lay at anchor, having just made her port from a voyage from South America, being at that time laden with copper and cochineal,—a most valuable prize she had proved,—and as she was found to be a surprising fast sailer, the owner had resolved to fit her out as a privateer.

She was not a large vessel, being of about a hundred and sixty tons, but she was very beautifully built. She was now armed with eight brass guns, of a calibre of six pounds each, four howitzers aft, and two cohorns on the taffrail.

"You have a very sweet little craft here, Elrington," said Captain Levee, after he had walked all over her, and examined her below and aloft. "She will sail better than before, I should think, for she then had a very full cargo, and now her top hamper is a mere nothing. Did the owner say how many men you had?"

"Fifty-four is, I believe, to be our full complement," I replied, "and I should think quite enough."

"Yes, if they are good men and true. You may do a great deal with this vessel, for you see she draws so little water, that you may run in where

I dare not venture. Come, we will now return to our lodgings, pack up, and each go on board of our vessels. We have had play enough, now to work again, and in good earnest."

"I was about to propose it myself," I replied, "for with a new vessel, officers and men not known to me, the sooner I am on board and with them the better. It will take some time to get everything and everybody in their places."

"Spoken like a man who understands his business," replied Captain Levee. "I wonder whether we shall be sent out together?"

"I can only say that I hope so," I replied, "as I should profit much by your experience, and hope to prove to you that, if necessary, I shall not be a bad second."

And as I made this reply, we arrived at the house where we had lodged.

Captain Levee was a man who, when once he had decided, was as rapid as lightning in execution. He sent for a dealer in horses, concluded a bargain with him in five minutes, paid his lodgings and all demands upon him, and before noon we were both on board of our respective vessels. But, previous to the seamen coming up for our boxes, I observed to him, "I should wish, Levee, that you would let me know, if it is only at a rough guess, what sum I may be indebted to you; as I may be fortunate, and if so, it will be but fair to repay you the money, although your kindness I cannot so easily return."

"I'll tell you exactly," said Levee. "If I take no prizes this cruise, and you do make money, why then we will, on our return, have another frolic somewhere, and you shall stand treat. That will make us all square, if I am not fortunate; but if I am, I consider your pleasant company to have more than repaid me for any little expense I may have incurred."

"You are very kind to say that," I replied; "but I hope you will be fortunate, and not have to depend upon me."

"I hope so too," he replied, laughing. "If we come back safe and sound, we will take a trip to Bath—I am anxious to see the place."

I mention this conversation, Madam, that I may make you acquainted with the character of Captain Levee, and prove to you how worthy a man I had as a companion.

It required about ten days to complete my little schooner with everything that I considered requisite, and the politeness of the owner was extremely gratifying. We were, however, but just complete, when the owner sent for me in a great hurry, and having taken me into a back room next to the counting-house, he locked the door, and said—

"Captain Elrington, I have been offered a large sum to do a service to some unfortunate people; but it is an affair which, for our own sakes, will demand the utmost secrecy: indeed, you will risk more than I shall; but at the same time I trust you will not refuse to perform the service, as I shall lose a considerable advantage. If you will undertake it, I shall not be ungrateful."

I replied that I was bound to him by many acts of kindness, and that he might confide in my gratitude.

"Well, then," he replied, lowering his voice, "the fact is this; four of the Jacobite party, who are hotly pursued, and for whose heads a large reward is offered, have contrived to escape to this port, and are here concealed by their friends, who have applied to me to land them at some port in France."

"I understand," I replied; "I will cheerfully execute the commission."

"I thank you, Captain Elrington; I expected no other answer from you. I would not put them on board Captain Levee's vessel for many reasons; but, at the same time, he knows that he is to sail to-morrow, and he shall wait for you and keep company with you till you have landed them; after which you may concert your own measures with him, and decide whether you cruise together or separate."

"Captain Levee will of course know that I have them on board?"

"Certainly; but it is to conceal these people from others in his ship, and not from him, that they are put on board of your vessel. At the same time, I confess I have my private reasons as well, which I do not wish to make known. You can sail to-morrow?"

"I can sail to-night, if you wish," I replied.

"No; to-morrow night will be the time that I have fixed."

"At what time will they come on board?"

"I cannot reply to that till to-morrow. The fact is, that the government people are on a hot scent; and there is a vessel of war in the offing, I am told, ready to board anything and everything which comes out. Captain Levee will sail to-morrow morning, and will in all probability be examined by the government vessel, which is, I understand, a most rapid sailer."

"Will he submit to it?"

"Yes, he must; and I have given him positive orders not to make the least attempt to evade her or prevent a search. He will then run to Holyhead, and lay-to there for you to join him, and you will proceed together to the port which the people taken on board shall direct, for that is a part of the agreement they have made with me."

"Then of course I am to evade the king's vessel?"

"Certainly; and I have no doubt but that you will be able so to do. Your vessel is so fleet, that there will be little difficulty: at all events, you will do your best: but recollect, that although you must make every attempt to escape, you must not make any attempt at resistance—indeed, that would be useless against a vessel of such force. Should you be in a position which might enable them to board you, you must find some safe hiding-place for your passengers; for I hardly need say, that if taken with them on board, the vessel will be confiscated, and you will run some danger of your life. I have nothing more to say to you just now, except that you may give out that Captain Levee sails to-morrow, and that you are to follow him in ten days. Your powder is on board?"

"Yes; I got it on board as soon as we hauled out in the stream."

"Well, then, you will call here to-morrow morning about eleven o'clock, not before, and (I hardly need repeat it), but I again say—secrecy,—as you value your life."

As soon as I had left the owner, I went down to the wharf, stepped into the boat, and went on board Captain Levee's vessel, which, I have omitted to state, was named the Arrow. I found him on board, and very busy getting ready for sea.

"So you are off to-morrow, Levee?" said I, before all the people on the deck.

"Yes," he replied.

"I wish I was, too; but I am to remain ten days longer, I find."

"I was in hopes we should have cruised together," replied Captain Levee; "but we must do as our owner wishes. What detains you?—I thought you were ready."

"I thought so too," I replied; "but we find that the head of the mainmast is sprung, and we must have a new one. I have just come from the owner's, and must set to work at once, and get ready for shifting our mast. So, fare you well, if I do not see you before you sail."

"I am to see the owner to-night," replied Levee. "Shall we not meet then, and take a parting glass?"

"I fear not, but I will come if I can," I replied; "if not, success to the Arrow!"

"And success to the Sparrow-Hawk!" replied Levee, "and God bless you, my good fellow."

I shook hands with my kind friend, and went over the side of the lugger into my boat, and then pulled for my own vessel. As soon as I got on board, I sent for officers and men, and said to them—

"We are to shift our mainmast for one that is three feet longer, and must work hard, that we may be able to sail as soon as possible. I cannot allow any of you to go on shore till the work is finished; when it is done, you will have leave as before till we sail."

That afternoon I sent down the topsail-yard and topmast, unbent the mainsail, main-topsail, and gaff—sent down the topmast and running-rigging on deck—cast loose the lanyards of the lower rigging, and quite dismantled the mainmast, so as to make it appear as if we were about to haul to the wharf and take it out. The men all remained on board, expecting that we should shift our berth the next day.

On the following morning I laid out a warp to the wharf; as if intending to haul in; and at the time appointed, I went on shore to the owner, and told him what I had done.

"But," he said, "I find that you will have to sail this night as soon as it is dark. How will you get ready?"

I replied that at nightfall I would immediately replace everything, and in an hour would be ready for sea.

"If such be the case, you have done well, Mr Elrington, and I thank you for your zeal on my behalf, which I shall not forget. Everything has been arranged, and you must come up here with some of your seamen as soon as you are ready to sail. Your men, or rather four of them, must remain in the house. The four gentlemen who are to be embarked will be dressed in seamen's attire, and will carry down their boxes and trunks as if they were your men taking your things on board. You will then remain a little distance from the wharf in the boat till your own men come down, and if there is no discovery you will take them on board with you; if, on the contrary, there is any suspicion, and the officers of the government are on the watch, and stop your men, you will then push off with the passengers, slip your cable if it is necessary, and make all sail for Holyhead, where you will fall in with the Arrow, which will be waiting there for you. Is the Arrow still in sight?"

"No," I replied; "she was out of sight more than an hour ago, and from our masthead we could see the topgallant sails of the vessel of war bearing N.N.W."

"Keep a look-out upon her, and see how she bears at dark," replied the owner, "for you must not fall in with her if possible. I think you had better return on board now, that you may keep your people quiet."

When I arrived on board the schooner, I told my officers that I did not think that we should shift the mast as proposed, and that everything must be got ready for refitting. I did not choose to say more, but I added that I was to go on shore in the evening to smoke a pipe with the owner, and then I should know for certain. I employed the men during the whole of the day in doing everything in preparation which could be done without exciting suspicion; and as soon as it was dark I called the men aft, and told them that I thought it was very likely, from the Arrow not having made her appearance, that we might be sent to join her immediately, and that I wished them to rig the mainmast, and make everything ready for an immediate start, promising them to serve out some liquor if they worked well. This was sufficient, and in little more than an hour the mast was secured, the rigging all complete, and the sails ready for bending. I then ordered the boat to be manned, and telling the officers that they were to bend the sails, and have everything ready for weighing on my return on board, which would be in an hour, or thereabouts, I pulled on shore, and went up to the owner's, taking four men with me, and leaving three men in the boat. I ordered these three men to remain till the others came down with my trunks and effects, and not, to leave the boat on any consideration.

When I arrived at the owner's, I told him what I had done, and he commended my arrangements. In the back room I found four gentlemen dressed in seamen's clothing, and as there was no time to be lost, they immediately shouldered the trunks and valises; desiring my own men to remain with the owner to bring down anything that he might wish to send on board, I left them in the counting-house. The gentlemen followed me with their loads down to the boat, and when I got there the men told me that some people had come down and asked whose boat it was, and why they were lying there, and that they had told the people that the captain had taken four men with him to bring down his things, and that they were waiting for him; so it was lucky that I said to my men what I did.

We hastened to put the trunks into the boat, and to get in ourselves after we had received this intelligence, and then I shoved off from the wharf, and laid about a stone's throw distant for my other men. At last we heard them coming down, and shortly afterwards we perceived that they were stopped by other people, and in altercation with them. I knew then that the officers were on the alert, and would discover the stratagem, and therefore desired my men and the gentlemen, who had each taken an oar in readiness, to give way and pull for the schooner. As we did so, the king's officers on search who had stopped my four men came down to the wharf and ordered us to come back, but we made no reply. As soon as we were alongside, we hoisted the things out of the boat, veered her astern by a tow-rope, slipped the cable, and made sail. Fortunately it was very dark, and we were very alert in our movements. We could perceive lights at the wharf as we sailed out of the river, and it was clear that we had had a narrow escape; but I felt no alarm on account of the owner, as I knew that although they might suspect, they could prove nothing. When about three miles out we hove-to, hoisted in the boat, and shaped our course.

All I had now to fear was the falling in with the ship of war in the offing, and I placed men to keep a sharp look-out in every direction, and told the officers that it was necessary that we should avoid her. When last seen, about an hour before dark, she was well to windward, and as the wind was from the northward, she would probably sail faster than we could, as a schooner does not sail so well free as on a wind. We had run out about four hours, and were steering our course for Holyhead, when suddenly we perceived the ship of war close to us, and to leeward. She had been lying with her mainsail to the mast, but she evidently had made us out, for she filled and set top-gallant sails.

I immediately hauled my wind, and as soon as she had way, she tacked and followed in pursuit, being then right astern of us, about half a mile off. It was very dark, and I knew that as our sails were set, and we bore from her, it would be difficult for her to keep us in sight, as we only presented what we call the feather-edge of our sails to her. I therefore steered on under all sail, and, finding that the schooner weathered on her, I kept her away a little, so as to retain the same bearings, and to leave her faster.

In an hour we could not make out the ship, and were therefore certain that she could not see us; so as I wanted to get clear of her, and be at Holyhead as soon as possible, I lowered down all the sails and put my helm up, so as to cross her and run to leeward under bare poles, while she continued her windward chase. This stratagem answered, and we saw no more of her; for, two hours afterwards, we fell in with the Arrow, and, hailing her, we both made sail down the Bristol Channel as fast as we could, and at daybreak there was no vessel in sight, and of course we had nothing more to fear from the Liverpool cruiser.

As we now sailed rapidly along in company, with the wind on our quarter, it was high time for me to look to my passengers, who had remained on deck in perfect silence from the time that they had come on board. I therefore went up to them, and apologised for not having as yet paid them that attention that I should have wished to have done under other circumstances.

"Captain," replied the oldest of them, with a courteous salute, "you have paid us every attention; you have been extremely active in saving our lives, and we return you our sincere thanks."

"Yes, indeed," replied a young and handsome man who stood next him, "Mr Elrington has saved us from the toils of our enemies; but now that we are in no fear from that quarter, I must tell him that we have hardly had a mouthful of food for twenty-four hours, and if he wishes to save our lives a second time, it will be by ordering a good breakfast to be prepared for us."

"Campbell speaks the truth, my dear Sir," said the one who had first spoken. "We have lately gained the knowledge of what it is to hunger and thirst; and we all join in his request."

"You shall not wait long," I replied; "I will be up again in a moment or two." I went down into the cabin, and, ordering my servant to put on the table a large piece of pressed Hamburg beef; a cold pie of various flesh and fowl combined, some bread and cheese, and some bottles of brandy and usquebaugh, I then went up again, and requested them all to descend. Hungry they certainly were, and it was incredible the quantity that they devoured. I should have imagined that they had not been fed for a week and I thought that if they were to consume at that rate, my stock would never last out, and the sooner they were landed the better. As soon as they left off eating, and had finished two bottles of usquebaugh, I said to them, "Gentlemen, my orders are to land you at any port of France that you should prefer. Have you made up your minds as to which it shall be, for it will be necessary that we shape a course according to your decision?"

"Mr Elrington, on that point we would wish to advise with you. I hardly need say that our object is to escape, and that falling in with and being captured by a ship of war, and there are many out in pursuit of us and other unfortunate adherents to the house of Stuart, would be extremely disagreeable, as our heads and our bodies would certainly part company, if we were taken. Now, which port do you think we should be most likely to reach with least chance of interruption?"

"I think," I replied, "as you pay me the compliment to ask my opinion, that it would be better to run down the Bay of Biscay, and then put in the port of Bordeaux, or any other, where you could be landed in safety; and my reason is this: the Channel is full of cruisers looking after those of your party who are attempting to escape; and my vessel will be chased and searched. Now, although we might sail faster than any one vessel in the Channel, yet it is very possible that in running away from one, we may fall into the jaws of another. And besides, we are two privateers, and cruising off Bordeaux will excite no suspicion, as it is a favourite cruising-ground; so that, if we were boarded, there would be little danger of discovery; but, of course, as long as I can prevent that, by taking to my heels, I shall not be boarded by any one. The only objection to what I propose is, that you will be confined longer in a vessel than you may like, or than you would be if you were to gain a nearer port."

"I agree with the captain of the vessel," said a grave-looking personage, who had not yet spoken, and whom I afterwards discovered to be a Catholic priest, "the staunchest adherent to the cause could not have given better advice, and I should recommend that it be followed."

The others were of the same opinion; and, in consequence, I edged the schooner down to the Arrow, and hailed Captain Levee, stating that we were to run to Bordeaux. After that I prepared for them sleeping accommodations as well as I could, and on my making apologies, they laughed, and told me such stories of their hardships during their escape, that I was not surprised at their not being difficult. I found out their names by their addressing one another, to be Campbell, McIntyre, Ferguson, and McDonald; all of them very refined gentlemen, and of excellent discourse. They were very merry, and laughed at all that they had suffered; sang Jacobite songs, as they were termed, and certainly did not spare my locker of wine. The wind continued fair, and we met with no interruption, and on the fourth evening, at dusk, we made the mouth of the Garonne, and hove-to, with our heads off shore, for the night. Captain Levee then came on board, and I introduced him to my passengers. To my surprise, after some conversation, he said—"I have now escorted Captain Elrington, according to the orders I received, and shall return to Liverpool as soon as possible; if, therefore, gentlemen, you have any letters to send to your friends announcing your safety, I shall be most happy to present them in any way you may suggest as most advisable."

That Captain Levee had some object in saying this, I was quite certain; and therefore I made no remark. The passengers thanked him for his proposal; and, being provided with writing materials, they all wrote to their friends, and put their letters into Captain Levee's hands, who then bade them farewell, and went on deck with me.

"Of course, you were not serious in what you said, Captain Levee?" I inquired, as we walked forward.

"No," he replied; "but I considered it prudent to make them believe so. Although Englishmen, they are enemies to our country, so far as they are enemies to our government, and, of course, wish no harm to the French, who have so warmly supported them. Now, if they knew that I remained here waiting for your coming out of the river, they would say so, and I might lose the chance of a good prize, as nothing would sail, if they knew that the coast was not clear. Now, I shall part company with you in an hour, and make all sail for England, as they may suppose, but, without fail, to-morrow night I shall be off here again, about five leagues from the port, with my sails furled; therefore, stay in the river as long as they will let you, as, while you are in port with the flag of truce, vessels may sail out."

"I understand you, and will do all I can to assist your views, Captain Levee. Now, we will go down again. I will give you a receipt for a coil of rope, which you will send your boat for, and write a letter to the owners, after which you will wish me good bye, and make sail."

"Exactly," Captain Levee replied, who then ordered his boat to go for a coil of three-inch, and bring it on board.

We then descended to the cabin, and I wrote a letter to the owner, and also a receipt for the coil of rope, which I delivered to Captain Levee. The boat soon returned from the lugger, the rope was taken on board, and then Captain Levee wished me farewell, and made his polite adieus to the gentlemen, who followed him on deck, and waited there till he had hoisted in his boat, and made all sail.

"How long will she be before she arrives at Liverpool with this wind?" inquired Mr Campbell.

"She will carry her canvass night and day," I replied; "and, therefore, as she sails so fast, I should say in five or six days."

"Well, I am grateful that we have such an early and safe opportunity of communicating with our friends in England; we might have waited two months otherwise."

"Very true," replied the priest, "but Heaven has assisted our anxious wishes. Let us be grateful for all things."

My passengers watched the lugger until she was nearly out of sight. I dare say that their thoughts were, that those on board of her were going to the country of their birth, from which they were exiles, probably for ever: they did not speak, but went down below, and retired to their beds. At daylight the next morning I ran the schooner in; and as soon as I was within three miles of the coast, I hoisted the white flag of truce, and stood for the mouth of the river Garonne. I perceived that the batteries were manned, but not a shot was fired, and we entered the river.

When we were a mile up the river, we were boarded by the French authorities, and my passengers, who had dressed themselves in their proper costume, informed the officer in the boat who they were, upon which he was very polite, and, calling a pilot out of the boat, the schooner was taken charge of by him, and we very soon afterwards, having wind and tide in our favour, were anchored alongside of two large merchant vessels and a French privateer of sixteen guns, which I instantly recognised as our old antagonist off Hispaniola, in the action in which the Revenge was captured, and Captain Weatherall lost his life. However, I kept my knowledge to myself, as the French officer and the Jacobite gentlemen were present. As soon as we had anchored, the passengers were requested to go into the boat, and the French officer and I to accompany them, that I might report myself to the governor, and we pulled away to the town, one of my boats following with the passengers' luggage.

On our landing, there was a great crowd assembled, and they looked very hard at me, as I was dressed in my lace coat and a cocked-up hat, also bound with broad gold lace. On our arrival in the presence of the governor, we were received with much urbanity; and as I had brought the Jacobite gentlemen in my schooner, it was presumed that I was favourable to the cause, and I was very politely treated. The governor invited us all to dine with him on that day. I made some excuse, saying, that I was anxious to return to Liverpool, that I might fit out for the coast of Africa, in which service I was to be employed by my owners; but the passengers insisted upon my staying a day or two, and the governor added to their solicitations his own.

I therefore accepted, not only because I was glad to have an opportunity to see so celebrated a town, but because it would meet the views of Captain Levee. We took leave of the governor, and went to an hotel, and I then sent my boat on board for necessaries, and hired a handsome apartment in the hotel. I had not been there half an hour, when the priest came to me and said, "Captain, you are not aware of the rank and consequence of the three gentlemen whom you have been so successful in escorting to a place of safety. I am requested by them to make you a handsome remuneration for your kindness and skilful conduct on this occasion."

"Sir," I replied, "this must not be. I am most happy in having assisted in the escape of unfortunate gentlemen; and all the pleasure I feel at having so done would be destroyed if I were to accept of what you offer. It is useless to repeat it; and if you do, I shall consider it an insult, and immediately repair on board of my vessel. You will therefore tender my best thanks and my refusal, with ardent wishes for their future welfare."

"After what you have said, Captain Elrington, I will, of course, not resume the offer. I will tell my fellow-passengers what you have said, and I am sure that they will, as I do, admire your high sense of honour."—The priest shook me by the hand, and then quitted my apartment. I did not see the other passengers till it was the hour to go to dine at the governor's, when they embraced me cordially, and the one calling himself Campbell said, "Should you ever be in distress or a prisoner in this country, recollect you have a friend who is ready to serve you. Here is an address to a lady, to whom you must write, and say that you wish the assistance of your passenger to Bordeaux—that will be sufficient—I trust you may never require it."

We had a pleasant dinner at the governor's, and among the people invited to meet us, I perceived the French captain of the privateer. I knew him immediately, although he did not recognise me. We had some conversation together, and he spoke about his cruises in the West Indies, and asked me whether I knew Captain Weatherall. I said there was a Captain Weatherall who commanded the Revenge privateer, and who was killed when his vessel was taken.

"Exactly," said the captain; "he was a brave man, and fought nobly, and so did all his people—they fought like devils."

"Yes," I replied, "they fought as long as they could, but Captain Weatherall was very short-handed. He had but fifty-five men on board at the commencement of the action."

"More than that, I'm sure," replied the French captain.

"He had not, I assure you," I replied; "he had lost so many in an attack on shore, and had so many away in prizes."

Our conversation had attracted general notice, and a French army officer observed, "Monsieur speaks so positively, that one would imagine that he was actually on board."

"And so I was, Sir," replied I, "and have my wounds to show for it. I knew this officer immediately I saw him, for I was close to Captain Weatherall at the time that this officer expostulated with him before the action; and I crossed my sword with him during the combat."

"You have convinced me that you were on board," replied the captain of the privateer, "by your mentioning the expostulations previous to the combat taking place. I am delighted to have met with so brave an enemy, for every man on board that vessel was a hero."

The conversation was then general, and many particulars were asked; and I will do, the French captain the justice to say, that he was very correct in all his statements, and neither vaunted his own success, nor did us less than justice.

The party then broke up to go to the theatre, and afterwards we repaired to the hotel. I remained there two days more, and on the last of these two days I had promised to sup with the French captain of the privateer, who had called upon me, and behaved very politely. The following day, after noon, when the tide served, I was to sail. Accordingly, after the theatre was over, I went with the French captain to his house, in company with two or three more. Supper was on the table when we arrived there, and we went into the room, waiting for the presence of the captain's lady, who had not gone to the theatre, and to whom I had not been introduced. After a few minutes she made her appearance, and as she entered the room, I was struck with her extreme beauty, although she was past the meridian of life. I thought I had seen her face before, and as she came forward with her husband, it at once rushed into my mind that she was the widow of the French gentleman who had so gallantly fought his vessel, and who fell by my hand—the lady who was nursing her son at the King's Hospital at Jamaica, and who had been so inveterate against me. Our eyes met, and her cheeks flushed; she recognised me, and I coloured deeply as I bowed to her. She was taken with a faintness, and fell back. Fortunately her husband received her in his arms.

"What is the matter, my love?" he said.

"Nothing; but I am taken with a vertigo," replied she; "it will go off directly. Make my excuses to the company, while I retire for a few minutes."

Her husband went out of the room, and after a minute or two came back, saying that Madam was not well enough to return to the room, and begged that they would admit her excuse, and sit down to supper without her. Whether his wife had informed him of who I was, I know not; but nothing could exceed the civility of the French captain towards me during the supper. We did not, however, remain very late, as the lady of the house was indisposed.

I found out, as I walked home with another French officer, that the captain of the privateer had fallen in with the French lady on her return from Jamaica, where her son died in the hospital, and had married her; and that, moreover, unlike most French husbands, he was most ardently attached to her.

I had breakfasted the next morning, and packed up my clothes preparatory to going on board, and had just returned from a visit of leave-taking with the governor, when who should walk up into my apartment but the French captain of the privateer, accompanied by three or four French officers of the army. I perceived by his looks when he entered that he was a little excited, but I met him cordially. He began a conversation about his action with Captain Weatherall, and instead of speaking handsomely as he had done before, he used expressions which I considered offensive, and I at once took him up by observing that, being under a flag of truce, it was impossible for me to notice what he said.

"No," he replied; "but I wish we were once more on the high seas together, for I have a little debt of gratitude to pay off."

"Well," I replied, "you may have; and I should not be sorry to give you an opportunity, if it were possible."

"May I inquire whether you intend to go home as a cartel, and carry your flag of truce to Liverpool?"

"No, Sir," I replied; "I shall haul down my flag of truce as soon as I am out of gun-shot of your batteries I understand what you mean, Sir. It is very true that your vessel carries nearly double the number of guts that mine does, but nevertheless I shall haul down my flag of truce, as I say I will."

"Not if I follow you down the river, I presume?" he said with a sort of sneer.

"Follow me if you dare," I cried; "you will meet with your master, depend upon it."

"Sacré!" replied he, in a passion, "I will blow you out of the water; and if I take you I will hang you for a pirate."

"Not the last, certainly," I said coolly.

"Look you, Sir," he cried, shutting his fist upon the palm of his other hand, "if I take you I will hang you; and if you take me, you may serve me in the same way. Is it a bargain, or are you a coward?"

"Gentlemen," I said to the officers present, "you must feel that your countryman is not behaving well. He has insulted me grossly. I will, however, consent to his terms on one condition, which is, that he will permit one of you, after he has sailed, to make known the conditions upon which we fight to his wife; and that one of you will pledge me his honour that he will impart these conditions as soon as we are gone."

"Agree to do so—pledge yourself to do so, Xavier," cried the French captain to one of the officers present.

"Since you wish it, certainly," he said.

"You pledge yourself to make the conditions known to Madam, as soon as we have sailed?"

"I do, upon the honour of an officer and a gentleman," replied he, "painful as it will be to me."

"Then, captain," I replied, "I agree to your conditions, and one or the other of us shall hang."

You may suppose, Madam, that I must have been in a state of great irritation to have consented to such terms. I was so, and could not brook such insult in the presence of the French officers. Moreover, as you will observe, in my conversation I did not commit myself in any way. There was nothing dishonourable. I told him that I should haul down my flag of truce, and I also told him that he would meet with his master, which was true enough, as he would meet with the Arrow, commanded by Captain Levee, as well as with my vessel; while he thought that he would have to fight with my inferior vessel alone, and, making sure of conquest, he purposely insulted me, to make me accept such conditions as would administer to the revenge of his wife, who had evidently worked him up to act in such a manner; and I accepted them, because I hoped the fate would be his if Captain Levee joined me, and if not, I was determined that I never would be taken alive.

After I had agreed to his conditions, they all took a very ceremonious leave, and I bowed them out with great mock humility. I then bade farewell to my passengers, who lodged in the same hotel, and went down to my boat, and pulled on board. As soon as the tide served, the pilot came on board, and we got under weigh. I observed a great bustle, and a hurrying to and fro of boats on board of the French privateer, and we had not gone above two miles down the river, before I perceived the men were aloft and lowering her sails. I told my officers that I had received a challenge from the French privateer, and had accepted it, and that we must get everything ready for action. They were much astonished at this, as the disparity of force was so great, but they went cheerfully to their duty, as did the men, among whom the news was soon spread.

# Chapter Ten.

**Captain Levee and I engage with the French Privateer—We come off victorious—My revenge against the French Lady—We take our Prize to Liverpool.**

The wind was light, and we did not gain the mouth of the river till near sun-down, when the pilot left us; and as soon as we were three miles in the offing, I hauled down the flag of truce in the sight of the French privateer, who was following us close, and was not more than four miles from us. To avoid mistake, I had agreed with Captain Levee that should I be coming out after dark, I would carry a light at the peak, and this light I now hoisted. It enabled the French privateer to follow me, and appeared only as a mark of contempt towards him. I stood on in the direction where I was to find Captain Levee, and could make out the Frenchman following me, and gradually nearing me. As it became dark, I made more sail to keep him further off till I had joined the Arrow, but the light at my peak pointed out to him where I was. All this seemed a mystery to my officers and men, until, having run out about four leagues, I desired them to keep a sharp look-out for the Arrow.

About half-past eight o'clock we perceived her lying-to; she had furled her sails after dark, as usual. The light I bore told her who I was, and I ran close to her, and, hailing Captain Levee, desired him to prepare for action, and that I would come on board to speak to him. This, of course, created a great bustle on board of the Arrow, and I hastened on board that they might not show any lights. I then informed Captain Levee of all that had passed, and that the Frenchman was not more than five miles from us. We agreed that I should still keep up the light, and bear away a little to draw the Frenchman to leeward of the port, and also to leeward of the Arrow;—that the Arrow should lower her sails again, so as not to be perceived until I had drawn the Frenchman past him, and that then I should commence the action under sail, and fight till the Arrow came up to my assistance. This being arranged, I hastened on board of my schooner, and, keeping away four points, I waited for the coming up of my antagonist. In half an hour we could perceive him through the gloom, not more than a mile from us, under all sail, standing steadily for the light which we carried at our peak.

As I had already discovered that my little schooner sailed faster than my opponent, I allowed her to come up within a quarter of a mile of me, when I rounded-to; and, desiring my men to aim at his rigging, so as to dismantle him, poured in my broadside of grape and langridge, and then shifted my helm and resumed my course, putting more sail on, so as to increase my distance to what it was before. This manoeuvre I executed three times with success, and I had the satisfaction of perceiving that his foretop-mast was shot away; but when I rounded-to the fourth time, he did the same, and we exchanged broadsides. The effect of his superior artillery was evident, for my rigging and sails were much damaged; happily nothing so serious as to impede our speed, and I again put before the breeze as before, and increased my distance previous to again rounding-to; for, as the water was very smooth, I knew that if I was crippled she would lay me by the board immediately, and I might be taken and hanged before the Arrow could come up to my assistance. I therefore continued a running fight at such a distance as rendered me less liable to suffer from his guns.

It is true that this distance made my guns even more ineffective, but I was decoying my Frenchman off from the land, and placing the Arrow between him and his port, so that his return would be intercepted. This continued for about an hour, when I perceived that the Frenchman had got up a new foretop-mast, and had set the sail upon it. He now ran out his bow-chasers, and continued to fire upon me with them alone, not choosing to lose ground by rounding-to, to give me a broadside; and as his canvass was all out, and I was occasionally rounding-to to dismantle him, we retained much the same distance from one another. At last a shot from his bow-chaser struck off the head of my mainmast, and my gaff came down.

This was serious. We hastened to reef the mainsail and hoist it up again upon the remainder of the mast, but having no gaff-topsail our speed was necessarily decreased, and the enemy appeared to be gradually closing with us. I looked out for the Arrow, but could perceive no signs of her; indeed it was too dark to see farther than half a mile. Finding that on the point of sailing we were on I had no chance, I determined to alter my course, and put my schooner right before the wind so that I might set the square mainsail, which would give time for the Arrow to arrive; indeed at this time I was in a state of great anxiety. However, I had made up my mind not to be taken alive, and to sell my life as dearly as I could.

When the enemy perceived that we had put before the wind, he did the same, and, as we were about half a mile from each other, we continued to exchange broadsides as we ran, she gradually nearing us so as to make her heavy artillery more effective. This portion of the contest continued for an hour, during which my little schooner had received much injury, and we were constantly repairing damages. At last, much to my delight, the day began to dawn, and I then discovered the Arrow about a mile and a half from us, right astern, under a press of sail.

I pointed her out to my officers and men, who were inspired with fresh courage at the sight. The enemy also perceived her, and appeared determined to bring the combat to an issue previous to her coming up, and I feared that, at all events, I might swing at the yard-arm, let the issue of the coming combat be what it might. She neared, steering a course so as to cut me off, and I continued to pour in my broadsides to cripple her if possible, as she did not now fire, but ran steadily for me, and my chances were bad.

Anxious that the Arrow should close as soon as possible, I hauled down my square mainsail, that we might not run from her, and prepared for an obstinate resistance if boarded. At last the Frenchman was within a cable's length, and at this critical moment the Arrow was about a mile to windward. We poured in our last broadside, and hastened to seize our pikes and cutlasses to repel the boarders, when to my satisfaction I found that one of our shot had cut his gaff in two. I immediately rounded to the wind; and as my antagonist was within pistol-shot of me, with her men all ready for the leap on board, I put my helm down, went round in stays, and crossed her so near to windward that you might have thrown a biscuit on board.

This manoeuvre prevented his boarding, and I may say saved my life, for his gaff being shot away he could not heave in stays to follow me, but was obliged to wear round after me, which increased his distance at least a cable's length to leeward. A furious broadside, however, which he poured in, crippled me altogether. Everything came running down upon the decks, and I was left a complete wreck; but I was to windward of him, and although he might sink me, he could not board or take possession until he had refitted his after-sail.

But now his time was come. A fresh antagonist, with equal weight of metal, was close to him, and he had to decide whether he would fight or run. Whether he conceived that running was useless, which it certainly was, or was determined to take us both or die, I know not; certain it is that he did not put his vessel before the wind, but waited with determination the coming up of the Arrow. Captain Levee passed under the Frenchman's stern, raking him with a broadside that almost unrigged him, and then engaged him to leeward, so as to cut off all chance of his escape.

The Frenchman returned the fire with spirit, and I took my men from my guns that we might set some sail upon the vessel, for after the Arrow commenced her fire no further notice was taken of me by the Frenchman. After a contest well maintained for half an hour, the mainmast of the Frenchman went by the board, and this almost settled the question, as he could not keep his vessel to the wind, and consequently she fell off; and received a raking fire from the Arrow. At last her bowsprit was between the main and fore rigging of the Arrow, and her decks were swept by the Arrow's raking fire. I had got some sail up forward, and was anxious to be at the close of the action. I perceived that the Frenchman was attempting to board the lugger, and was pouring all his people on the forecastle, and I therefore edged down to him that I might, with my people, board him on the quarter, which would place him, as we say, between two fires. The conflict was at its highest, the French attempting and the Arrow's crew repelling them, when I laid my schooner on her quarter, and leaped on board of her with my few remaining men. The Frenchmen turned to repel my attack, and thus weakened their party opposed to the Arrow's men; the consequence was, that they were first beaten back, and then boarded by Captain Levee and his crew.

As soon as I had gained the deck of the Frenchman, I thought of nothing but to single out the French captain. At first I could not see him, but as his crew retreated from Captain Levee and his men, I perceived him, pale and exhausted, but still attempting to rally them. As my object was to take him alive, I rushed in advance at him, wrestled, and threw him on his back on the deck. There I held him, while the combatants, fighting and retreating, tumbled over us one after another, and bruised us severely with their weight. At last the French were beaten below, and I had time to breathe; calling to two of my men, I desired them to take charge of the French captain, and, as they valued their lives, not to let him escape, or destroy himself but to take him into our vessel and guard him carefully in my cabin. Having done this, I went to Captain Levee, and we embraced.

"You did not come a minute too soon," I said, wiping the blood from my face.

"No, indeed; and, but for your clever manoeuvre you would have been beaten. Your vessel is a mere nutshell compared to this;—you did well, more than well, to maintain the combat so long. Have you lost many men?"

"We had ten sent below before we boarded; what may have followed since I do not know: I have the French captain safe in my cabin."

"I saw the men hand him over:— well, now to repair damages, and then I will tell you what you shall do. I must send on board and help you; the Arrow has not suffered much considering, and I can spare the men. As soon as we have cleared up the decks a little, we will breakfast together, and talk the matter over."

It required two hours before we could clear the decks of our vessels, for we had separated, and the Arrow had taken charge of the prize. Before I took the boat to go on board the Arrow, I went down into my cabin, where the French captain lay bound and watched by two of the men.

"You are prepared to pay the penalty agreed upon, Monsieur?" said I.

"I am, Sir," he replied. "I now understand what you meant when you said that I should meet with my match. I have no one to blame but myself. I urge you to the conditions, expecting an easy and certain conquest with my superior vessel. I have fallen into my own net, and there's an end of the matter—except that when things go wrong, a woman is certain to be at the bottom of it."

"I am aware, Sir," I replied, "that your wife instigated you to act as you did, or you would never have so behaved. In attempting to revenge the death of one husband she has lost two."

"*C'est vrai,*" replied the Frenchman, composedly, and I then quitted the cabin, and went on board of the Arrow.

"Well, Elrington," said Captain Levee, "what do you intend to do with the French captain? Is he to pay the forfeit, and awing at the yard-arm?"

"I don't like hanging a man, especially a brave man, in cold blood," I replied. "It was all his wife's doing, and he has confessed as much."

"He would certainly have hanged you," replied Levee.

"Yes, that I believe; but it would have been that he might have a quiet life at home—not from any resentment against me. Now I have no feeling of that kind to actuate me."

"What will you do, then?"

"Not hang him, certainly; and yet I should like to punish her."

"She deserves it," replied Captain Levee. "Now, Elrington, will you approve of my suggestion?"

"Let me hear it."

"It is this: they do not know that I have assisted in taking the privateer, as they have no idea that I am here. As soon as we have refitted her and your vessel, I will remain where I am. You shall run into the mouth of the Garonne, with your colours flying, and the English Jack over the French flag on board of the prize. This will lead them to suppose that you have taken the vessel without assistance. When just out of gun-shot, heave-to, fire a gun, and then swing an effigy to the yard-arm, and remain there, to make them suppose that you have hung the French captain. At nightfall you can make sail and rejoin me. That will punish her, and annoy them generally."

"I will do so; it is an excellent device, and she will never know the truth for a long time to come."

We remained all that day refitting; in the evening I made sail, in company with the French schooner, which was manned by Captain Levee, and stood in shore. At break of the following day I ran in, standing for the harbour, without my colours being hoisted, and then it occurred to me that I would make their disappointment greater, by allowing them first to imagine that the victory was theirs; so, when about six miles off, I hoisted French colours on the French schooner, and French colours over English on board of my own.

I continued to stand on till within two miles and a half of the batteries, and could see crowds flocking down to witness the supposed triumphant arrival of their privateer into port; when of a sudden I hauled my wind, hove-to, brailed up my sails, and changed the colours, firing a gun in bravado. Allowing them half an hour to comment upon this disappointment, I then fired another gun, and hoisted up to the yard-arm the figure of a man, composed of clothes stuffed with hay, made to represent the French captain; and having so done, I remained during the whole forenoon, with my sails brailed up, that they might have a clear view of the hanging figure. At last we perceived a large boat, with a flag of truce, coming out of the river. I remained where I was, and, allowing it to come alongside, I perceived in it the French officer who had pledged himself to give the conditions of the combat to the lady; and seated by him was the French captain's wife, with her head sunk down on her knees, and her face buried in her handkerchief.

I saluted the officer as he came on deck. He returned my bow, and then said, "Sir, the fortune of war has proved in your favour, and I perceive that the conditions of the issue of the combat have been adhered to on your side. Against that I have not a word to say, as my friend would have as rigidly adhered to them. But, Sir, we war not with the dead, and I have come off at the request of his miserable wife, to beg that you will, now that your revenge is satisfied, deliver up to her her husband's body, that it may receive the rites of the Church, and Christian burial. You surely, as a brave man, will not deny this small favour to a woman whom you have twice deprived of her husband?"

"Sir," I replied, "on condition that his lady will step on board and make the request herself, I will comply with it, but on no other terms."

"It will be most painful, and her feelings might well have been spared such a trial as to meet your face again, and make the request in person; but, as you insist upon it, I will make known your terms."

As he went into his boat I ran down into the cabin, and desired them to cast loose the French captain, saying to him, "Sir, your wife is here requesting your body, which she believes to be swinging at the yard-arm, for I have put that trick into execution to punish her. I never intended to take your life, and I shall now do more, I shall give you not only life but liberty—such shall be my revenge."

The French captain stared as if confounded, but made no reply. I then went on deck, where I found the lady had been lifted up the side. They led her to me, and she fell on her knees, but the effort was too much for her, and she fainted away. I ordered her to be taken down into the cabin, and, without any explanation, desired the French officer to accompany her, not wishing to be present at the unexpected meeting. I therefore remained on deck, and ordering the men to lower down the effigy they did so, laughing at the French seamen in the boat, who for the first time perceived, for they had not looked up before, that it was only a sham captain. I looked over the side, and told them that the captain was alive and well, and would be in the boat very soon, at which they were greatly rejoiced. In the mean time the explanation took place in the cabin, and after a few minutes the French officer came up, and expressed his satisfaction at what I had done.

"You have given a lesson, Sir, without being guilty of barbarity. Your conduct has been noble."

He was soon followed by the French captain and his lady, who was now all gratitude, and would have kissed my hands, but I prevented her, and said, "Madam, at least now you have no occasion to hate me.

If I was so unfortunate, in self-defence, as to slay your first husband, I have restored to you your second. Let us, then, part in amity."

The French captain squeezed my hand, but said nothing. I begged they would take some refreshment, but they were too anxious to return and undeceive their friends, and requested permission to go into the boat. Of course I consented, and as the boat pulled away the crew gave three huzzas, as a compliment to us. When they were a mile in shore, I hauled down the colours of both vessels, and made sail out to rejoin Captain Levee, which I did in the evening, and then related all that had passed.

He was much pleased with the result of the affair, and we then, having consulted, considered it advisable to run back to Liverpool with the prize, for she required so many hands to man her as to render us by no means efficient vessels. Moreover, I have omitted to state that, while I was in the Garonne, the Arrow had taken two good prizes, which she had manned and sent to Liverpool. We therefore made sail to the northward, and in a week were again in port, with our prize. We found that the other vessels had arrived safe, and the owner was much pleased with the result of this short and eventful cruise.

# Chapter Eleven.

**I cause myself to be dismissed from my Owner's Service—Am arrested—Conveyed to London, and confined in the Tower—Am visited by a Romish Priest, and through his interference obtain my Liberation—Set off to Liverpool, and find my Owner and Captain Levee—Their surprise—Miss Trevannion.**

When I called upon our owner, which I did as soon as I had dropped my anchor and furled sails, he embraced me, and then led me into the back room next to his counting-house.

"My dear Elrington," said he, "well as you managed to get off the Jacobite gentlemen, there is a strong suspicion on the part of the government that they were on board of your vessel, and that I was a party to their escape. Whether they will take any measures now that you have returned I know not; they may have gained some intelligence, or they may worm out something, by their emissaries, from those who compose your crew, and if so we must expect their vengeance. Now tell me where you landed them, and all the events of your cruise, for I have heard but little from those who brought in the prizes taken by the Arrow. Captain Levee is too busy with his own vessel and the prize to come on shore for these two hours, and I wish to talk with you alone upon this affair."

After I had narrated all that had passed, and the manner in which the French privateer had been captured, the owner said—

"If the government spies, and there are plenty of them about, find out from your crew that you landed passengers at Bordeaux, depend upon it you will be arrested and examined, without you get out of the way till the affair has blown over. Now the men will narrate in the taverns the curious history of this French privateer, and in so doing cannot fail to state that you were on shore in France. Now, Elrington, you have run the risk to oblige me, and I must keep you out of difficulty; and, if you feel inclined to hide yourself for a time, I will of course pay all your expenses."

"No," I replied; "if they find out what has taken place, and wish to get hold of me in consequence, I think it will be better to brave it out. If I hide away, it will make them more anxious to have me, and will confirm their suspicions that I am what they are pleased to call a traitor; a reward will be offered for my apprehension, and at any time that I do appear the reward will cause me to be taken up. If, on the contrary, I brave it out, and, if I am asked, say at once that I did land passengers, at all events they will not make it high treason; so, with your leave, I will stay. I hardly need say that I shall take the whole responsibility on myself, and declare that I took them on board without your knowledge; that you may rest assured of."

"On consideration, I think that your plan is the best," replied my owner. "I am grateful for your offer of screening me, which I would not permit, were it not that I shall be useful to you if any mischance takes place, and, if in prison, could be of no service."

"Then, Sir," I replied, "the wisest course will be for you at once to dismiss me from the command of the privateer, in consequence of your having been informed that I carried passengers and landed them in France. That step will prove you a friend to the government, and will enable you, after a time, to get me out of my scrape more effectually."

"You are sacrificing yourself, Elrington, and all for me."

"Not so, Sir. I am only securing a friend in case of need."

"That you certainly are," replied my owner, squeezing my hand. "Well, it will be the best plan even for you, and so let it be."

"Then I will now return on board, and tell the officers that I am dismissed. There is no time to be lost; and here comes Captain Levee; so for the present, Sir, farewell."

On my return on board, I called up the officers and men, and told them that I had offended the owner, and that he had dismissed me from the command of the privateer. One of the officers inquired what I had done: and I said, before the men, that it was for landing the passengers in France. They all condoled with me, and expressed their sorrow at my leaving them, and I believe they were sincere. It was fortunate that I did as I had done, for I found that the government emissaries were on board at the time that I made the communication, and had already gained the information from some of my crew. I ordered my chest and bedding to be put into the boat, and, as soon as they were ready, I gave up the command to the first officer, and bidding them all farewell went down the side, and pulled on shore, repairing to my former lodgings.

I had not been there two hours before I was arrested and taken to prison. I was, however, very comfortably lodged, because I was a state-prisoner, and I presume that more respect is paid to a man when he is to be drawn and quartered, and his head set above the Tower gates, than a petty malefactor. The next day I was summoned before what was called the Commission, and asked whether I had not landed some people in France? I replied immediately that I had done so.

"Who were they?" was the next inquiry.

"They stated themselves to be Roman Catholic priests," replied I, "and such I believed them to be."

"Why did I do so?"

"Because, in the first place, they paid me one hundred guineas each; and, in the second, because I considered them mischievous, dangerous men, conspiring against the government, and that the sooner they were out of the country the better."

"How did I know that they were traitors?"

"All Roman priests were traitors in my opinion, and I hated them as bad as I did the French; but it is difficult to deal with a priest, and I thought that I was performing a good service in ridding the country of them."

"Who else was privy to the affair?"

"No one; I had made the arrangement with them myself; and not an officer or man on board knew anything about it."

"But my owner, Mr Trevannion, was he a party to it?"

"No, he was not; and on my return he dismissed me from the command of the privateer, as soon as he found out that I had landed the priests in France."

A great many more questions were put to me, all of which I answered very cautiously, yet without apparent hesitation; and, after an examination of four hours, the president of the Commission told me that I had been, by my own acknowledgment, aiding and abetting the escape of malignant traitors, and prevented them meeting their just fate on the scaffold. That, in so doing, I had been guilty of treason, and must abide the sentence of the supreme Commission in London, whither I should be sent the following day. I replied that I was a loyal subject; that I hated the French and Romish plotters, and that I had done what I considered was best; that if I had done wrong, it was only an error in judgment; and any one that said I was a traitor lied in his throat.

My reply was taken down, and I was sent back to prison.

The following afternoon the gaoler came into my room, accompanied by two persons, one of whom informed me that I was delivered over to their custody to be taken to London. I was led out, and at the door I found three horses, upon one of which I was desired to mount. As soon as I was in the saddle, a rope was passed from one leg to the other under the horse's belly, so as to prevent my escape; and my horse was led between the other two, upon which my keepers rode, each having a hand-rein made fast from my horse's bridle to his own. A crowd was assembled round the entrance of the gaol, and among the lookers-on I perceived Captain Levee and my owner; but of course I thought it imprudent to take any notice of them, and they did not make any recognition of me.

I hardly need say, my dear Madam, how very revolting it was to my feelings to be thus led away like a felon; but at the same time I must acknowledge the courtesy of my conductors, who apologised for being compelled to take such measures of security, and on the way showed great kindness and good-feeling.

Everything being arranged, we proceeded on our journey: but it was late when we set off, owing to one of my conductors being sent for by the commissioner, and having to wait for letters for nearly three hours. As it may be supposed, we could not travel at speed, and we seldom went faster than a walk, which I was sorry for, as I was anxious that the journey should be over and my fate decided as soon as possible.

Almost an hour after dark, a party of men rushed from the side of the road, and some seizing the bridles of the horses the others threw the two conductors off their saddles by taking them by the leg and heaving them over on the other side. This was done so quickly, that the two men, who were well armed, had not time to draw out a pistol or any other weapon of defence; and as soon as they were on the ground they were immediately seized and overpowered. The faces of the men who had thus assailed the king's officers were blackened so as to disguise them, but from their voices I knew them to be the men and officers of the privateer. "Now then, Captain Elrington," said one of them, "be off with you as fast as possible, and we will take care of these fellows."

I still remained in my saddle, and, although somewhat flurried with the surprise of the attack, I had had time to recover myself; and had decided upon my mode of behaviour. I felt, as I had said to the owner when we consulted together, that an escape now would be only putting off the evil day, and that it was better to meet the case boldly at once; so I rose in my stirrups, and said to the men in a loud voice, "My good fellows, I am much obliged to you for your exertions in my behalf; as it proves your good-will, but I cannot and will not take advantage of them. By some mistake I am accused of being a traitor, when I feel that I am a true and loyal subject, which I have no doubt will be fully established upon my arrival in London. I cannot, therefore, take advantage of this opportunity to escape. I respect the laws of my country, and I beg you to do the same. Oblige me by releasing the two gentlemen whom you have made your prisoners, and assist them to remount their horses, for I am resolved that I will go to London and be honourably acquitted. Once more, my lads, many thanks for your kind intentions; and now I wish you farewell; and if you would do me a great favour, you will disperse peaceably, and leave us to proceed on our journey."

The men perceived that I was in earnest, and therefore did as I requested, and in another minute I was again alone with my two keepers.

"You have behaved honourably, Sir, and perhaps wisely," observed one of my conductors, as he was about to remount his horse. "I will not ask you who those people were, although I have no doubt but you recognised them yourself."

"No," I replied, "I did not. I guessed from whence they came, but I did not recognise any one individual."

I gave this cautious answer, although I had recognised Captain Levee and one of my own officers.

"Well, Captain Elrington, you have proved to us that you may be trusted, and therefore, on your pledging your word that you will not escape, we shall have a great pleasure in removing all unpleasant precautions."

"I certainly have proved that I would not escape, and will readily give you my assurance that I will not alter my mind."

"That is sufficient, Sir," replied the officer; and he then cut away the rope which bound my legs, and also took off the two leading reins attached to the other horses. "We shall now," he said, "proceed not only more pleasantly, but more rapidly."

My conductors then mounted their horses, and we set off at a good trot, and in an hour arrived at the place where we were to put up for the night. We found supper prepared for us, and good beds. My conductors now left me free of all restraint, and we retired to our beds. The next day we continued our journey in the same manner. My companions were pleasant and gentlemanlike men, and we discoursed freely upon every topic; no one could have imagined that I was a state-prisoner.

We arrived, at London on the fifth day, and I was then delivered over to the keeper of the Tower, according to the instructions that my conductors had received. They bade me farewell, and promised that they would not fail to represent my conduct to the authorities, and gave me hopes of a speedy release. I had the same idea, and took possession of the apartments prepared for me (which were airy and well ventilated) with almost cheerfulness.

On the third day of my arrival a Commission was sent to the Tower to examine me, and I gave the same replies as before. They were very particular in obtaining the descriptions of the persons of those whom I had landed in France, and I answered without disguise. I afterwards found out that I had done a very foolish thing. Had I misrepresented their persons, it would have been supposed that they really were four Catholic priests, but from my exact description they discovered that I had rescued the four traitors (as they termed them) that they were the most anxious to secure and make an example of; and their annoyance at this discovery had so angered them against me that my subsequent conduct could not create any feeling favourable towards me.

Three weeks elapsed, and I was wearied of confinement. My gaoler told me that he feared my case was a bad one; and, after another week had passed, he said that I was condemned as aiding and abetting treason. I must say that I little expected this result, and it quite overthrew me. I asked my gaoler what was his authority. He said that so many people had assisted and effected the escape of the rebels without one having been convicted of having so done except myself on my own avowal, that they deemed it absolutely necessary that an example should be made to deter others from aiding those who were still secreted in the country; and that in consequence it had been decided by the Privy Council that I should be made an example of. He told me much more which I need not repeat, except that it proved the malignant feeling that was indulged by the powers in authority against those who had assisted their defeated opponents, and I felt that I had no chance, and prepared my mind to meet my fate.

Alas, my dear Madam, I was but ill prepared to die,—not that I feared death, but I feared what must be my condition after death. I had lived a reckless, lawless life, without fear of God or man; all the religious feelings which had been instilled into me by my good tutor (you know my family history, and I need say no more) during my youth had been gradually sapped away by the loose companionship which I had held since the time that I quitted my father's house; and when I heard that I was to die my mind was in a state of great disquiet and uncomfortable feeling. I wished to review my life, and examine myself; but I hardly knew where to begin.

All was chaos and confusion. I could remember many bad actions, but few good ones. I felt that I was like a vessel without a rudder, and without a pilot; and after hours and hours of deep thought I would give up the task of examination in stern despair, saying to myself, "Well, if it must be so, it must." I felt an inclination to defy that Heaven which I felt would never be opened to me. This was the case for more than a week after I heard of my condemnation, until I began to reflect upon the nature of our creed, and the terms of salvation which were offered; and as I thought over them I felt a dawn of hope, and I requested the gaoler to furnish me with a Bible. I read it day and night, for I expected every morning to be summoned to execution. I felt almost agony at times lest such should be the case; but time passed on, and another fortnight elapsed, during which I had profited by my reading, and felt some contrition for my many offences and my life of guilt, and I also felt that I could be saved through the merits of Him who died for the whole world. Day after day my faith became more lively, and my mind more at ease. One morning the gaoler came to me, and said that there was a priest who wished to see me. As I understood he was a Roman, I was about to refuse; but on consideration I thought otherwise, and he was admitted. He was a tall, spare man, with a dark Spanish countenance.

"You are, I believe," said he, "Captain Elrington, who effected the escape of some of our poor friends, and who are now condemned for your kind act?"

"I am, Sir," replied I.

"I am aware," said he, "that your profession of faith is not mine, and do not, therefore, come to talk with you on serious points, without you should wish it yourself; my object is, being indebted as we are to you for saving our friends, to offer to be of any use that I can to you, in executing any wishes, or delivering any messages, which you may wish to give, should you suffer for your generous conduct, and you may trust anything to me with safety, that I swear to you;" and he took a crucifix from the folds of his garment, and kissed it, as he said so.

"I thank you for your kind offer, Sir," replied I, "but I have nothing to trouble you with. I have long quitted my family, who know not whether I am alive or dead, for reasons that I need not explain. I am under an assumed name, and it is my intention to suffer under that name, that my family may not be disgraced by my ignominious death, or be aware that I have perished on the scaffold."

"Perhaps you are right," replied the priest; "but let us talk upon another point; have you no friends that could exert themselves in your favour so as to procure your pardon and release?"

"None," replied I, "except those who, I am sure, are exerting themselves to the utmost of their power, and to whom no message from me is necessary."

"Do you know nobody at court," said the priest, "no person of rank in the government—or I may say opposed to the government—for people now-a-days are not what they seem or pretend to be?"

"I have no knowledge of any titled person," replied I; "when I parted with one of the gentlemen whom I landed at Bordeaux he gave me the name of a lady of quality at Paris, desiring me, if in difficulty, to apply to him through her; but that was if in difficulty in France; of course she could do nothing for me in this country."

"Have you the name of the lady?"

"Yes," replied I; "it is on the first leaf of my pocket-book. Here it is."

The priest read the name, and then said—

"You must write immediately a few words, acquainting her with your position. I will see the letter safely delivered before the week is over."

"What good can she possibly do me?" replied I.

"I cannot say; but this I know, that if anything is to be done, it will be. Write immediately."

The priest called the gaoler and requested writing materials, which were brought, and in a few minutes I had done as he requested.

"There, Sir, I have written to please you; but I candidly state that I consider it a useless attempt."

"Were I of your opinion, I should not have advised you to write," replied he. "There are wheels within wheels that you have no conception of; in these troubled times. What I most fear is that it may arrive too late."

The priest took his leave of me, and I was left to my own thoughts. When I considered that the address of this lady had been given to me by the very man whom they were so anxious to secure as a traitor, I at once decided that no benefit could arrive from any interference on her part; and I therefore, after a quarter of an hour, dismissed the whole subject from my thoughts, and commenced my reading of the sacred writings. The following morning, when the gaoler came in, I could not help observing to him, that as I had been condemned so many days I felt much surprise at the delay of my execution. His reply was, that he heard that others were in custody upon the same charge, and that they waited for their convictions, that we might all suffer at the same time; for the order for my execution had come on the Friday last, but had been countermanded on the afternoon of the same day. Although this satisfied me that I had no hopes of escape, yet I was pleased that I had obtained more time for preparation, and I renewed my reading with ardour. Another week passed, when the gaoler, with a solemn face, and much apparent concern, came in, and informed me that the other parties arrested had been tried before the Commission, and had been condemned, and that it was expected that the execution would take place either on the morrow or the day after. The announcement did not affect me much. I had made up my mind that I should suffer, and had to a degree weaned myself from life. I considered how all hopes of my ever enjoying the delight of my family and kindred ties had flown away, and I looked with disgust upon my career as a privateersman—a career of recklessness and blood, so denounced by the sacred writings which I had before me. I reflected, that if I were to leave the prison I should have no other means of sustenance, and should probably return to my former life, and load my soul with a still heavier weight of crime; and, although I felt an occasional bitter pang at the idea of leaving the world so young—a world which I could not hate—still I was, after a few hours' communing and reflection, resigned to my fate, and exclaimed with sincerity, "Thy will be done." I think, Madam, you may have observed that, sinful as I was, my whole career proved that I was not a hardened sinner. Good was not driven entirely out of me, but was latent, notwithstanding all my excesses, and the bad company which had influenced me.

I now prayed, and prayed earnestly, and I thought that my prayers were heard. Such was my state of mind on the day before the one appointed for my execution, when the gaoler and one of the sheriff's officers came into my cell, accompanied by the Roman Catholic priest whom I have before mentioned. I perceived by the countenance of the gaoler, who was a humane man, that he had no unpleasant news.

The sheriff's officer delivered to him an order for my liberation, and to my astonishment I was told by the gaoler that my pardon was signed, and that I was free. I was stupified with the intelligence, and I stood without making any reply. The priest waved his hand to them as a hint to leave the room, which they both did. As they left, my eyes followed them, and then I cast them down upon the Bible which lay before me on the table, and, slipping down from the bench upon my knees, I covered up my face and prayed. My prayers were confused— I hardly knew what I said—but I knew that they were intended to be grateful to Heaven for my unexpected preservation from an ignominious death. After a time, I rose up, and perceived the priest, whose presence I had till then forgotten. He had been kneeling at the other side of the table praying with me, and I am sure for me—and he was rising up just after I had.

"I trust, Captain Elrington," said he, after a pause, "that the peril you have been in will influence your future life; and that this severe trial will not be thrown away upon you."

"I trust not, Sir," replied I. "I feel that it has been good for me to have been afflicted, I believe that I have been indebted to your exertions for my deliverance."

"No further than having seen your letter duly and speedily delivered. I could do no more, for with all will I have no power; and that was little to do for one who so generously assisted our friends in their distress."

"Am I then to believe that I am indebted to the interest of a French lady, residing at the court of Versailles, for my deliverance?"

"Even so—this may appear strange to you, Captain Elrington, but such is the case. Understand, that in these troubled times the ruling monarch of this country cannot distinguish his friends from his enemies. He can only trust to professions, and they are not always sincere. There are many in the council at this time who, if the Pretender, as he is called, had succeeded, would long before this have joined him, and who had wished him success, although they dared not venture to assist him. The interest of the lady in question with these people has prevailed over the true adherents of the Hanoverian king, and thus through this lady have you obtained your release. I state this to you in confidence; to publish what I have told you would be to betray your friends. Can I be of any further service to you? For you can leave your prison as soon as you please."

"None, I thank you, good Sir," replied I; "I have money more than sufficient to reward my gaoler, and to defray my expenses to Liverpool."

"You have my best thanks and sincere wishes for your happiness. Then I will not intrude upon you any more, except to give you my address in case of need. You have made warm friends by your conduct, and if ever you require their assistance it will not be withheld."

The priest gave his address upon a piece of paper and then came to me.

"Our creeds are not exactly the same, but you will not, my son, refuse my blessing?" said he, putting his hand upon my head.

"Oh, no," said I, dropping on my knees, "I receive it all in thankfulness."

"May God bless you, my son," said he; with emotion—and he then quitted the cell.

What with the previous excitement when my liberation was announced, and the parting with the kind priest, my feelings were so powerful, that, as soon as I was alone, I gave vent to them in a flood of tears. As soon as I was more composed, I rose from the bench, put my necessaries into my valise, and summoned the gaoler, to whom I made a handsome present, thanking him for his kindness during my incarceration. I then shook hands with him, feed the turnkey who had attended upon me, and in a minute more I was clear of the Tower gates. How my heart heaved when I was once more in the open air.

I looked around me, and perceived that many men were busy in erecting a scaffolding. My heart sank as I beheld them, as I felt certain what it was for; but, to verify my opinion, I turned to an old woman who had a sort of stall from which she dispensed mead to the populace, and inquired of her for what the scaffold was being erected.

"It's for the men who are to be executed to-morrow for aiding the Jacobites to escape," said she. "Won't your worship take a glass of mead this morning?"

"I am not thirsty," I replied, as I walked hastily away with my valise upon my shoulders.

A stranger to this part of London, I hardly knew where to direct my steps; I walked past the square before the Tower, until I came into a street called Catherine Street, where a tavern met my view, and into it

I entered immediately,—glad, as it were, to hide myself; for I felt as if all the world looked upon me as a person just discharged from prison. I obtained good entertainment there, and slept there that night. The next morning, the host having provided me two good horses, and a youngster to take them back, I set off for Liverpool, and after five days' travel without adventure I arrived at the town, and proceeded direct to the house of Mr Trevannion, my owner. I took my valise off the boy's horse, and having paid him for his attendance I knocked at the door, for it was late in the evening, and dark, when I arrived. The door (for it was at his private house door, which was next to the counting-house door, that I knocked) was opened; and the woman who opened it shrieked, and let drop the candle, exclaiming, "Help, O God—a ghost, a ghost!" for it appeared that the news had arrived at Liverpool from a messenger who had been sent express after I had been condemned, stating that there was no hope, and that I was to suffer on the Monday previous; and this was the Saturday evening on which I had arrived. Mr Trevannion's clerk, hearing a noise in the passage, came out with another candle, and, seeing me, and the woman lying on the floor in a swoon, stared, staggered to the door of the room where his master was sitting, and the door being ajar he fell back with great force into the room, dropping under the table between Mr Trevannion and Captain Levee, who was sitting with him, smoking, as was very often their wont. This brought out Captain Levee with one of the table-candlesticks, who, upon seeing me, ran to me, and embracing me warmly, cried out, as the clerk made his escape—

"Here is Elrington alive and well, Sir!"

At this announcement Mr Trevannion came out, and threw himself into my arms, saying—

"I thank God for all his mercies, but, above all, that I have not been the cause of your death, my dear Elrington. Come in," he exclaimed, in a faltering voice; and as soon as he gained his seat he laid his head down and sobbed with excitement and joy.

I followed Captain Levee into the room, and was taking a chair, when I perceived there was another person present besides Captain Levee and Mr Trevannion, which was the daughter of the latter; that is, I presumed as much, for I knew that he was a widower, and had one daughter living, out of a family of three children. She appeared to be about seventeen years of age, and had just come from a Protestant convent, as they called establishments where young women were educated at Chester. Mr Trevannion was still with his face covered, and not yet recovered from his burst of feeling, when this young gentlewoman came up to me, and said—

"Captain Elrington, you have behaved nobly to my father; accept my hand and my friendship."

I was so dazzled from coming out of the dark, and so excited from what had just passed, that I was almost bewildered; but I accepted the offered hand, and bowed over it, although I declare that at the time I could not distinguish her features, although I perceived that her person was slight and elegant. As she retreated to her seat, Mr Trevannion, who had recovered from his emotion, said—

"I thought that at this moment your head was exhibited over the gates of Temple-bar. The idea, as Captain Levee will tell you, has haunted me; for I felt, and should always have felt, that I was the cause of your death. God bless you, my dear Sir, and may I have an opportunity of showing you my gratitude and regard for your noble conduct towards me, and the sacrifice which you would have made. You need not tell me, for I know too well, that you took all the onus and blame of the affair upon your own shoulders, and preferred death to impeaching me."

"My dear Elrington," said Captain Levee, "I told our crew, and you have proved me a true prophet, that you never would peach, but die game. We were talking of you, supposing you dead, when you came in. I must tell you, that more than once Mr Trevannion had made up his mind to deliver himself up, and acknowledge the truth, but I prevented him, as it would have been a useless sacrifice."

"You did; but, nevertheless, it was so heavy on my conscience, that had it not been for your perseverance, and the thoughts of leaving my poor girl here an orphan in the world, I certainly should have so done, for I felt life to be a burden."

"I am very glad that you did not, Sir," I replied; "my life is of little value; I have no one to support, no one to love, and no one to lament me if I fall. A shot from the enemy may soon send me out of the world, and there will only be a man the less in it, as far as people are interested about me."

"That is not the case now, at all events," replied Mr Trevannion; "but pray tell us how it is that you have escaped."

"I have not escaped," I replied; "here is my pardon, with the sign-manual."

"And how was it obtained?" exclaimed Captain Levee; "all intercession made through some of the strongest friends of the government was in vain,—that I can assert; for you must not suppose that we have been idle down here. We did not leave London till after you were condemned, and every entreaty to see you, or to communicate by letter, was denied to us."

"I had better, then, begin at the beginning, and state all that occurred. I will first thank you, my dear Levee, for your kind assistance, which I would not avail myself of; as I calculated (wrongly, I own) that it would be wiser to remain a prisoner; and I considered that my very refusal to escape would be admitted by the government as a proof of my innocence. I did not know that I had to deal with such malignant people."

I then commenced my narrative, which occupied the remainder of the evening, and, having received their congratulations, we had a pipe or two, and, as I was fatigued, we retired to bed. I slept little on this, I may say, first night of rest and quiet, after my liberation. I was happy, and yet perplexed. During the time of my imprisonment, it had occurred to me that the life of a privateersman was not one which I could follow up with a good conscience; and I had, on my journey down to Liverpool, made up my mind that I would give it up. I knew this might annoy Mr Trevannion, and that I should have to meet with the ridicule of Captain Levee, and I was thinking whether it were possible, in the first place, that I could give some well-grounded excuse; and, in the next, what other means of gaining my livelihood I could substitute in its stead. My restlessness induced me to get up earlier than usual, and I went out for an hour's walk upon the wharfs. I saw my little schooner riding on the stream, and, as she gently rose and dipped to the swell which ran in with the tide, she looked so beautiful that my resolutions were already giving way. I would look at her no longer; so I turned from the river, and walked back to the owner's house. It was still early when I went into the eating-hall, where I found Miss Trevannion alone.

# Chapter Twelve.

**I state my newly-awakened scruples as to the lawfulness of a Privateersman's Life to Mr Trevannion, but nevertheless undertake another Cruise—Save a Youth from drowning, who he proves to be—Conflict with a French Privateer—Take her and deliver a Prize—Return to Liverpool—Resign the Command of the Sparrow-hawk, and agree to superintend Mr Trevannion's Business.**

Miss Trevannion, my dear Madam, was taller than your sex usually are, her figure slight, and still unformed to a certain degree, but promising perfection. Her hair was very dark, her features regular and handsome, her complexion very pale, and her skin fair as the snow. As she stood in silence, she reminded you of a classical antique statue, and hardly appeared to breathe through her delicate lips; but when she was animated with conversation, it almost reminded you of the Promethean fire which poets state was stolen from Heaven to animate a piece of marble. Then the colour came in her cheeks, intelligence played on her countenance, and everything which at first sight appeared wanting, was, like magic, found to light up her face. Her smiles were the sweetest I ever beheld, and one of those smiles she bestowed upon me as I entered the room and paid her my obeisance. The night before, I had not observed her much;—I was too busy with her father and Captain Levee, and she sat remote from the table and distant from the light, and she never spoke but when she took my hand and thanked me, as I mentioned before. I thought then that her voice was like a silver bell, but made no other remark upon her. We had, however, exchanged but few words before her father came in, accompanied by Captain Levee, and we sat down to our morning's repast of chocolate.

After we had broken our fast, Captain Levee hastened away, on board of his vessel. My imprisonment had detained him from sailing, and Mr Trevannion was anxious that he should be off as soon as possible to make up for lost time, as the expenses of the vessel were heavy.

"Farewell, Elrington, for the present," said he; "I shall come to you on board of your schooner some time during the day." When Captain Levee was gone—for, to tell the truth, I was afraid of his ridicule—I thought it a good opportunity to give my thoughts to my owner, and as I had nothing to say which his daughter might not hear, I began as follows:

"Mr Trevannion, I think it right to state to you that during my imprisonment a great change has come over my feelings upon certain points. I am not ashamed to acknowledge that it has been occasioned by the death which stared me in the face, and from my having seriously communed with myself, and examined, more than I perhaps have done during the whole of my former life, the sacred writings which are given us as our guide. The point to which I refer is, that I have come to a conviction that privateering is not a lawful or honourable profession, and with these feelings I should wish to resign the command of the schooner which you have had the kindness to give me."

"Indeed, Elrington," replied Mr Trevannion. "Well, I should not have thought to have heard this from you, I confess. Much as I respect your scruples, you are too scrupulous. I can hardly imagine that you have turned to the sect of the Quakers, and think fighting is contrary to the Scriptures."

"No, Sir, not so far as that. I consider war, as a profession, both necessary and honourable, and a nation is bound to be prepared for any foreign attack, and to act upon the defensive, or on the offensive, if it is necessary. It is not that. I do not consider the soldier who fights for his country is not doing his duty, nor the seamen who are employed by the state are not equally justified in their profession. What I refer to is privateering. That is, vessels fitted out for the purpose of aggression by private merchants, and merely for the sake of profit. They are not fitted out with any patriotic motives, but merely for gain. They are speculations in which the lives of people on both sides are sacrificed for the sake of lucre—and had you witnessed such scenes of bloodshed and cruelty as I have, during my career, such dreadful passions let loose, and defying all restraint, you would agree with me that he who leads such miscreants to their quarry has much to answer for. Were it possible to control the men on board of a privateer as the men are controlled in the king's service it might be more excusable; but manned, as privateers always will be, with the most reckless characters, when once they are roused by opposition, stimulated by the sight of plunder, or drunken with victory, no power on earth can restrain their barbarity and vengeance, and a captain of a privateer who attempted would, in most cases, if he stood between them and their will, unless he were supported, fall a victim to his rashness. All this I have seen; and all I now express I have long felt, even when younger and more thoughtless. You know that I did give up privateering at one time, because I was shocked at the excesses to which I was a party. Since that I have accepted the command of a vessel, for the idea of being captain was too flattering to my vanity to permit me to refuse; but reflection has again decided me not to engage in it further. I hope this communication will not displease you, Mr Trevannion. If I am wrong in my opinion at all events I am sincere, for I am giving up my only source of livelihood from a sense of duty."

"I know that you are sincere, Elrington," replied Mr Trevannion, "but at the same time I think that you are much too strait-laced in your opinions. When nations are at war, they mutually do all the mischief that they can to each other, and I cannot see what difference there is between my fitting out a privateer under the king's authority, or the king having vessels and men for the national service. The government fit out all the vessels that they can, and when their own funds are exhausted they encourage individuals to employ their capital in adding to the means of distressing the enemy. If I had property on the high seas, would it be respected any more than other English property by the enemy? Certainly not; and, therefore, I am not bound to respect theirs. The end of war is to obtain an honourable peace; and the more the enemy is distressed, the sooner are you likely to obtain one. I do not, therefore, consider that privateering is worse than any other species of warfare, or that the privateersman is a whit more reckless or brutal than soldiers or men-of-war's men in the hour of victory in the king's service."

"There is this difference, Sir," replied I; "first, in the officers commanding; although glad to obtain prize-money, they are stimulated by nobler feelings as well. They look to honour and distinction; they have the feeling that they are defending their king and country, to support them and throw a halo on their exertions; and they have such control over their men, that, although I admit they are equally inclined to excess as the privateersman, they are held in check by the authority which they dare not resist. Now, Mr Trevannion, privateersmen seek not honour, and are not stimulated by a desire to serve the country; all they look to is how to obtain the property of others under sanction; and could they without any risk do so, they would care little whether it was English property or not, provided that they put the money into their pockets. If I held this opinion as a seaman on board of a privateer, what must I feel now, when I am the leader of such people, and the responsibility of their acts is thrown upon my shoulders, for such I feel is the case!"

"I think," replied Mr Trevannion, "that we had better not discuss this question any further just now. Of course you must decide for yourself; but I have this favour to ask of you. Trusting to your resuming the command of the vessel, I have no one to replace you at present, and I hope you will not refuse to take the command of her for one more cruise: should you on your return and on mature reflection be of the same opinion as you are now, I certainly shall no longer press you to remain, and will do all I can to assist you in any other views you may have."

"To that, Sir, I can have no objection," replied I; "it would be unfair of me to leave you without a captain to the vessel, and I am therefore ready to sail in her as soon as you please, upon the understanding that I may quit her, if I am of the same opinion as I am now, upon my return to port."

"I thank you, my dear Sir," said Mr Trevannion, rising; "that is all I request. I must now go to the counting-house."

So saying, he left the room, but his countenance showed that he was far from pleased.

Miss Trevannion, who had been a silent listener to the conversation, as soon as her father had closed, the door after him, thus spoke:

"Captain Elrington, the opinion of a young maiden like me can be of little value, but you know not how much pleasure you have given me by the sentiments you have expressed. Alas! That a man so good, so generous, and so feeling in every other respect, should be led away by the desire of gain, to be the owner of such a description of property. But in this town wealth is everything; the way by which it is obtained is not thought of. My father's father left him a large property in vessels employed wholly in the slave-trade, and it was through the persuasions of my poor mother that my father was induced to give up that nefarious traffic. Since that his capital has been chiefly employed in privateering, which, if not so brutal and disgraceful, is certainly nearly as demoralising. I have been home but a short time, and I have already ventured to express my opinion, certainly not so forcibly and so well as you have, upon the subject; but I was laughed at as a tender-hearted girl, who could not be a fit judge of such matters. But now that you, a captain of one of his vessels, have expressed your dislike to the profession, I think some good may arise. If my father were a poor man, it would be more excusable, if excuse there can be; but such is not the case. He is wealthy, and to whom has he to leave his wealth but to me, his only child? Captain Elrington, you are right—be firm—my father's obligations to you are very great and your opinion will have its influence. I am his daughter—his only daughter—his love for me is great, I know, and I also have my power over him. Supported as I have been by you, I will now exert it to the utmost to persuade him to retire from further employment of his means in such a speculation.

"I thanked you yesterday, when I first saw you, for your noble behaviour; I little thought that I should have again, in so short a time, to express my thanks." Miss Trevannion did not wait for any reply from me, but then quitted the room.

I must say, that, although so young a person, I was much pleased at Miss Trevannion's approval of my sentiments. She appeared, from the very short acquaintance I had had with her, to be a person of a firm and decided disposition, and very different from the insipid class of females generally met with. Her approval strengthened my resolution; still, as I had promised her father that I would go another cruise in the privateer, I left the house and went on board to resume the command. My return was joyfully hailed by the officers and men, which is not always the case. I found her, as may be supposed, ready for sea at a minute's warning, so that I had nothing to do but embark my effects, which I did before the noon was passed, and then went on shore to Mr Trevannion, to receive his orders. I found him with Captain Levee in the back room; and I told Mr Trevannion that I had resumed the command, and was ready to sail as soon as he pleased.

"We must make up for lost time, Elrington," replied he; "I have ordered Captain Levee to cruise to the northward of the Western Isles, occasionally working up as far as the Scilly Isles. Now I think you had better take your ground in the Channel, between Dunkirk and Calais. There is as much to be made by salvage in recapturing English vessels in that quarter as there is in taking the enemy's vessels; and I am sure," added Mr Trevannion, smiling, "you will think that legitimate warfare."

At this Captain Levee laughed, and said, "I have been told what you said to Mr Trevannion, Elrington. I said that it was the effects of being condemned for high treason, and would wear off in a three-months' cruise."

"Good impressions do wear off very soon, I fear," replied I; "but I hope that it will not be the case in this instance."

"We shall see, my good fellow," replied Captain Levee; "for my part I hope they will, for otherwise we shall lose the best privateersman I ever fell in with. However, it's no use bringing up the question now; let us wait till our cruises are over, and we meet again. Good bye, Elrington, and may you be fortunate. My anchor is short stay apeak, and I shall be under sail in half an hour."

Captain Levee sailed at the time that he mentioned; I remained at anchor till the next morning, and then once more was running down the Irish Channel before a stiff breeze. I forgot to mention that while at Mr Trevannion's I had looked at the address of the Catholic priest who had announced to me my release from prison, and had left copies of it, as well as of that of the lady at Paris, in the care of Mr Trevannion. It was now cold, autumnal weather, and the Channel was but rough sailing-ground. During the first fortnight we were fortunate enough to make two recaptures of considerable value, which arrived safely in the Thames, after which we had a succession of gales from the southward, it being the time of the equinox, which drove us close to the sands of Yarmouth, and we even had difficulty in clearing them and getting into sea-room by standing to the eastward. The weather still continued very bad, and we were lying-to under storm sails for several days, and at last found ourselves a degree and a half to the northward, off the coast of Norfolk, when the weather moderated, and the wind changed to the northward. It was a fine clear night, but with no moon, and we were running before the wind to regain our cruising-ground; but the wind again shifted and baffled us, and at last it fell light, and, being on a wind, we did not make more than four miles an hour, although there was very little sea. About one o'clock in the morning I had gone on deck, and was walking to and fro with the first officer, Mr James, when I thought that I heard a faint halloo from to windward.

"Stop," said I; "silence there forward."

I listened, and thought that I heard the cry again. "Mr James," said I, "did you not hear some one shout?"

"No, Sir," replied he.

"Wait, then, and listen."

We did so, but I could not hear it repeated.

"I am certain that I heard a voice as if on the waters," said I. "Perhaps some one has fallen overboard. Turn the hands up to muster, and haul the fore-sheet to windward."

The men were mustered, but no one was missing.

"It was your fancy, Sir," observed the first officer.

"It may have been," replied I; "but I am still in my own mind persuaded that such was the case. Perhaps I was mistaken."

"Shall we let draw the fore-sheet, Sir?" said Mr James.

"Yes, we may as well; but the wind is lighter than it was. I think we shall have a calm."

"It will be as much as she can do to stem the tide and hold her own," observed Mr James. "Let draw the fore-sheet, my lads."

Somehow or another I had a feeling which I could not surmount, that I certainly had heard a faint shout; and although, admitting such to be the case, there was little chance of being of service to any one, I felt a reluctance to leave the spot, and as I walked the deck silent and alone this feeling became insurmountable.

I remained on deck till the tide turned, and then, instead of taking advantage of it so as to gain to the southward, I put the schooner's head the other way, so as to keep as near as I could to the spot where I heard the voice, reducing her sail so as just to stem the tide. I cannot now account for my anxiety, which, under the circumstances, I most certainly never should have felt, unless it was that Providence was pleased to interpose on this occasion more directly than usual. I could not leave the deck; I waited for daylight with great impatience, and as the day dawned I had my telescope in my hand looking round the compass.

At last, as the sun rose from the fog on the horizon, something attracted my eye, and I made it out to be the two masts of a vessel which had sunk in about six fathoms of water. Still I could see nothing except the masts. However, to make sure, I made sail on the schooner, and stood towards them. A short tack enabled us to fetch, and in half an hour we passed the wreck about a half-musket-shot to windward, when we perceived an arm lifted up out of the water, and waved to us.

"There is somebody there," said I, "and I was right. Quickly, my lads; fore-sheet to windward, and lower down the stern-boat."

This was done in a minute, and in a short time the boat returned, bringing with them a lad about sixteen years old, whom they had found in the water, clinging to the masts of the vessel. He was too much exhausted to speak or move. He was put into bed, covered up with blankets, and some warm spirits and water poured down his throat. We then hoisted up the boat, and made sail upon the schooner, and I went down below to breakfast, rejoicing that I had acted upon the impulse which I had felt, and had thus been instrumental in saving the life of a fellow-creature. A few minutes after he was put into bed the lad fell into a sound sleep, which continued during the whole of the day. The next morning he awoke greatly recovered, and very hungry, and as soon as he had eaten he rose and dressed himself.

I then sent for him, as I was impatient to see him and learn his history. When he entered the cabin, it struck me I had seen his features before, but where I could not say. To my inquiries he stated that the brig was the Jane and Mary, of Hull, laden with coals; that they had started a wooden end during the gale, and that she had filled so rapidly that they got the boat from off the boom to save their lives, but from the heavy sea running, and the confusion, the boat had been bilged against the bulwarks, and went down as they were shoving off; that he had supported himself by one of the oars, and was soon separated from his companions who floated around him; that during this time the brig had sunk, and he, clinging to the oar, had been drawn towards her as she sank, and carried some feet under water. On his rising he perceived the top-gallant masts above water, and had made for them, and on looking round he could not see any of the rest of the crew, who must have all perished; that he had been two days on the mast, and was perished with cold. Finding that his feet, which hung down on the water, were much warmer than the other portions of his body exposed to the wind, he had sunk himself down in the water, and remained there, and had he not done so he must have perished.

I asked him how long he had been at sea, and he said he had only gone one voyage, and had been but three months on board. There was something in his manner so superior to the condition of apprentice (which he stated himself to be) on board of such a vessel, and I felt such an interest, which I could not account for, towards the lad, that I then asked who were his friends. He replied, stammering, that he had not a friend in the world except a brother older than himself by many years, and he did not know where he was.

"But your father's name? Is he alive, and who is he? You must tell me that, or I shall not know where to send you."

The youth was very confused, and would not give me any answer.

"Come, my lad," I said, "I think as I have saved your life I deserve a little confidence, and it shall not be misplaced. I perceive that you have not been brought up as a lad for the sea, and you must therefore trust me."

"I will, Sir," he replied, "if you will not send me back to my father and mother."

"Certainly not against your will, my good lad," I replied, "although I shall probably persuade you all I can to return to them. I presume you ran away from your home?"

"Yes, Sir, I did," replied he; "for I could not possibly stay there any longer, and my brother did so before me, for the same reason that I did."

"Well, I promise you, if you will confide in me, that I will not force your inclinations; so now tell me who are your father and mother, and why you left home. You want a friend now, and without confidence you cannot expect friendship."

"I will tell you all, Sir," he replied, "for I see by your face that you will not take advantage of me."

He then commenced, and you may imagine my surprise, my dear Madam, when I found that it was my own brother Philip, whom I had left a child of ten years old, who was addressing me. He had, as he had asserted, left his home and thrown himself on the wide world for the same reason which I had; for his spirit, like mine, could not brook the treatment which he received. I allowed him to finish his narrative, and then made myself known to him.

You may imagine the scene, and the delight of the poor fellow, who, as he encircled me in his arms, clinging to me with the tears of joy on his cheeks, told me that his great object had been to find me out, and that, although he had no idea what had become of me, he thought it most likely that I had taken to a seafaring life.

I now felt certain that Providence had specially interposed in this business, and had, for its own good reasons, created those unusual feelings of interest which I described to you, that I might be the saviour of my brother; and most grateful was I, I can assure you. I had now a companion and friend, one to love and to cherish. I was no longer alone in the world and I do not know when I had felt so happy for a long while.

I left my brother below in the cabin, and went on deck to acquaint the officers with this strange meeting. The intelligence soon ran through the vessel, and of course the poor shipwrecked boy became an object of unusual interest. That whole day I was interrogating and receiving intelligence from him relative to our family. I made him describe his sisters and every member of it, even the servants and our neighbours were not forgotten, and for the first time since I had quitted home, I knew what had occurred during the six years of my absence. From the accounts he gave me, I certainly had no inclination ever to return as long as certain parties were in existence; and my brother declared that nothing but force should ever induce him. The more I talked with him, the more I was pleased with him. He appeared of a frank, noble disposition, full of honour and high sentiments, winning in his manners, and mirthful to excess. Indeed, his handsome countenance implied and expressed as much, and it did not deceive.

I hardly need say that he took up his quarters in my cabin, and, having procured for him more suitable apparel, he looked what he was,—the perfect young gentleman. He was soon a general favourite on board, not only with the officers but with the men. One would have thought that the danger and distress we had found him in would have sickened him for the sea for ever; but it was quite the contrary. He delighted in his profession, and was certainly born to be a sailor. I asked him what he felt when he had remained so long clinging to the mast; if he had not given up all hopes of being saved? And he replied no, that he had not; that he did not know how long he might have had to remain there, but that he had never abandoned the idea of being taken off by some vessel or another, and that he thought that he might have continued there for twenty-four hours longer without being exhausted, as after he had sunk himself into the water he felt warm, and no exertion was necessary. It is of such buoyant spirits as these, Madam, that seamen should be made.

You cannot have an idea of the pleasure which I experienced at this falling in with my brother Philip. It appeared to have given a new stimulus to my existence; even privateering did not appear so hateful to me, after I had heard him express his delight at being likely to be so employed, for such he stated had long been his ardent wish. Two days afterwards we had regained our cruising-ground, and perceived a French privateer steering for the port of Calais, in company with a large merchant vessel which she had captured. The wind was light, and we discovered her at daybreak, just as the fog cleared away, she being then about mid-channel, and not more than five miles distant. We made all sail, and soon were within gun-shot. The Frenchman appeared determined not to part with his prize without a trial of strength, but as the captured vessel was the nearest to us, I decided to retake her first, and then fight him if he wished. I therefore steered to lay the prize by the board. The Frenchman, a lugger of twelve guns, perceiving our intention, made also for the prize to defend her, he steering up for her close-hauled, we running down to her free, the prize lying between us, and sheltering each of us from the other's guns. It is difficult to say whether the Frenchman or we were the first to touch her sides with our respective vessels; I rather think that the

Frenchman was a second or two before us. At all events they were quicker than we were, and were on the deck first, besides having the advantage of the assistance of their men already on board, so that we were taken at a great disadvantage. However, we did gain the deck by boarding at two points, forward and aft, and a fierce contest ensued. The French were more numerous than we were, but my men were better selected, being all very powerful, athletic fellows. Philip had boarded with the other party forward, which was led by my chief officer. My party, who were abaft, not being so numerous, were beaten back to the taffrail of the vessel, where we stood at bay, defending ourselves against the furious assaults of the Frenchmen. But if we lost, the other party gained, for the whole body of the Frenchmen were between us and them, and those who faced Philip's party were driven back to abaft the mainmast. It so happened that Philip was thrown down on the deck, and his men passed over him; and while in that position, and unable to rise from the pressure upon him, he heard a calling out from below: this told him that the English prisoners were in the hold; and as soon as he could rise he threw off the hatches, and they rushed up, to the number of twenty-three stout fellows, to our support, cheering most manfully, and by their cheers announcing to the French that we had received assistance. This gave fresh courage to my men, who were hard pressed and faint with their great exertion. We cheered, and rushed upon the enemy, who were already weakened by many of them having turned round to resist the increased impetus from forward. Our cheers were replied to by Philip's party and the prisoners, and the French were losing the day. They made another desperate rush upon Philip's men, and succeeded in driving them back to before the main-hatches; but what they gained forward, they lost abaft, as we pushed on with vigour. This was their last attempt. The main-hatch being open, several of them in the confusion fell into it, others followed them of their own accord, and at last every one of them was beaten down from the deck, and the hatches were put over them, with three cheers.

"Now for the privateer—she is our own," cried Philip; "follow me, my men," continued he, as he sprang upon the bulwarks of the prize, and from thence into the main rigging of the lugger alongside.

Most of my men followed him; and as there were but few men left on board of the lugger, she was soon in our possession, and thus we had both the enemy and the prize without firing a cannon-shot. It was strange that this combat between two privateers should thus be decided upon the deck of another vessel, but such was the fact. We had several men badly wounded, but not one killed. The French were not quite so fortunate, as seven of their men lay dead upon the decks. The prize proved to be the Antelope West-Indiaman, laden with sugar and rum, and of considerable value. We gave her up to the captain and crew, who had at afforded us such timely assistance, and they were not a little pleased at being thus rescued from a French prison. The privateer was named the Jean Bart, of twelve guns, and one hundred and fifteen men, some away in prizes. She was a new vessel, and this her first cruise. As it required many men to man her, and we had the prisoners to encumber us, I resolved that I would take her to Liverpool at once; and six days afterwards we arrived there without further adventure. Philip's gallant conduct had won him great favour with my officers and men, and I must say that I felt very proud of him.

As soon as we had anchored both vessels, I went on shore with Philip to Mr Trevannion's to give him an account of what had occurred during the short cruise, and I hardly need say that he was satisfied with the results, as we had made three recaptures of value besides a privateer. I introduced Philip to him, acquainting him with his miraculous preservation, and Mr Trevannion very kindly invited him for the present to remain in his house. We then took our leave, promising to be back by dinner-time, and I went with Philip to fit him out in a more creditable way; and having made my purchases and given my orders, (it being then almost two o'clock *post meridiem*,) we hastened to Mr Trevannion's, that we might be in time for dinner. I was, I must confess, anxious to see Miss Trevannion, for she had often occupied my thoughts during the cruise. She met me with great friendliness and welcomed me back. Our dinner was very agreeable, and Philip's sallies were much approved of. He was, indeed, a mirthful, witty lad, full of jest and humour, and with a good presence withal. Mr Trevannion being called out just as dinner was finished, Miss Trevannion observed—"I presume, Mr Elrington, that your good fortune and the reputation you have acquired in so short a time, have put an end to all your misgivings as to a privateersman's life?"

"I am not quite so light and inconstant, Miss Trevannion," replied I; "I rejoice that in this cruise I have really nothing to lament or blush for, and trust at the same time we have been serviceable to our country; but my opinion is the same, and I certainly wish that I had fought under the king's pennant instead of on board of a privateer."

"You are, then, of the same mind, and intend to resign the command?"

"I do, Miss Trevannion, although I admit that this lad's welfare makes it more important than ever that I should have some means of livelihood."

"I rejoice to hear you speak thus, Mr Elrington, and I think my father's obligations to you are such, that if he does not assist you, I should feel ashamed of him—but such I am certain will not be the case. He will forward your views, whatever they may be, to the utmost of his power—at the same time, I admit, from conversations I have had with him, that he will be mortified at your resigning the command."

"And so shall I," said Philip, "for I do not agree with you or my brother: I see no more harm in privateering than in any other fighting: I suppose, Miss Trevannion, you have been the cause of my brother's scruples, and I tell you candidly to your face, that I do not thank you for it."

Miss Trevannion coloured up at this remark, and then replied, "I do not think, Mr Philip, that I have had the pleasure of seeing your brother more than three times in my life, and that within this last six weeks, and sure I am that we have not had a quarter of an hour's conversation altogether. It is, therefore, assuredly, too much to say that I am the cause, and your brother will tell you that he expressed these opinions before I ever had had any conversation with him."

"That may be," replied Philip, "but you approved of his sentiments, and that concluded the business, I am sure, and I don't wonder at it. I only hope that you won't ask me to do anything I do not wish to do; for I am sure that I could never refuse you anything."

"I am glad to hear you say so, Mr Philip; for if I see you do that which I think wrong, I shall certainly try my influence over you," replied Miss Trevannion, smiling. "I really was not aware that I had such power."

Here Mr Trevannion came in again, and the conversation was changed; and shortly afterwards Miss Trevannion left the room. Philip, who was tired of sitting while Mr Trevannion and I took our pipes, and who was anxious to see the town, also left us; and I then stated to Mr Trevannion that having now completed the cruise which I had agreed that I would, I wished to know whether he had provided himself with another captain.

"As you appear so determined, my dear Elrington, I will only say that I am very sorry, and will not urge the matter any longer. My daughter told me since your absence that she was certain you would adhere to your resolution; and, although I hoped the contrary, yet I have been considering in which way I can serve you. It is not only my pleasure but my duty so to do; I have not forgotten, and never will forget, that you in all probability saved my life by your self-devotion in the affair of the Jacobites. When you first came to me, you were recommended as a good accountant, and, to a certain degree, a man of business; and, at all events, you proved yourself well acquainted and apt at figures. Do you think that a situation on shore would suit you?"

"I should endeavour to give satisfaction, Sir," I replied; "but I fear that I should have much to learn."

"Of course you would; but I reply that you would soon learn. Now, Elrington, what I have to say to you is this: I am getting old, and in a few years shall be past work; and I think I should like you as an assistant for the present, and a successor hereafter. If you would like to join me, you shall superintend the more active portion of the business; and I have no doubt but that in a year or two you will be master of the whole. As you know, I have privateers and I have merchant vessels, and I keep my storehouses. I have done well up to the present; not so well, perhaps, now, as I did when I had slave-vessels, which were most profitable; but my deceased wife persuaded me to give up that traffic, and I have not resumed it, in honour of her memory. These foolish women should never interfere in such matters; but let that pass. What I have to say is, that if you choose after a year to join me as a partner, I will give you an eighth of the business, and as we continue I will make over a further share in proportion to the profits; and I will make such arrangements as to enable you at my death to take the whole concern upon favourable terms."

Mr Trevannion knocked the ashes out of his pipe, and, as he concluded,—"I am," I replied, "as you may imagine, Sir, much gratified and honoured at your proposal, which I hardly need say that I willingly accept. I only hope you will make allowance for my ignorance at first setting off, and not ascribe to any other cause my imperfections. You may assure yourself that good-will shall never be wanting on my part, and I shall work day and night, if required, to prove my gratitude for so kind an offer."

"Then, it is settled," said Mr Trevannion; "but what are we to do with your brother Philip?"

"He thinks for himself, Sir, and does not agree with me on the question in point. Of course, I have no right to insist that my scruples should be his; indeed, I fear that I should have little chance in persuading him, as he is so fond of a life of adventure. It is natural in one so young. Age will sober him."

"Then you have no objection to his going on board of a privateer?"

"I would rather that he was in any other service, Sir; but as I cannot control him I must submit, if he insist upon following that profession. He is a gallant, clever boy, and as soon as I can, I will try to procure him a situation in a king's ship. At present he must go to sea in some way or the other, and it were, perhaps, better that he should be in good hands (such as Captain Levee's for instance) on board of a privateer, than mix up with those who might demoralise him more."

"Well, then, he shall have his choice," replied Mr Trevannion. "He is a smart lad, and will do you credit wherever he may be."

"If I may take the liberty to advise, Sir," replied I, "I think you could not do better than to give the command of the Sparrow-hawk to the chief officer, Mr James; he is a good seaman and a brave man, and I have no doubt will acquit himself to your satisfaction."

"I was thinking the same; and as you recommend him he shall take your place. Now, as all this is settled, you may as well go on board and make known that you have resigned the command. Tell Mr James that he is to take your place. Bring your clothes on shore, and you will find apartments ready for you on your return, for in future you will of course consider this house as your residence. I assure you that, now that you do not leave me, I am almost glad that the affair is arranged as it is. I wanted assistance, that is the fact, and I hold myself fortunate that you are the party who has been selected. We shall meet in the evening."

Mr Trevannion then went away in the direction of his daughter's room instead of the counting-house as usual, and I quitted the house. I did not go immediately down to the wharf to embark. I wanted to have a short time for reflection, for I was much overpowered with Mr Trevannion's kindness, and the happy prospects before me. I walked out into the country for some distance, deep in my own reflections, and I must say that Miss Trevannion was too often interfering with my train of thought.

I had of course no fixed ideas, but I more than once was weighing in my mind whether I should not make known to them who I was, and how superior in birth to what they imagined. After an hour passed in building castles, I retraced my steps, passed through the town, and, going down to the wharf, waved my handkerchief for a boat, and was soon on board. I then summoned the officers and men, told them that I had resigned the command of the vessel, and that in future they were to consider Mr James as their captain. I packed up my clothes, leaving many articles for my successor which were no longer of any use to me, but which he would have been compelled to replace.

Philip I found was down in the cabin, and with him I had a long conversation, he stated his wish to remain at sea, saying that he preferred a privateer to a merchant vessel, and a king's ship to a privateer. Not being old enough, or sufficient time at sea to be eligible for a king's ship, I agreed that he should sail with Captain Levee, as soon as he came back from his cruise. He had already sent in a good prize. As soon as my clothes and other articles were put into the boat, I wished them all farewell, and was cheered by the men as I pulled on shore.

My effects were taken up to Mr Trevannion's house by the seamen, to whom I gave a gratuity, and I was met by Mr Trevannion, who showed me into a large and well-furnished bed-room, which he told me was in future to be considered as my own. I passed away the afternoon in arranging my clothes, and did not go down to the parlour till supper-time, where I found Miss Trevannion, who congratulated me upon my having changed my occupation to one more worthy of me. I made a suitable reply, and we sat down to supper. Having described this first great event in my life, I shall for the present conclude.

---

# Chapter Thirteen.

**After staying a year with him, Mr Trevannion proposes to take me into Partnership, but I decline the offer from conscientious motives—Miss Trevannion treats me with unmerited coldness—This and her Father's anger make me resolve to quit the House—What I overhear and see before my departure—The Ring.**

You may now behold me in a very different position, my dear Madam; instead of the laced hat and hanger at my side, imagine me in a plain suit of grey with black buttons, and a pen behind my ear; instead of walking the deck and balancing to the motion of the vessel, I am now perched immoveably upon a high stool; instead of sweeping the horizon with my telescope, or watching the straining and bending of the spars aloft, I am now with my eyes incessantly fixed upon the ledger or day-book, absorbed in calculation. You may inquire how I liked the change. At first, I must confess, not over-much, and, notwithstanding my dislike to the life of a privateersman, I often sighed heavily, and wished that I were an officer in the king's service. The change from a life of activity to one of sedentary habits was too sudden, and I often found myself, with my eyes still fixed upon the figures before me, absorbed in a sort of castle-building reverie, in which I was boarding or chasing the enemy, handling my cutlass, and sometimes so moved by my imagination as to brandish my arm over my head, when an exclamation of surprise from one of the clerks would remind me of my folly, and, angry with myself; I would once more resume my pen. But after a time I had more command over myself; and could sit steadily at my work. Mr Trevannion had often observed how absent I was, and it was a source of amusement to him; when we met at dinner, his daughter would say, "So I hear you had another sea-fight this morning, Mr Elrington;" and her father would laugh heartily as he gave a description of my ridiculous conduct.

I very soon, with the kind assistance of Mr Trevannion, became master of my work, and gave him satisfaction. My chief employment consisted in writing the letters to correspondents. At first I only copied Mr Trevannion's letters in his private letter-book; but as I became aware of the nature of the correspondence, and what was necessary to be detailed, I then made a rough copy of the letters, and submitted them to Mr Trevannion for his approval. At first there were a few alterations made, afterwards I wrote them fairly out, and almost invariably they gave satisfaction, or, if anything was added, it was in a postscript. Mr Trevannion's affairs, I found, were much more extensive than I had imagined. He had the two privateers, two vessels on the coast of Africa trading for ivory and gold-dust and other articles, two or three vessels employed in trading to Virginia for tobacco and other produce, and some smaller vessels engaged in the Newfoundland fisheries, which, when they had taken in their cargo, ran to the Mediterranean to dispose of it, and returned with Mediterranean produce to Liverpool. That he was a very wealthy man, independent of his large stakes upon the seas, was certain. He had lent much money to the guild of Liverpool, and had some tenanted properties in the county; but of them I knew nothing, except from the payment of the rents. What surprised me much was, that a man of Mr Trevannion's wealth, having but one child to provide for, should not retire from business—and I once made the remark to his daughter. Her reply was: "I thought as you do once, but now I think differently. When I have been on a visit with my father, and he has stayed away for several weeks, you have no idea how restless and uneasy he has become from want of occupation. It has become his habit, and habit is second nature. It is not from a wish to accumulate that he continues at the counting-house, but because he cannot be happy without employment. I, therefore, do not any longer persuade him to leave off, as I am convinced that it would be persuading him to be unhappy. Until you came, I think the fatigue was too great for him; but you have, as he apprises me, relieved him of the heaviest portion of the labour, and I hardly need say that I am rejoiced that you have so done."

"It certainly is not that he requires to make money, Miss Trevannion; and, as he is so liberal in everything, I must credit what you assert, that it is the dislike to having no employment which induces him to continue in business. It has not yet become such a habit in me," continued I, smiling; "I think I could leave it off with great pleasure."

"But is not that because you have not yet recovered from your former habits, which were so at variance with a quiet and a sedentary life?" replied she.

"I fear it is so," said I, "and I believe, of all habits, those of a vagrant are the most difficult to overcome. You used to laugh at me the first few months that I was here. I presume that I am a little improved, as I have not been attacked lately?"

"My father says so, and is much pleased with you, Mr Elrington, if my telling you so gives you any satisfaction."

"Certainly it does, because I wish to please him."

"And me, too, I hope?"

"Yes, most truly, Miss Trevannion; I only wish I had it in my power to show how much I study your good opinion."

"Will you risk my father's displeasure for it?" replied she, looking at me fixedly.

"Yes, I will, provided—"

"Oh! There is a proviso already."

"I grant that there should not have been any, as I am sure that you would not ask me to do anything which is wrong. And my proviso was, that I did not undertake what my conscience did not approve."

"Your proviso was good, Mr Elrington, for when a woman would persuade, a man should be particularly guarded that he is not led into error by a rash promise. I think, however, that we are both agreed upon the point. I will therefore come at once to what I wish you to do. It is the intention of my father, in the course of a few days, when you shall have accomplished your year of service, to offer to take you into partnership; and I am certain it will be on liberal terms. Now I wish you to refuse his offer unless he gives up privateering."

"I will do so at all risks, and I am truly glad that I have your encouragement for taking such a bold step."

"I tell you frankly that he will be very indignant. There is an excitement about the privateering which has become almost necessary to him, and he cares little about the remainder of his speculations. He is so blind to the immorality to which it leads, that he does not think it is an unlawful pursuit; if he did, I am sure that he would abandon it. All my persuasion has been useless."

"And if a favourite and only daughter cannot prevail, what chance have I, Miss Trevannion?"

"A better chance, Mr Elrington; he is partial to me, but I am a woman, and he looks upon my observations as a woman's weakness. The objections raised by a man, a young man, and one who has so long been actively engaged in the service, will, therefore, carry more weight; besides, he has now become so accustomed to you, and has had so much trouble taken off his hands, and, at the same time, has such implicit confidence in you, that I do not think, if he finds that he has to choose between your leaving him and his leaving off privateering, he will hesitate in relinquishing the latter. You have, moreover, great weight with him, Mr Elrington; my father is fully aware of the deep obligation he is under to your courage and self-devotion in the affair of the Jacobite refugees. You will, therefore, succeed, if you are firm; and, if you do succeed, you will have my gratitude, if that is of any importance to you; my friendship you know you have already."

The entrance of Mr Trevannion prevented my reply. We had been waiting for his return from a walk, and dinner had been ready some time. "I have just seen some of the men of the Arrow," said Mr Trevannion, taking off his hat and spencer, "and that detained me."

"Has Captain Levee arrived, then, Sir?" said I.

"No; but he has sent in a prize—of no great value—laden with light wares. The men in charge tell me he has had a rough affair with a vessel armed *en flute*, and that he has lost some men. Your brother Philip, as usual, is wounded."

I should here observe, that during the year which had passed away the two privateers had been several times in port—they had met with moderate success, barely sufficient to pay their expenses; my brother Philip had always conducted himself very gallantly, and had been twice wounded in different engagements.

"Well, Sir," replied I, "I do not think that the loss of a little blood will do any harm to such a hot-headed youth as Master Philip; but I hope in a short time to give him an opportunity of shedding it in the service of the king, instead of in the pursuit of money. Indeed," continued I, as I sat down to table, "the enemy are now so cautious, or have so few vessels on the high seas, that I fear your privateering account current will not be very favourable, when balanced, as it will be in a few days, notwithstanding this cargo of wares just arrived."

"Then we must hope better for next year," replied Mr Trevannion. "Amy, my dear, have you been out to-day?"

"Yes, Sir; I was riding for two hours."

"Have they altered your pillion yet?"

"Yes, Sir; it came home last night, and it is now very comfortable."

"I called at Mrs Carleton's, who is much better. What a fop that Mr Carleton is—I don't know what scented powder he uses, but it perfumed the whole room. Had not Mrs Carleton been such an invalid, I should have opened the window."

Mr Trevannion then turned the conversation to some political intelligence which he had just received, and this engaged us till the dinner was over, and I returned to the counting-house, where I found the men who had brought in the prize, and who gave me a letter from Philip, stating that his wound was of no consequence.

The communication of Mr Trevannion took place, as his daughter had assured me it would, on the anniversary of my entering into Mr Trevannion's counting-house. After dinner, as we, as usual, were smoking our pipes, Mr Trevannion said: "Elrington, you have been with me now one year, and during that time you have made yourself fully master of your business;—much to my surprise, I acknowledge, but still more to my satisfaction. That I have every reason to be satisfied with you, you may imagine, when I tell you that it is now my intention to take you into partnership, and I trust by my so doing that you will soon be an independent man. You know the capital in the business as well as I do. I did say an eighth, but I now propose to make ever to you one-fourth, and to allow your profits of every year (deducting your necessary expenses) to be invested in the business, until you have acquired a right to one half. Of future arrangements we will speak hereafter."

"Mr Trevannion," replied it, "that I am truly grateful for such unexpected liberality I hardly need say, and you have my best thanks for your noble offer; but I have scruples which, I must confess, I cannot get over."

"Scruples!" exclaimed Mr Trevannion, laying down his pipe on the table. "Oh! I see now," continued he, after a pause; "you think I am robbing my daughter. No, no, the labourer is worthy of his hire, and she will have more than sufficient. You carry your conscientiousness too far, my dear fellow; I have more than enough for Amy, out of the business altogether."

"I am aware of that, Sir," added I, "and I did not, therefore, refer to your daughter when I said that I had scruples. I must be candid with you, Sir. How is it that I am now in your employ?"

"Why, because you had a dislike to privateering, and I had a debt of gratitude to pay."

"Exactly, Sir; but whether you had been pleased to employ me or not, I had made up my mind, as you well know, from conscientious motives, not to continue on board of a privateer."

"Well, I grant that."

"The same motives, Sir, will not allow me to be a sharer in the profits arising from such sources. I should consider myself equally wrong if I did so, as if I remained on board. Do not be angry with me, Sir," continued I; "if I, with many thanks, decline your offer of being your partner, I will faithfully serve you upon any salary which you may consider I may merit, and trust to your liberality in everything."

Mr Trevannion made no reply; he had resumed his pipe, and continued to smoke it, with his eyes fixed upon the mantel-piece. As soon as his pipe was out, he rose, put on his hat, and walked out of the room, without making any further observation. I waited a few minutes, and then went back to the counting-house.

That Mr Trevannion was seriously offended I was convinced; but I valued the good opinion of his daughter more than I did that of Mr Trevannion; indeed, my feelings towards her had, during the year that I had been in the house, gradually become of that nature that they threatened much my peace of mind. I cannot say that I loved her in the usual acceptation of the term,—adoration would better express what I felt. She was so pure, so perfect, such a model of female perfection, that I looked up to her with a reverence which almost quelled any feeling of love. I felt that she was above me, and that, with her wealth, it would be madness for one in my present position to aspire to her. Yet with this feeling I would have sacrificed all my hopes and present advantages to have obtained her approving smiles. It is not, therefore, to be wondered at that I risked Mr Trevannion's displeasure to gain her approbation; and when I resumed my seat at my desk, and thought of what had passed, I made up my mind to be once more an outcast in the world rather than swerve from the promise which I had made to her. I knew Mr Trevannion to be a very decided man, and hasty when offended. That he was seriously offended with me there was no doubt. I found that he had quitted the house immediately after he had left the room. I had hoped that he had gone to his daughter's apartments, and that a conversation with her might have produced a good effect; but such was not the case.

In about half an hour Mr Trevannion returned, and as he walked into the back room adjoining the counting-house, he desired me to follow him. I did so. "Mr Elrington," said he, sitting down, and leaving me standing at the table, "I fear, after what has passed, that we shall not continue on good terms. You have reproached me, an old man, with carrying on an unlawful business; in short, in raising your own scruples and talking of your own conscience, you have implied that I am acting contrary to what conscience should dictate. In short, you have told me, by implication, that I am not an honest man. You have thrown back in my face my liberal offer. My wish to oblige you has been treated not only with indifference, but I may add with contumely;—and that merely because you have formed some absurd notions of right and wrong in which you will find no one to agree with you, except, perhaps, priests and women. I wish you well, Mr Elrington, nevertheless. I am truly sorry for your infatuation, and wished to have served you, but you will not be assisted by me."

Here Mr Trevannion paused, but I made no reply. After a time, wiping the perspiration from his forehead with his handkerchief, for he evidently was in a state of great excitement, he continued:

"As you do not choose to join me from conscientious scruples, I cannot but imagine that you do not like to serve me from similar motives, for I see little difference between the two (and here, Madam, there was some force in his observation, but it never occurred to me before); at all events, without weighing your scruples so exactly as to know how far they may or may not extend, I feel that we are not likely to get on pleasantly together. I shall always think that I am reproached by you when anything is said connected with the privateers, and you may have twinges of conscience which may be disagreeable to you. Let us, therefore, part quietly. For your services up to the present, and to assist you in any other engagements you may enter on, take this—"

Mr Trevannion opened a lower drawer of the table, and put before me a bag containing, as I afterwards discovered, 250 gold jacobuses.

"I wish you well, Mr Elrington, but I sincerely wish that we had never met."

Mr Trevannion then rose abruptly, and, before I could make my reply, brushed past me, went out at the door, and again walked away at a rapid pace down the street. I remained where I stood; my eyes had followed him as he went away. I was completely surprised. I anticipated much anger, much altercation; but I never had an idea that he would be so unjust as to throw off in this way one who for his sake had gone through a heavy trial and come out with honour. My heart was full of bitterness. I felt that Mr Trevannion had treated me with harshness and ingratitude.

"Alas!" thought I, "such is the world, and such will ever be the case with such imperfect beings as we are. How vain to expect anything like consistency, much less perfection, in our erring natures! Hurt but the self-love of a man, wound his vanity, and all obligations are forgotten."

I turned away from the bag of money, which I was resolved not to accept, although I had not at the time twenty guineas at my own disposal. It was now within half an hour of dark; I collected all my books, put some in the iron safe, others as usual in my desk, and having arranged everything as completely as I could, I locked the safe, and enclosed the keys in a parcel, which I sealed. Putting Mr Trevannion's name on the outside, I laid the parcel on the table in the room where we had had our conference, by the side of the bag of money.

It was now dark, or nearly so, and leaving the confidential porter, as usual, to shut up the house, I went up to the sitting-room with the expectation of seeing Miss Trevannion, and bidding her farewell. I was not disappointed; I found her at her netting, having just lighted the lamp which hung over the table.

"Miss Trevannion," said I, advancing respectfully towards her, "I have fulfilled my promise, and I have received my reward,"—she looked up at me—"which is, I am dismissed from this house and your presence for ever."

"I trust," said she, after a pause, "that you have not exceeded my wishes. It appears to me so strange, that I must think that such is the case. My father never could have dismissed you in this way for merely expressing an opinion, Mr Elrington. You must have gone too far."

"Miss Trevannion, when you meet your father, you can then ascertain whether I have been guilty of intemperance or rudeness, or a proper want of respect in making the communication,—which I did in exactly the manner you yourself proposed, and my reward has been such as I state."

"You have a better reward, Mr Elrington, if what you assert is really correct; you have the reward of having done your duty; but I cannot imagine that your dismissal has arisen from the mere expression of an opinion. You'll excuse me, Mr Elrington, that, as a daughter, I cannot, in justice to a much-respected father, believe that such is the case."

This was said in so cold a manner, that I was nettled to the highest degree. Miss Trevannion had promised me her gratitude, instead of which I felt that she was doubting my word, and, as it were, taking the side of her father against me. And this was the return from her. I could have upbraided her, and told her what I felt; namely, that she had taken advantage of my feelings towards her to make me a cat's-paw to obtain her end with her father; and that now, having failed, I was left to my fate, without even commiseration; but she looked so calm, so grave, and so beautiful, that I could not do it. I commanded my wounded feelings, and replied:

"Since I have the misfortune to meet the displeasure of the daughter as well as of the father, Miss Trevannion, I have not another word to say, but farewell, and may you prosper."

My voice faltered as I said the last words, and, bowing to her, I quitted the room. Miss Trevannion did not even say farewell to me, but I thought that her lips appeared to move, as quitting the room I took my last look upon her beautiful face. I shut the door after me, and, overpowered by my feelings, I sank upon a settee in the ante-room, in a state of giddy stupor. I know not how long I remained there, for my head turned and my senses reeled; but I was aroused from it by the heavy tread of Mr Trevannion, who came along the corridor without a light, and not perceiving me opened the door of the sitting-room where his daughter still remained. He threw the door to after he had entered, but it did not quite close, leaving a narrow stream of light through the ante-room.

"Father," said Miss Trevannion in my hearing, "you look warm and excited."

"I have reason so to be," replied Mr Trevannion, abruptly.

"I have heard from Mr Elrington the cause of it," replied Miss Trevannion; "that is, I have heard his version of it. I am glad that you have come back, as I am most anxious to hear yours. What has Mr Elrington said or done to cause such irritation and his dismissal?"

"He has behaved with insolence and ingratitude," replied Mr Trevannion; "I offered him partnership, and he refused, unless I would give up privateering."

"So he stated; but in what manner was he insolent to you?"

"Insolent!—told me that he acted from conscientious motives, which was as much as to say that I did not."

"Was his language very offensive?"

"No, not his language—that was respectful enough; but it was the very respect which made it insolent. So I told him that as he could not, from scruples of conscience, join me in privateering, of course his scruples of conscience could not allow him to keep the books, and I dismissed him."

"Do you mean to say, my dear father, that he, in a respectful manner, declined entering into partnership from these scruples which you mention; that he gave you no other offence than expressing his opinion, and declining your offer?"

"And what would you have more?" replied Mr Trevannion.

"I wish to know where was the insult, the ingratitude, on his part which you complain of?"

"Simply in refusing the offer. He ought to have felt grateful, and he was not; and he had no right to give such reasons as he did; for the reasons were condemning my actions. But you women cannot understand these things."

"I rather think, my dear father, that we cannot; for I cannot perceive either the insult or the ingratitude which you complain of, and such I think will be your own opinion when you have had time to reflect, and are more cool. Mr Elrington expressed nothing more to-day, when he stated his dislike to privateering from conscientious motives, than he did after his return from his confinement in the Tower, when he gave up the command of the privateer on those very grounds; and then, when still warm with gratitude to him for his self-devotion, you did not consider it an insult, but, on the contrary, took him still nearer to you into your own house. Why, then, should you consider it an insult now? Neither can I see any ingratitude. You made him an offer, the value of which, in a worldly point of view, he could not but appreciate, and he declined it from conscientious motives; declined it, as you acknowledge, respectfully; proving that he was ready to sacrifice his worldly interests to what he considered his duty as a Christian. When Mr Elrington told me that you had dismissed him, I felt so certain that he must have been guilty of some unpardonable conduct towards you to have induced you to have resorted to such a step, that I did not credit him when he asserted the contrary. I could not believe, as a daughter, anything so much to the prejudice of my own father, and so much at variance with his general conduct. I now feel that I have been most unjust to Mr Elrington, and conducted myself towards him in a way which I bitterly regret, and hope by some means to be able to express my contrition for—"

"Amy—Amy," said Mr Trevannion, severely, "are you blinded by regard for this young man, that you side against your own father? Am I to understand that you have given your affections without my sanction or approval?"

"No, Sir," replied Miss Trevannion; "that I do respect and regard Mr Elrington is true, and I cannot do otherwise for his many good qualities and his devotion towards you; but if you would ask me if I love him, I reply that such a thought has not yet entered my head. Without a knowledge of who he is, or his family, and without your approval, I should never think of yielding up my affections in so hasty a manner; but I may say more: these affections have never been solicited by Mr Elrington. He has always behaved towards me with that respect, which, as the daughter of his patron, I have had a right to expect; but in no instance has he ever signified to me that he had any preference in my favour. Having assured you of this, my dear father, I cannot but say that I consider that he has, in this instance, not only been treated with injustice by you, but also by me."

"Say no more," replied Mr Trevannion. As he said this, I heard footsteps in the passage, and was about to retreat to my own room; but, as the party came without a light, I remained. It was the porter, who knocked at the sitting-room door, and was requested to come in by Mr Trevannion.

"If you please, Sir, Mr Elrington is gone out, I believe, and I found this packet directed to you on the table of the inner room, and also this bag of money, which I suppose you forgot to put away before you left."

"Very well, Humphrey, leave them on the table."

The man did so, and quitted the room, not perceiving me in the dark as he passed through the ante-room.

"He has not taken the money," observed Mr Trevannion. "He might have done so, as he ought to be paid for his services."

"I presume, my dear father, that his feelings were too much hurt by what passed," said Miss Trevannion. "There are obligations which cannot be repaid with gold."

"These, I perceive, are the keys of the safe; I did not think that he would have gone away this night."

I now considered it high time to quit the ante-room, where I had been irresistibly detained by the conversation which took place. I hastened to my own chamber, determined that I would leave the house the next morning before any one was stirring. I gained it in the dark, but, having the means of striking a light, I did so, and packed up all my clothes ready for my departure. I had just fastened down my valise, when I perceived a light on the further end of the long corridor which led to my apartment. Thinking it might be Mr Trevannion, and not wishing to see him, I blew out my own light and retreated to a small dressing-room, within my chamber, communicating by a glass door. The light evidently approached, and at last I perceived the party was entering my room, the door of which was wide open. It was Miss Trevannion who entered, and, turning round with her chamber-light in her hand, appeared to survey the apartment with a mournful air. She perceived my valise, and her eyes were fixed upon it for some time; at last she walked up to the dressing-table, and, sitting on the stool before it, leant down her head upon her hands and wept.

"Alas!" thought I, "if those tears were but for me; but it is not so—she has been excited, and her tears have come to her relief."

After a time she raised her head from the table, and said, "How unjust have I been—and I shall see him no more!—if I could but beg his pardon, I should be more happy. Poor fellow!—what must he have felt at my harsh bearing. Oh! My father, I could not have believed it. And what did I say?—that I had no feeling for—well, I thought so at the time, but now—I am not quite sure that I was correct, though he—well, it's better that he's gone—but I cannot bear that he should have gone as he has done. How his opinion of me must have changed! That is what vexes me—" and again she bent her head down on the table and wept.

In a moment she again rose, and took her candle in her hand. Perceiving on the dressing-table a small gold ring which I had taken off my finger the day before, and had forgotten, she took it up and examined it. After a little while she laid her light down on the table, and put the ring upon her finger.

"I will keep it till I see him again," murmured she; and then taking her light she walked slowly out of the room.

The knowledge I had gained by this unintentional eaves-dropping on my part, was the source of much reflection; and as I lay on the bed without taking off my clothes, it occupied my thoughts till the day began to break. That I still retained the good opinion of Miss Trevannion was certain, and the mortification I had endured at our final interview was now wholly removed. It was her duty to suppose her parent not in fault till the contrary was proved. She had known her father for years—me she had only known for a short time—and never before had she known him guilty of injustice. But her expressions and her behaviour in my room—was it possible that she was partial to me, more partial than she had asserted to her father when she was questioned?—and her taking away the ring!

# Chapter Fourteen.

### A Conspiracy, which ends satisfactorily to all Parties—Privateering is abandoned, and Captain Levee and Philip serve the King.

The night passed away in attempts at analysing the real feelings of Miss Trevannion, and also my own towards her; and now that I was to be separated from her, I discovered what I really had not before imagined, that my future happiness was seriously endangered by my sentiments towards her; in short, dear Madam, that I was most seriously in love.

"And now," thought I, "of what avail is it to have made this discovery now, except it were to convince me, as Miss Trevannion had said, that it were better that I were gone."

I did not fail to call to mind her observation about my unknown parentage and family, and this I reflected upon with pleasure, as it was the chief objection raised by her, and, at the same time, one that I could proudly remove, from my birth being really more distinguished than her own. Should I make it known? How could I?—we should, probably, never meet again. All this, and much more, was canvassed in my mind during the night, and also another question of more real importance, which was, what I was to do, and where I was to go? On this last point I could not make up my mind, but I determined that I would not leave Liverpool for a day or two, but would take up my quarters at my old lodgings, where I had lived with Captain Levee.

As the day dawned, I rose from the bed, and, taking my valise on my shoulder, I went softly down-stairs, opened the street-door, and, shutting it again carefully, I hastened down the street as fast as I could. I met nobody, for it was still early, and arrived at the lodging-house, where I had some trouble to obtain admittance; the old lady at last opening the door in great dishabille.

"Captain Elrington! Is it possible," exclaimed she, "why, what's the matter?"

"Nothing, Madam," replied I, "but that I have come to take possession of your lodgings for a few days."

"And welcome, Sir," replied she; "will you walk up-stairs while I make myself more fit to be seen. I was in bed and fast asleep when you knocked; I do believe I was dreaming of my good friend, Captain Levee."

I went up-stairs and threw myself on the old settee which was so familiar to me, and somehow or another, in a few minutes I was in a sound sleep. How long I might have slept on I cannot tell, but in less than an hour I was waked up by loud talking and laughter, and a few seconds afterwards found myself embraced by my brother Philip and Captain Levee. The Arrow had anchored at break of day, and they had just come on shore. I was delighted to see them, as every one is when he meets with friends when he is in distress. I briefly stated how it was that they found me there, and when breakfast was on the table, I entered into full details of what had passed, with the exception of Miss Trevannion having entered my room—that I considered too sacred to repeat to any one.

"You know, my dear Elrington," said Captain Levee, "that I have not the scruples which you have relative to privateering, but still I respect the conscientious scruples of others. There is no excuse for Mr Trevannion's conduct, and I cannot think but there is something else at the bottom of all this. You haven't been making love to his daughter, or, what would amount to the same thing, she has not been making advances to you?"

"I have not dared the first, Levee, and you do not know her, to suppose her capable of the latter."

"Well, if she had done so, there would have been no harm done," replied he; "but I will say no more as you look so grave. Philip and I will now call upon Mr Trevannion; and while I engage the old gentleman, Philip shall run alongside of the young maiden, and between the two we shall get our bearings and distance, and know how the land lies—and I will tell you more, Elrington, although I have no objection to be captain of a privateer, I certainly consider the command of a king's ship more reputable; and if I could manage to get the Arrow hired into the king's service (I still remaining in command of her), I should prefer it being so. At all events, I'll side with you, and that will drive the old gentleman on a dead lee-shore. Come along, Philip—we shall be with you in two hours, Elrington." With these words Captain Levee left the room, followed by my brother.

It was nearly three hours before they returned, and then I received the following narratives: Captain Levee, as he sat down, said, "Now, Philip, we'll hear your account first."

"Well, mine is soon told," replied Philip; "I had made up my mind how to act, and did not tell Captain Levee what I intended to do. When Mr Trevannion met us in the room behind the counting-house he appeared very much flurried: he shook hands with Captain Levee, and offered me his hand, which I refused, saying, 'Mr Trevannion, I have just seen my brother, and I hardly need say that nothing will induce me to remain in your employ. I will, therefore, thank you for my wages at your convenience.'

"'Hey-day, young man,' cried he, 'you give yourself strange airs. Well, Sir, you shall have your discharge; I can do without such snip-jacks as you are.'

"'Snip-jacks! Mr Trevannion,' replied I; 'if I must say it, we are better born and better bred than you or any of your connexions, and you were honoured by our service.'"

"You said that, Philip?—then you were wrong!"

"I told the truth."

"Still, you should not have said it; we took his service, and therefore—"

"We are not snip-jacks," interrupted Philip, "and his calling names brought on the reply."

"You must admit the provocation, Elrington," said Captain Levee.

"Well, go on, Philip."

"'Indeed,' said Mr Trevannion, in a great passion; 'well, then, I will soon rid myself of the obligation. Call this afternoon, Master Philip, and you shall receive your wages. You may now quit the room.'

"I did so, and put my hat a-cock to annoy him."

"So far his narrative is quite correct," said Captain Levee;—"now go on."

"Well," said Philip, "instead of turning out of the house, I turned into it, and went to the young lady's sitting-room. I opened the door softly, and found her with her hand up to her head, looking very sedate and sorrowful. 'Master Philip,' said she, 'you startled me; I am glad to see you—when did you arrive?'

"'This morning, Miss Trevannion.'

"'Well, sit down and bear me company for a time. Have you seen your brother?'

"'I have, Miss Trevannion,' replied I, still remaining on my feet, 'and I have just seen your father. I come now to bid you farewell. I have left the privateer, and shall never join her again; perhaps I may never see you again either, which, believe me, I am truly sorry for.'

"She covered her eyes with her hand, as she leant on the table, and I saw a tear fall as she said—'It is a sad business altogether, and has distressed me very much. I hope your brother does not think that I blame him; tell him that I do not in the least, and that he must forget my behaviour to him when we parted. I did him injustice, and I beg his pardon. Tell him so, Philip.'"

"Did she say those words, Philip?"

"Yes, word for word, and looked like an angel when he said so. I replied that I would certainly deliver her message, but that I must not remain, for fear of Mr Trevannion finding me with her, as he ordered me to quit the house."

"'Indeed,' said she; 'what can be the matter with my poor father?'

"'Why, Miss Trevannion,' said I, 'he was very angry, and he had reason, for I was very saucy, and that's the truth.'

"'Why, Philip, what did you say to him?'

"'Oh, I hardly know,' replied I, 'but I know that I said more than I ought; for I was very angry at my brother's dismissal. Good bye, Miss Trevannion.'

"Miss Trevannion was taking a ring off her finger as I said good bye, and I thought she was going to give it me as a keepsake; but, after a little hesitation, she put it on again, and then held out her hand, saying, 'Good bye, Master Philip, let us not part in anger, at all events.' I took her hand, bowed, and turned away to quit the room; when I was at the door I looked round, and she was sitting with her face in her hands and I think she was weeping. I went out into the street, and waited for Captain Levee, and there's an end of my story."

"Well, now I'll give you my portion, Elrington —As soon as Philip went out of the room, Mr Trevannion said, 'That's a most impudent boy, and I am glad that he is gone. You are of course aware that his brother has left me, and the cause of our disagreement?'

"'Yes, Sir,' replied I, drily, 'I have heard the whole particulars.'

"'Did you ever hear of such ridiculous scruples?' said he.

"'Yes, Sir, I heard them before, and so did you, when he gave up the command of the privateer, and I respected them, because I knew that Mr Elrington was sincere. Indeed, his observations on that head are undeniably true, and have had great weight with me; so much so, that I intend to enter into the king's service as soon as I possibly can.'

"I wish you had seen the look of Mr Trevannion when I said this—he was stupefied. That I, Captain Levee, who had commanded his vessels so long—I, the very *beau idéal* of a privateersman, a reckless, extravagant dare-devil, should also presume to have scruples, was too much for him. 'Et tu, Brute,' he might have exclaimed, but he did not; but he stared at me without speaking for some time; at last he said, 'Is the golden age arrived, or is this a conspiracy?'

"'Neither one nor the other, Sir,' I replied; 'I follow privateering because I can do no better; but as soon as I can do better, I shall leave it off.'

"'Perhaps,' said Mr Trevannion, 'you would wish to resign the command at once. If so, I beg you will not make any ceremony.'

"'I have not wished to put you to any inconvenience, Mr Trevannion,' replied I, 'but as you kindly beg me to use no ceremony, I will take advantage of your offer, and resign the command of the Arrow this day.'"

"Surely, Levee, you have not done so?"

"Yes, I have," replied Captain Levee, "and I have done so, in the first place, out of friendship to you, and, in the second, because I wish to be employed in the king's service, and my only chance of obtaining that wish is doing what I have done."

"How will that effect your purpose?"

"Because the men have sailed so long with me, that they will not sail under any other person, if I tell them not. Mr Trevannion will find himself in an awkward position, and I think we can force him to hire his vessel to government, who will gladly accept such a one as the Arrow."

"That I believe, if from her reputation alone," replied I. "Well, Levee, I thank you very much for this proof of sincere friendship. The plot thickens, and a few days will decide the question."

"Very true, and now let me finish my story. 'I am afraid,' said Mr Trevannion, in a very sarcastic tone, 'that I shall not be able to find any one to replace you in this moral age, Captain Levee; but I will try.'

"'Sir,' I replied, 'I will now answer your sarcasm. There is some excuse for ignorant seamen before the mast, who enter on board of privateers; they are indifferent to blood and carnage, and their feelings are blunted: there is some excuse even for decayed gentlemen like me, Mr Trevannion (for I am a gentleman born), who, to obtain a maintenance without labour, risk their lives and shed their blood; but there is no excuse for those who, having already as much wealth and more than they can require, still furnish the means and equip vessels of this description to commit the destruction which they do, for the sake of gain. There is a sermon, Sir, for you from a captain of a privateer, and I now wish you good morning.' I then got up, and, making a profound bow, I quitted the room before Mr Trevannion made any reply, and here I am. Now all we have to do is to wait quietly, and see what takes place; but first, I shall go on board the Arrow, and let them know that I have quarrelled with the owner. The men are not very well pleased as it is with their want of success these two last voyages, and it will require but little to blow up the discontent into a mutiny. Come, Philip, I shall want you to assist me. We shall be back to dinner, Elrington.''

When I was again alone, I had time to consider what had passed. What I chiefly dwelt upon was the interview, between Philip and Miss Trevannion—her message to me—her hesitation—and keeping the ring. I could not help surmising that our feelings towards each other were reciprocal, and this idea gave me infinite delight, and repaid me for all that had passed. Then my brother's hasty declaration to her father, that we were better born and bred than he was, would certainly be repeated by him to his daughter, and must make an impression. And what would Mr Trevannion do? Would he give way to the unanimous opinion against him? I feared not, at least without another struggle. All these questions occupied my thoughts till the return of Captain Levee and Philip from the privateer. They had well managed their business. The crew of the Arrow had come to an unanimous resolution that they would not sail with any other captain but Captain Levee; and that if he did resign the command of the vessel, as soon as their wages were paid, and they received their share of prize-money, they would leave, and enter into the king's service.

That afternoon Mr Trevannion sent for the officer next in command, to give him the command of the vessel; but as he went over the side, the men, expecting that he was sent for for that purpose, told him that they would serve under no one but Captain Levee, and that he might acquaint the owner with their determination. This put the finishing blow to Mr Trevannion. As soon as this was communicated to him, he was wild with rage in being thus thwarted in every way. As I afterwards was informed, he went even to his daughter, acquainted her with all that had passed, and gave vent to his indignation, accusing her of being a party in the conspiracy. But this was to be his last effort: the excitement had been too great, and after dinner he felt so unwell that he went to bed. The next morning he was in a raging fever, and at times delirious. The fever was so violent that the doctors had much to do to reduce it, and for ten days Mr Trevannion was in great danger. At last it was got under, leaving him in a state of great weakness and exhaustion, and his recovery was anything but rapid. Humphrey, the porter, had brought us this intelligence; as now there was no one to transact the business of the house, and the poor fellow did not know what to do, I desired him to apply to Miss Trevannion for directions, and told him that, although I would not enter the house, I would, if she wished it, see to the more important concerns which could not be neglected. She was then attending her father, and sent me a message, requesting, as a favour to her, that I would assist all I could in the dilemma. I consequently sent for the books, and gave orders, and made the necessary arrangements, as I had done before I had been dismissed by Mr Trevannion.

It was nearly five weeks before Mr Trevannion had sufficiently recovered to mention anything about business to him, and then it was that he learnt from his daughter that I had carried it on for him during his illness, and that everything had gone on as well as if he had acted for himself. Although Miss Trevannion had not expressed a wish that I should call, she had sent Humphrey for my brother Philip, to let us know the dangerous state in which her father was, and after that Philip called every day, and was the bearer of messages to me. As her father recovered, she told Philip that he had expressed himself very strongly as to his conduct towards me, and had acknowledged that I was right in my scruples, and that he was astonished that he had not viewed privateering in the same light that I did. That he felt very grateful for my considerate and kind conduct in conducting the business during his illness, and that as soon as he was well enough he would call upon me, to beg my pardon for his conduct towards me. Miss Trevannion also told him that her father had said that he considered his illness a judgment upon him, and a warning to open his eyes to his sacrifice of principle to the desire of gain, and that he received it accordingly with humility and thankfulness; that it was his intention to offer the privateer vessels to government, and if they did not hire them, he should dispose of them in some other way. This was very agreeable intelligence, and was the source of much conversation between Captain Levee and me.

About a fortnight afterwards, Mr Trevannion, who was still weak, sent me a billet, in which he said that he was afraid that his anxiety to see me and his being still confined to his room, rather retarded his recovery, and begged as a favour that I would accept his acknowledgment in writing, and come to see him. That I consented to do, and repaired to his house accordingly. I found him in his room, sitting in his dressing-gown, and he had evidently suffered much.

"Mr Elrington," said he, "I trust to your excellent nature to accept my apologies for the very unjust treatment you have received at my hands. I am ashamed of myself and I can say no more."

"I beg, Mr Trevannion, that you will say no more; I accept the return of your friendship with pleasure," replied I; "I am sorry that you have been so ill."

"I am not," replied he; "it is good for us to be chastised at times. My sickness has opened my eyes, and made me, I trust, a better man. May I ask a favour of you?"

"Most certainly, Sir," replied I.

"It is that you will execute a commission for me, which is to go to London on my account, see the government people who control the naval affairs, and offer the Arrow as a hired vessel. You know all her qualifies so well, and have kept her accounts so long, that you will be able to furnish them with all necessary information. I should wish Captain Levee to go with you, and, if you possibly can, make it a condition that he is taken into the king's service, and appointed the captain of her."

"I will do so with pleasure," replied I.

"One more favour I have to beg, Mr Elrington. When I so foolishly quarrelled with you, you left a bag of money, to which you were fully entitled from your good services, upon the table in the inner room. I trust now that you will not mortify me by refusing it, or I shall think that you have not really forgiven me."

I bowed assent.

"I thank you, Mr Elrington—thank you very much. Now I shall soon get well. To-morrow, perhaps, you will have the kindness to come and see me again. I feel rather overcome at present. Remember me kindly to Philip. Good-bye for to-day," said Mr Trevannion holding out his emaciated hand. "God bless you."

I took his hand and quitted the room, shutting the door softly. Mr Trevannion was quite alone when I was with him. Humphrey, the porter, had shown me up-stairs to the room.

Anxious as I was to see Miss Trevannion, I did not venture into the sitting-room, but passed the door and went down-stairs; when I was going out of the street-door, Humphrey followed me, and said Miss Trevannion wished to see me. I went back again with a beating heart, a sensation I had not felt before, when about to go into her presence. She was standing by the table.

"Mr Elrington," said she, as I bowed upon entering, "I did not think that you could carry your resentment against me so far as to leave the house without asking to see me; but if you do not wish to see me, 'tis a duty I owe to myself to wish to see you, if only for a moment, that I may beg your pardon for my conduct towards you when we last parted. I have suffered much since that, Mr Elrington; do not make me suffer more by continuing your resentment. Recollect I am but a weak woman, and must not be judged so severely as one of your own sex."

"I have nothing to pardon that I am aware of, Miss Trevannion," replied I; "I did not intrude upon you just now, because being no longer an inmate of the house, and not having parted with you in complete amity, I thought it would be presumptuous in me so to do."

"You are very generous, Mr Elrington," replied she; "now take my hand, and I promise never to be so hasty again."

I took the proffered hand, and raised it respectfully to my lips. I had never done so before; but Miss Trevannion showed no signs of displeasure, or attempted to withdraw it.

"Do you think my father looks very ill, Mr Elrington?" said she.

"From his appearance, I think that he must have suffered much."

"I am most thankful that you have come to see him, Mr Elrington. You have no idea how his mind was troubled, and how he longed to be reconciled to you. I trust he has made his peace."

"I have always had too much respect for your father, and gratitude for his kindness to me, to have made that a work of difficulty."

"You rejoice me much—make me very happy, Mr Elrington," replied Miss Trevannion, as the tears dropped fast from her eyes. "You must excuse me," said she; "I have become very weak and nervous during my father's illness—and sitting up with him so much,—but it is over now."

"You have had much anxiety, I see, Miss Trevannion; you are pale and thin to what you were."

"Did my father—? But I have no right to ask such questions."

"You would inquire, Miss Trevannion, whether anything was said as to future arrangements?"

Miss Trevannion made a sign of assent.

"I have promised to execute a commission for him, and am going to London, accompanied by Captain Levee."

"To get rid of those wretched privateers, is it not?"

"Yes it is, and I am to come to-morrow to arrange further: but I think you want to return to your father's room, so I will now take my leave."

"You are considerate, Mr Elrington; I did want to go up-stairs; but before I go I have some property of yours to place in your hands."

I bowed, thinking that she referred to the ring, which I perceived on her finger, and was annoyed that she was in such haste to return it. But, on the contrary, she went to the buffet and brought out the bag of gold jacobuses, which she laid on the table.

"You are very proud, Mr Elrington, not to take what was fairly your due," said Miss Trevannion, smiling.

"It is much more than I have ever earned," replied I; "but your father made me promise not to refuse it a second time, and of course I shall now take it."

My heart was much lightened when I found that it was the gold, and not the ring.

"Then good-bye, Mr Elrington; to-morrow I shall see you, of course."

Miss Trevannion then left the room and hastened up-stairs to her father, and I went home to my lodgings. I narrated the substance of what had passed between Mr Trevannion and me to Captain Levee and Philip, and also that I had been kindly received by Miss Trevannion.

"Well, I like the reconciliation and arrangement very much," said Captain Levee; "and as you have such a bag of gold, and I have not fifty guineas in the world, you shall stand treat in London, Elrington."

"That I will with pleasure; it will only be discharging an old debt, Levee. Philip shall go with us."

"But," said Captain Levee, "do you not think they will recognise their state-prisoner, and be cautious of a Jacobite?"

"They may remember the name," said I, "but my person was seen but by few. I do, however, think it would be advisable, as I shall have to sign papers, to take another."

"I think so, too," replied Captain Levee; "what shall we call you?"

"Let me see; I'll have a good name. I had a relative of the name of Musgrave; I think I will borrow his name. What say you, Philip? Will you be, for the future, Philip Musgrave?"

"Yes, brother, with all my heart. The name appears to fit me better than that of Elrington."

Thus, Madam, did I resume my real name without any suspicion on the part of Captain Levee; but I could not well sign government papers with an assumed one.

On the following day I called upon Mr Trevannion, who received me with great affection, and it was arranged that I should set off in three days, which time would be required for preparation, and to make the necessary purchases. To supply funds for the journey, Mr Trevannion gave me another bag of jacobuses, of the same amount as the former, saying that he wished us to appear bravely when we arrived in London, and that he should require no account of the expenditure, only that if the contents of the bag were not sufficient, he would supply more. This was nothing more but an excuse on his part to be generous; for one quarter of the money would have been sufficient for all needful expenses. I told him that I had taken the name of Musgrave, as that of Elrington might be remembered to the injury of the proposal, and he said that it was well thought of by me. Miss Trevannion had entered the room when I mentioned that to her father, and afterwards had quitted it. After I had taken leave of Mr Trevannion, I went down to the sitting-room, where I found his daughter waiting for me. We had much friendly discourse, and at one time she said, "I heard you say that you had taken the name of Musgrave for your intended journey. Do you intend to retain that name when you return?"

"Why should I?" replied I.

"Because," replied she, "perhaps it is your real name. Excuse a lady's curiosity, but is not that the fact?"

"Miss Trevannion," replied I, "my real name must at present remain a secret."

"That is to say, it will no longer be a secret if intrusted to me? I thank you, Sir, for the compliment."

"I do not intend to imply that, Miss Trevannion; I fully believe that you can keep a secret."

"If you fully believe so, you might, then, reply to my question; the more so, as I now pledge myself to keep your secret most faithfully."

"Then, Miss Trevannion, my real name is Musgrave," replied I.

"I thank you for your confidence, Mr Musgrave, which shall not be misplaced. I might now follow up my inquiries as to why you changed your name, with many other queries; but I am too discreet for that— the time may come when I shall know all; but I am content with your proof of confidence, and thank you for it."

Miss Trevannion never was so lively and communicative with me before, as she was this morning; there was a friendliness without any of her usual reserve, and I left her more full of admiration and devotion than ever.

In three days more our preparations were made, and, taking leave of Miss Trevannion and her father, who was recovering, and had admitted company to his room, we set off on horseback, as we had done before, and attended by the same two men of Captain Levee's who had served us on a former journey to London. We had no adventure whatever on this journey which could be worth narrating, and I shall therefore say that we arrived in good health and spirits, and took up our abode at once at our former lodging-house, instead of going to the inn. We were welcomed by the hostess, who had her house almost empty. The following day I made inquiries, and, in consequence, went to the Navy Office, and, requesting to see one of the head clerks, informed him of the occasion of my coming up to London. He was very civil, and replied that the government were in want of vessels, and he had no doubt but they would have the Arrow, as she was well-known as a strong privateer. I then inquired whether they thought it likely that Captain Levee might be taken into the service, stating what an excellent crew the Arrow had, and that they would not remain in her, unless they were commanded by him, in whom they had great confidence.

The clerk replied that it might be done certainly,—"but," added he— "Sir, you cannot expect people to do such kind offices without they are rewarded."

I perfectly understood him, and replied, that, of course, I did not expect it; but I was so ignorant as to what ought to be done, that I begged that he would give me his advice, for which I should be most grateful.

"Well, well, you understand me, Mr Musgrave, and that is sufficient. I will be plain with you. It will cost 100 guineas to obtain what you want for Captain Levee, and of that money I shall not receive a doit."

"I shall be most happy to give that sum and half as much more to obtain my wish, Sir, and shall feel much obliged to you in the bargain; and while I am negotiating, I may as well state that I have a brother who sails with Captain Levee, who is most anxious to be with him, and sail as his lieutenant."

"That will cost another fifty guineas, Mr Musgrave."

"I am most willing," replied I.

"Well, we must first get the vessel hired into the service. You have your tonnage and equipment all on paper?"

"Everything that is requisite; and, moreover, every cruise she has made, the actions she has fought, and the prizes she has taken under the command of Captain Levee, and with the crew now on board."

"Furnish all these documents, Mr Musgrave, and leave it to me. I am to understand that you perfectly agree to the terms I have proposed?"

"Perfectly, Sir; and, if you please, I will sign a memorandum to that effect."

"No, no," replied he, "we never put such things down on paper. It is an affair of honour and good faith. You say your money is all ready."

"At a minute's warning."

"That is sufficient, Mr Musgrave. I will now wish you good morning. Send me the documents."

"I have them in my pocket, Sir."

"Better still; then the affair may be arranged this afternoon, and you may call to-morrow at about two in the afternoon; and you may as well bring the money with you, as you can but take it away again if everything is not to your satisfaction."

I returned to the lodgings quite delighted with the prospect of such a fortunate issue to my mission, and was in good time for dinner. I did not tell Captain Levee or Philip of what had passed, but merely that I considered that there was a good chance of success, and that I was to call on the following day. That night we went to the theatre, and saw a play performed, written by Shakespeare, in the time of Queen Elizabeth, and called the "Merry Wives of Windsor." We were much pleased with the character of *Falstaff*, a fat knight, full of humour. The next day, at the time appointed, I called upon the head clerk, who told me that everything was arranged according to my wishes; that the hiring of the vessel was according to her tonnage; and he considered that the price offered by the government was fair and liberal; so did I, and immediately accepted it. He then drew from his desk the articles of agreement between the government and the owner of the vessel, and, at the same time, the warrants for Captain Levee and Philip, to act as commander and lieutenant.

"Now, Mr Musgrave, all you have to do is to sign the first paper, and fulfil the other portion of our agreement."

I immediately pulled out the bag of money which I had brought with me, and, after counting it over, the clerk gave me his pen to sign the document, and handed to me the warrants for Philip and Captain Levee.

"You have behaved liberally in this affair, Mr Musgrave," said the gentleman, as he locked up the bag of money in his desk: "if at any time I can be of use to you, you may command me."

"I thank you, Sir," replied I; "I may by-and-by have to ask you to exert your influence in behalf of my brother, that he may obtain the command of one of the king's ships, and if you can help me, I shall be most grateful."

"Depend upon it I will," replied he, "and I beg you will use no ceremony on making the application."

He then shook hands with me, and I went home. Dinner was over when I came back, but the hostess had put away some victuals for me, and while I was eating them I gave them an account of my success, handing their warrants to Captain Levee and Philip. They could hardly credit me, even when the documents were in their hands, but, pledging them to secrecy, I told them by what means I had been so successful. Whereupon they thanked me, and we then went out to procure the uniforms suitable to their respective ranks, and this occupied us till the evening, when we agreed to go to the cockpit and see the fights between the various animals, with which Philip particularly was much delighted. As we had nothing to detain us in London, and it was necessary that the Arrow should immediately run round to the Nore, we determined, as the uniforms were to be ready on the following day, that the day after that we would return to Liverpool.

---

# Chapter Fifteen.

**We return to Liverpool—I have an interview with Miss Trevannion—Plutus interferes with Cupid, and I sail again for the coast of Africa.**

We set off, and arrived at Liverpool, without accident, late on the sixth night, when we repaired to our usual lodgings. The next day I called to tell Mr Trevannion that I had returned, and was informed by Humphrey that he was quite strong again, and very anxious to see me, although he had no idea that I should return so soon. Humphrey went up to announce my arrival, and Mr Trevannion admitted me immediately, although he was not yet out of bed.

"I fear that you have not been successful," said he as he took my hand.

"On the contrary, Sir, I have succeeded in everything," and I then gave him an account of what had happened.

"Well," replied he, "I am glad of it, and recollect I must be at the expense, as, without you had incurred it, the schooner would not, in all probability, have been hired. And now I want to consult with you about something else. Here is a letter from Captain Irving, of the Amy, brought home by the Chester Lass."

These were two vessels employed on the Gold Coast, which belonged to Mr Trevannion.

"Read it," said Mr Trevannion, "and give me your opinion."

I did so: Captain Irving stated that he had pushed the two vessels up a small river on the coast, which he had not known of before, and had fallen in with a black ruler, who had never yet treated with the English; but only with the Spaniards, for slaves. That his English commodities were quite new to the natives, and that, in consequence, he had made a most fortunate traffic with them, and had loaded a vessel with ivory, wax, and gold-dust to the amount of 1000 pounds, and that he had sent the Chester Lass, remaining himself to continue the barter before it was known to the other ships on the coast, which it would soon be. He continued, that he had not sufficient of the articles which were most valued by the natives, and requested that Mr Trevannion would immediately despatch another vessel with various goods enumerated, and that then he should be able to fill his own vessel as well as the one that he had despatched home; that the river was in such a latitude, and the mouth difficult to discover; that he sent a little sketch of the coast, which would facilitate the discovery—but that no time was to be lost, as the sickly season was coming on, and it was very unhealthy at that time.

As I folded up the letter, Mr Trevannion said:

"Now, here is an invoice of the whole cargo sent home by the Chester Lass. I reckon it worth about 7000 pounds."

I looked over the invoice, and agreed with Mr Trevannion that it was well worth that, if not more.

"This is most important, you will acknowledge, Musgrave," said Mr Trevannion; "but before I go any further, I trust that, now the only difficulty is got over, you will not refuse to be my partner; the only difference I intend to make, is, that I now offer you one-fourth instead of one-eighth. Silence gives consent," continued Mr Trevannion, as I did not immediately reply.

"I was so astonished at your munificent offer, Sir, that I could not well speak."

"Then it's agreed; so say no more about it," said Mr Trevannion, taking me by the hand, and pressing it warmly—"and now to business. My idea is, to send out the Sparrow-Hawk, being so fast a sailer. Of course, as a privateer, she has done her work; and as the government wish the complement of the Arrow to be increased, I think we cannot do better than to fill her up with some of the Sparrow-Hawk's men, leaving about twenty-five on board of her, and sending her out as soon as possible to the coast, with the articles which Captain Irving requests."

"I agree with you, Sir, that it will be the best plan."

"But whom to send is the difficulty," said Mr Trevannion. "Captain Paul, of the Chester Lass, is very ill, and not likely to be out of bed for some time; and even if he were well, I have no opinion of him in an affair of this moment. If, as Captain Irving says, he can fill the Amy, her cargo will be worth three times that of the Chester Lass; but, of course, the destination of the Sparrow-Hawk must be a secret, and I do not know whom to intrust her to. We require some one in whom we can put confidence."

"I agree with you, Sir," replied I; "and, if you have no objection, I think that the best plan will be for me to go myself; I shall be back again in ten weeks at the furthest."

"Well, as you will now have a strong interest in it, I really think so too. In fact, I don't know whom else we can trust."

"I agree with you, Sir, and I will go myself, and I think the sooner the better; but I do not know whether we can obtain all the goods requisite immediately."

"We can have them in five or six days," replied Mr Trevannion; "I sent Humphrey out to make inquiry."

"At all events, I must look to them myself; and there are many other things to manage, so I had better wish you a good morning now, Mr Trevannion, and in the evening I will call again, and let you know what I have done."

"Do so," said he, and I then took my leave.

I certainly was very much astonished as well as much pleased at Mr Trevannion's liberality relative to the partnership, and I could now look forward to competency in a few years at the furthest. Certainly, if Mr Trevannion had been hasty in his conduct towards me he had made most noble reparation. I first returned to the lodgings and told Captain Levee and Philip what had passed; they immediately proposed that we should all go together on board the Sparrow-Hawk, that I might make my arrangements, and that they might persuade some of the men to join the Arrow. I first picked out the men I wished to sail with me; and then they talked over the rest, who that evening went on shore for their wages, and the next morning joined the Arrow, as Captain Levee was anxious to get round to the Nore. The day after the men joined, the Arrow sailed, which I was not sorry for, as it left me more at leisure to expedite my own affairs. Philip promised to be my correspondent, and I bade them both farewell with regret. I called in the evening, as I had promised, upon Mr Trevannion, and he then gave me the deed of partnership, signed and dated the day when he first made the offer, and we had quarrelled; but I did not see Miss Trevannion; much to my regret, her father said that she was ailing. The business I had to transact, and fitting out the Sparrow-Hawk, so completely occupied me, that it was now three days that I had been at Liverpool without having seen her, and I was much annoyed at it, as I had called every day. My feelings towards her were now stronger than before. She was never out of my thoughts, and I hardly know how it was that I transacted business as I did. This evening I was determined, if possible, that I would see her, and find out why she avoided me, as it appeared to me that she did. When I called, therefore, I did not ask to see her father, but told Humphrey to find out where Miss Trevannion was, and say that I requested to speak with her.

Humphrey returned, and said that she was in the sitting-room, to which I instantly repaired.

"I am fearful that I have given you some unintentional cause of displeasure, Miss Trevannion," said I, as I entered, "for you have appeared to avoid me since my return."

"Indeed, Mr Musgrave, I have not," replied she; "I was most anxious to see you, and have thought it very unpolite, I may add, unkind, on your part not to have come to me."

"I have been in the house every day, and sometimes twice a day, with your father, Miss Trevannion, and have never met you. Once I inquired for you, and your father told me you were unwell, whereas Humphrey had but five minutes before told me that you were well and in good spirits."

"Humphrey told the truth, and so did my father. I was in good health and spirits, and in five minutes afterwards I was ill and unhappy."

"I trust I was no party to it, Miss Trevannion."

"You were a party to it, but not the great offender, who was my father. He had told me that upon your return he had installed you as his partner, and had done you the justice you had deserved; and then he told me that you were going out to the coast of Africa in the Sparrow-Hawk."

"It is very true, Miss Trevannion; but where is the offence?"

"The offence is this: my father no sooner does you justice than he wants more ivory and gold-dust, having more than enough already; but I told him it was as bad as privateering, for in either case he sends people out to sacrifice their lives, that he may gain more money. I have no patience with this foolish pursuit of wealth."

"After all your father's kindness to me, Miss Trevannion, I could do no less than accept the offer."

"You would have been more wise and more just to yourself to have refused it, Mr Musgrave. I read the letters to my father when they arrived, and you know what Captain Irving says about the unhealthiness of the climate. You have been my father's best friend, and he should not have treated you thus."

"I never did value life, Miss Trevannion; but really the kind interest you have expressed on this occasion makes me feel as if my poor life was of some value. To one who has been such a football of fortune as I have been, and who has hardly known a kind feeling towards him ever expressed, it is a gratification that I really appreciate, and, coming from one whom I respect and esteem more than any other person in the world, it quite overpowers me. Indeed, Miss Trevannion, I am truly grateful."

I was correct when I said that it overpowered me, for it did completely, and I was so oppressed by my feelings, that I reeled to a chair, and covered up my face with my hands. What would I have given to have dared to state what I felt!

"You are ill, Mr Musgrave," said Miss Trevannion, coming to me. "Can I offer you anything?"

I made no reply; I could not speak.

"Mr Musgrave," said Miss Trevannion, taking my hand, "you frighten me. What is the matter? Shall I call Humphrey?"

I felt her hand tremble in mine, and, uncertain what to think, I came to the resolution to make the avowal.

"Miss Trevannion," said I, after a pause, and rising from my chair, "I feel that this internal conflict is too great for me, and if it last it must kill me. I give you my honour that I have for months tried everything in my power to curb my desires and to persuade myself of my folly and rash ambition, but I cannot do so any longer. It were better that I knew my fate at once, even if my sentence should be my death. You will ridicule my folly, be surprised at my presumption, and, in all probability, spurn me for the avowal, but make it I must. Miss Trevannion, I have dared—to love you; I have but one excuse to offer, which is, that I have been more than a year in your company, and it is impossible for any one not to love one so pure, so beautiful, and so good. I would have postponed this avowal till I was able to resume my position in society, by the means which industry might have afforded me; but my departure upon this business, and the kind of presentiment which I have, that I may not see you again, has forced it from me. In a few days I leave you—be gentle with me for my involuntary offence—pity me while you condemn, and I will return no more."

Miss Trevannion did not reply; she breathed quick, and stood motionless. I gathered courage; I looked in her face, there was no displeasure—I approached her, she was half fainting, and put her hand upon my shoulder to steady herself. I put my arm round her waist, and led her to the sofa, and knelt at her feet, watching every change in her beautiful countenance. I took her hand and pressed it to my lips; by degrees I became more bold, and got by her side, and pressed her to my heart. She burst into tears, and wept with her head on my bosom.

"Do not be angry with me," said I, after a time.

"Do I appear as if I was angry with you?" replied she, raising her head.

"Oh, no; but I cannot believe my happiness to be real. It must be a dream."

"What is life but a dream?" replied she mournfully. "Oh, the coast of Africa! How I dread it!"

And so I confess did I from that moment; I had a presentiment, as I had told her, that something would go wrong, and I could not get over the feeling.

I shall no longer dwell upon what took place on that delightful evening, Madam; suffice to say, that Miss Trevannion and I were mutually pledged, and, after an exchange of thought and feeling, we parted, and when we did part I pressed those dear lips to mine. I went home reeling with excitement, and hastened to bed, that I might have unrestrained freedom of thought. I enacted the scene of the evening over and over again; recalled each motion, each look, every word which had passed, and, defying fever and presentiment of evil, imagined also our happy meeting to part no more. It was long before I could compose myself to sleep, and when I did, I need not say who it was that occupied my dreams. I called as soon as I could venture so to do on the following day, and had a long interview with my dear Amy. Before I went up to her father, I tried to soothe her anxiety upon my approaching voyage, and to persuade her that there was little or no danger to be apprehended in so short a stay. Willingly would I have given it up, but Mr Trevannion had so set his mind upon it, and I had, by my consent, rendered it so impossible for him to find a substitute in time, that I could not do so, and I persuaded Miss Trevannion that I was right in acting to my promise line question that came forward was, whether we should make known our engagement to her father at once, and this was decided in the negative. Much as he liked me, he was not yet prepared to receive me so suddenly as a son-in-law, and Amy was of opinion that the communication had better be postponed. To this, of course, I gave a willing assent. I was satisfied with the knowledge of her affection, which I felt would never change. As I was talking with her father, after my interview with Amy, he said:

"Really, Elrington, or Musgrave, I hardly know which to call you."

"Musgrave is my real name, Sir," replied I.

"Musgrave—Musgrave—where did I know a Musgrave?"

"We are from the north," replied I.

"Well," said he, "I was going to say, that I really wish I could find some one else to take your place in this voyage, for I do not much like your going."

"Do, my dear father," said Miss Trevannion, who was standing by him.

"Hey! Miss Amy, what have you to do with it, I should like to know, and how can it concern you whether Mr Musgrave goes or not?"

"I said so, Sir, because I know how you will feel his loss for so long a period. You know how you did feel his loss before, and I do not wish to see you working so hard, as you will have to do it without his assistance."

"Well, that's kindly thought, Amy, at all events; but still I fear that Mr Musgrave must go, and I must work by myself till he comes back; so it's no use saying any more about it."

Amy sighed and made no reply. On the third day after this interview, everything was ready, and on the following morning I was to sail. Mr Trevannion had so many directions to give, and kept me so wholly with him, that I could hardly find time to speak to his daughter. However, it was agreed that as I was to sail at daylight, that she would see me after her father had gone to bed. Our meeting took place— need I say that it was a tender one. We renewed our vows over and over again, and it was not till past midnight that I tore myself away. Old Humphrey looked very knowingly at me when he let me out of the street-door. I slipped a guinea in his hand and wished him good-bye. I hastened on board of the Sparrow-Hawk, and, desiring to be called before daylight, went down into the cabin. There I remained sitting at the table and thinking of Amy so long, that when the mate came down to wake me he found that I was still sitting there, having never been to bed during the whole of the night.

I started from my reverie and hastened on deck to get the schooner under weigh. It was soon done, although we were, comparatively speaking, short-handed. There was a fine breeze, and lightened as she now was, the little vessel flew through the water. Liverpool was soon out of sight, and we were dashing down the Irish Channel.

"She sails well now," said I to the second mate, a very clever man, and much hotter educated than most seamen, for he could navigate, as well as being a first-rate seaman.

"Yes, Sir," replied Olivarez, "she walks fast. She is not too deep now," replied he; "what a slaver she would make."

This man was not an Englishman, but a Brazilian Portuguese by birth, although he had long been out of his country. Having set her course, I went down below, that I might indulge in my castle-building more at my ease. The wind increased to a gale, but as it was from the northward, and bore us to our destination, it was welcomed. We soon crossed the Bay of Biscay, and were in more genial latitudes; and, after a rapid run of about four weeks, I found myself nearly in the latitude given to us of the river where the Amy was at anchor. I then hauled in for the shore, which was very low, and required being approached with caution. We saw some towering palm-trees at sunset, and then we hove-to; the next day we again stood in, and having ascertained our exact latitude at noon, we found ourselves about four miles to the northward of the river's mouth. We shaped a course, and in two hours I made out the marks given for our guidance in the rough sketch of Captain Irving, and thus satisfied that I was right, ran directly for the mouth of the river. Captain Irving was correct in saying it was difficult, for it was not until we were within a mile that we could find any opening; but at last we did, and at the same time perceived the masts of two vessels at some distance up the river. We stood in, and found that there was no bar at the river mouth, which was a very unusual circumstance on this coast. The soundings were gradual, and in an hour afterwards we anchored between the Amy and a fine schooner under British colours. Captain Irving recognised the Sparrow-Hawk, and immediately came on board. After the usual salutations, he told me that his vessel was half-laden, but that he waited for the articles he had sent for to enable him to complete his cargo. I told him that I had them on board, and he should have them as soon as he sent his boats. He stated that no vessels, except those engaged in the slave-trade, had ever come into this river, and that they only brought the cloth and other articles usual in the trade; but that his assorted cargo had astonished the people, and they were wild to possess things which they had never before seen. They had offered slaves in quantities, but finding that he would not take them in exchange, they had now brought down ivory and gold-dust. He told me how glad he was that I had come, as the river was very sickly, and was becoming more and more so every day; that out of twelve men he had already four down with fever.

I inquired of him what that vessel was on the other side of us. He replied it was a Liverpool slave-trader, and that the captain appeared to be a very good sort of man; that he never indulged in liquor, nor was given to profane language.

A few minutes afterwards the captain of the slaver came on board to pay his respects, and I asked him down in the cabin, and gave him beer and cheese, the two greatest luxuries in those climes. He appeared, as Captain Irving stated, a very quiet, well-behaved, serious person, which I was rather surprised at. When we repaired on deck, I observed, as the vessel was close to us, that there were two very large dogs on board, who, at the sight of the captain, bayed furiously. He told me that they were Cuba bloodhounds and that he never went on shore without them, as they were the most faithful and courageous animals, and he considered that he was safer with them than with half a dozen armed men. Shortly afterwards Captain Irving and he both took leave. As there were still some hours of daylight, Captain Irving sent his boats for the goods, and after that, as the evening fell, I went down below, as Captain Irving requested I would do, and by no means remain on deck after sun-down, as it was extremely unhealthy.

On the following day Captain Irving went on shore with his goods and trafficked most favourably. Indeed, as we afterwards found out, he had procured in exchange more ivory than his vessel would hold, besides much gold-dust. The day after, I went on shore with Captain Irving to call upon the king, as he called himself. He was seated in front of a hut made of palmetto leaves, with a lace coat on, but no other garment whatever, so that he made a curious appearance. After a little conversation, I went away, and, hearing that the slaver was taking her cargo on board, about a hundred yards further up, I walked in that direction. The slaves were brought down in about twenty at a time, all of them fastened by the neck to a long bamboo pole, which confined them all together. One string of them had been sent down and put into the boat, and another was standing ready for embarkation; when, as I cast my eyes over them and commiserated their misery, I observed a female whom I thought I had seen before. I looked again, and behold! It was Whyna, the princess who had been so kind to me in my captivity. I went up to her and touched her on the shoulder. She turned round, as well as the lashing to the pole would permit her, and on seeing me gave a faint scream. Without ceremony I took out my knife and released her, and led her away. She fell down at my feet and kissed them. The black man who had charge of the delivery of the slaves was very angry, and ran up to me, brandishing his long stick; but the captain of the schooner, who was on shore, and who had witnessed what I had done, saluted him with a kick in the stomach, which made him quiet enough. In few words I told the captain of the slaver that I was once in captivity, and this woman had befriended me, requesting him to name his price and I would willingly pay it.

"It's not worth mentioning, Sir," replied he; "women are as cheap as dirt; take her and welcome."

"Not so," replied I; "I must pay for her ransom."

"Well then, Sir," said he, "I am in great want of a telescope; you have one on board, will you let me have it?"

"Most certainly," replied I, "and many thanks into the bargain."

I lifted up the poor creature, who was badly emaciated and weak, and led her to the boat of the Amy and put her in. Captain Irving came down, and we returned on board. It was with great difficulty that, after I had given the poor creature some refreshment, which she was really in need of, I could recollect sufficient of her language to make myself understood by her; but by degrees words came to my memory, and as she spoke I recovered more. As well as I could make her out, the warriors had risen against the king on account of his barbarity, and had cut him to pieces; and that all his wives and servants had been sold as slaves. I promised her that she should not be a slave, but should come to my country and be taken care of.

She kissed my hands, and as she smiled her thanks, she reminded me of the Whyna of former times. I did not, however, think it advisable that she should come on board of the schooner, and I requested Captain Irving to take charge of her, and let her want for nothing, telling him that I intended that she should go home in his vessel. He willingly consented, and I hailed the schooner for a boat and went on deck. Whyna followed, but I told her I was obliged to go on board of the schooner, and that she had better go and lie down. As she probably thought that the Amy was my vessel, and that I was going away on a visit, she complied with my request, and went down with Captain Irving, who led her into a state-room which was not occupied.

As soon as I arrived on board the schooner, I sent the telescope which the captain of the slaver had begged for. Whyna had said to me, "I shall be your slave now," evidently expecting that she was to remain with me, but that I could not consent to. Miss Trevannion had heard from me my adventures when in captivity, and I would not on that account allow Whyna to be in the same vessel with me. The next day Captain Irving came on board to tell me that he had two more men down with the fever, and that he wished I could give them some assistance in getting his cargo on board, which I did, and before night the Amy was loaded up to the hatchways, and there still remained a considerable number of elephants' teeth on shore in the hut where he received them. I therefore determined, as his crew were evidently sickening fast, that he should sail immediately, and that I would take the remainder of the ivory on board of the schooner and follow him, giving him a rendezvous to wait at until I joined him, that we might proceed home in company. That night three of my men were ill.

I was on board of the Amy, and had been talking with Whyna, who wanted to know why I did not sleep on board of the vessel. I told her that I could not, but that we were to go to England directly, and that I was living on board of the schooner. Captain Irving weighed at daybreak, and in an hour was out of the river, and as I was as anxious to be clear of such an unhealthy spot, I manned my boats and went on shore for the ivory that was left. I found that it would take the whole of the day to embark it, as we had to go two miles further up the river than the depth of water would permit the vessel to do; for the ivory was in a hut close to the king's house. I had sent off four boat-loads, and it being then noon, I went off with the fifth myself, that I might get my dinner, leaving the second mate to attend on shore, and taking with me the first mate who messed in the cabin. As we were in the middle of the stream, the boat struck against a stump of a tree, as we supposed, and knocked so large a hole in the bow that she began to fill. I immediately ordered the men to pull for the nearest point, which was on the opposite side of the river, that we might ground the boat to prevent her sinking.

The first mate, who was a very active man, finding that the elephants' teeth prevented his reaching the bow of the boat, and stuffing into it some oakum which he had found in the stern sheets, sounded with the boat-hook, and finding that there was not more than three feet of water where we were pulling, jumped over the bows to push the oakum into the hole; but the poor fellow had not been a few seconds in the water, when he gave a shriek, and we perceived that a large shark had snapped him in two. This was a sad mishap, and the men, terrified, pulled as hard as they could, while two of them baled out the boat, to gain the shore, for we knew what fate awaited us if we sunk in the river. With great exertion we succeeded, running her up among the canes, which grew on that side of the river so thick that it was difficult to force your way through them.

We landed up to our knees in mud, and, throwing out the ivory, we found that a whole plank was rent out, and that it was impossible to repair our boat; and we were hidden by the canes from those who could have assisted us, had they known that we required their assistance, and we had no possible means of communication. At last I thought that if I could force my way through the canes to the point down the river, I could hail and make signals for assistance; and desiring the men to remain by the boat, I set of upon my expedition. At first I got on pretty well, as there were little paths through the canes, made, as I imagined, by the natives; and, although I was often up to my knees in thick black mud, I continued to get on pretty fast; but at last the canes grew so thick that I could hardly force my way through them, and it was a work of excessive labour. Still I persevered, expecting each second that I should arrive at the banks of the river, and be rewarded for my fatigue; but the more I laboured the worse it appeared to be, and at last I became worn out with fatigue, and quite bewildered. I then tried to find my way back, and was equally unsuccessful, and I sat down with anything but pleasant thoughts in my mind. I calculated that I had been two hours in making this attempt, and was now, quite puzzled how to proceed. I bitterly lamented my rashness, now that it was too late.

Having reposed a little, I resumed my toil, and was again, after an hour's exertion, compelled, from fatigues to sit down in the deep black mud. Another respite from toil, and another hour or more of exertion, and I gave myself up for lost. The day was evidently fast closing in—the light overhead was not near so bright as it had been; and I knew that a night passed in the miasma of the cane was death. At last it became darker and darker. There could not be an hour of daylight remaining. I determined upon one more struggle, and, reeking as I was with perspiration and faint with fatigue, I rose again, and was forcing my way through the thickest of the canes, when I heard a deep growl, and perceived a large panther not twenty yards from me. It was on the move as well as I was, attempting to force his way through the canes, so as to come to me. I retreated from him as fast as I could, but he gained slowly on me, and my strength was fast exhausting. I thought I heard sounds at a distance, and they became more and more distinct, but what they were my fear and my struggles probably prevented me from making out. My eyes were fixed upon the fierce animal which was in pursuit of me, and I now thanked God that the canes were so thick and impassable; still the animal evidently gained ground—until it was not more than five yards from me, dashing and springing at the canes, and tearing them aside with his teeth.

The sounds were now nearer, and I made them out to be the howling of other animals. A moment's pause, and I thought it was the baying of dogs; and I then thought that I must have arrived close to where the schooner was, and that I heard the baying of the bloodhounds. At last I could do no more, and I dropped, exhausted and almost senseless, in the mud. I recollect hearing the crushing of the canes, and then a savage roar, and then yells, and growls, and struggles, and fierce contentions—but I had fainted.

I must now inform the reader that about an hour after I had left the boat the captain of the slaver was pulling up the river, and was hailed by our men in our long-boat. Perceiving them on shore on that side of the river, and that they were in distress, he pulled towards them, and they told him what had happened, and that an hour previous I had left the boat to force my way through the cane-brakes, and they had heard nothing of me since.

"Madness!" cried he. "He is a lost man. Stay till I come back from the schooner."

He went back to the schooner, and taking two of his crew who were negroes, and his two bloodhounds, into the boat, he returned immediately, and as soon as he landed he put the bloodhounds on my track, and sent the negroes on with them. They had followed me in all my windings, for it appeared that I had travelled in every direction, and had come up with me just as I had sunk with exhaustion, and the panther was so close upon me. The bloodhounds had attacked the panther, and this was the noise which sounded in my ears, as I lay stupified and at the mercy of the wild beast. The panther was not easily, although eventually, overcome, and the black men coming up had found me and borne me in a state of insensibility on board the Sparrow-Hawk. The fever had come on me, and it was not till three weeks afterwards that I recovered my senses, when I learnt what I have now told the reader, and much more, with which I am about to make him acquainted.

When I recovered my senses, I found myself in the cabin of the Sparrow-Hawk. For some hours I was confused and wandering, but I rallied from time to time, till I could at last recognise the beams and carlines over my head. I was too weak to move, and I continued to lie on my back till I again fell asleep; how long I do not know, but it must have been for many hours, and then when I awoke I found myself much stronger.

I could now turn on my bed, and doing so I perceived a young man of the name of Ingram by my side in a doze, with his eyes shut. I called him in a faint voice, and he started up.

"I have been very ill," said I, "have I not?"

"Yes, Sir, indeed you have."

"I have been trying to recollect all about it, but I cannot as yet."

"It's not worth remembering, Sir," replied he. "Do you wish anything to drink?"

"No," replied I.

"Then you had better go to sleep again."

"I cannot do that. I feel as if I should like to get up. Where is Mr Thompson? I must see him."

"Mr Thompson, Sir," replied he; "don't you recollect?"

"What?"

"Why, Sir, he was bitten in two by a shark."

"Shark!" this was the key-note required, and my memory returned. "Yes, yes, I recollect now all, all. I recollect the panther and the cane-brakes. How was I preserved?"

"The bloodhounds killed the panther, and you were brought on board insensible, and have been in a raging fever ever since."

"It must be so," replied I, collecting my senses after a few moments of thought. "It must be so. How long have I been ill?"

"This is the twenty-first day."

"The twenty-first day!" cried I. "Is it possible? Are none of the men ill?"

"No, Sir, they are all well."

"But I hear the water against the bends. Are we not still at anchor?"

"No, Sir, the second mate got the schooner under weigh as he found you were so ill."

"And I have been ill twenty-one days! Why we must be near home?"

"We expect to make the land in a few days, Sir," replied Ingram.

"Thank Heaven for all its mercies," said I. "I never expected to see old England again. But what a bad smell there is. What can it be?"

"I suppose it is the bilge-water, Sir," replied Ingram. "People who are ill and weak always are annoyed by it; but I think, Sir, if you would take a little gruel, and then go to sleep again, it would be better."

"Well, I fear I am not very strong, and talking so much has done me no good. I think I could take a little gruel."

"Then, Sir, I'll go and get some made, and be back very soon."

"Do, Ingram, and tell Mr Olivarez, the second mate, that I would speak to him."

"Yes, I will," replied the man, and he left the state-room.

I waited some time listening for the arrival of the second mate, and then I thought that I heard odd noises in the hold before the bulkhead of the state-room in which I was lying, but I was still very weak, and my head swam. After a time Ingram came down with the gruel, into which he put some sugar and a spoonful of rum, to flavour it, as he said. He offered it to me, and I drank it all, for I had an appetite; but whether it was that I was very weak, or the rum he put in was more than he said, it is certain that I had hardly given him back the basin than I felt so drowsy that I turned away from him, and was soon again in forgetfulness.

This Ingram was a young man who had been apprenticed to an apothecary, and had taken to the sea. He was well educated, and a very merry fellow, and I had chosen him as one who could attend upon me in the cabin, and at the same time be otherwise useful if required, as he was a very good seaman, and very active. When I awoke again I felt convinced that I must have slept through the night, as it was broad daylight, as before, but Ingram was not by my bedside. There was no bell in the state-room, and I was obliged to await his coming. I felt much stronger than the day before, and now proposed getting out of bed as soon as Ingram should come down into the cabin. I now remembered that the second mate had not come down to me, and heard noises and murmurings in the hold as I had the day previous, which surprised me, and I became more anxious for the return of Ingram. At last he came, and I told him that I had been awake more than an hour.

"How do you feel yourself, Sir?" said he.

"Quite strong. I should like to get up and dress. Perhaps I may be able to get on deck for a quarter of an hour."

"I think," replied he, "that you had better wait, and hear what I have to tell you, Sir. I would not tell you yesterday, because I thought it would be too much for you; but as I see you are really better to-day, I must say that I have strange things to tell you."

"Indeed!" cried I, with surprise. "Strange things. By the bye, why did not Olivarez come to me yesterday?"

"I will explain all to you, Sir, if you will lie down and listen to what I have to say, and take the news quietly."

"Very well, Ingram, I will do so. Now pray go on."

"You were brought on board in a state of fever and insensibility by the captain of the slaver. He said, as he lifted you over the side, that you were a dead man. We all thought the same, and you were taken down into the cabin with that persuasion on the part of the whole crew. Your delirium and fever increased, and every hour it was expected that you would give up the ghost. Now, Sir, two days afterwards the slaver sailed with his cargo, and we were left alone in the river. Olivarez, who of course commanded, talked to the men. He said that you were as good as dead already, and that he thought that this was a fair opportunity for their making money. He proposed that the ivory still on shore should be changed for slaves, which he said the negroes would gladly do, and that we should run with our cargo to the Brazils. He said that it would be useless our remaining in the river, as we should all lose our lives in the same way that you had done, and that he thought, as commanding the schooner, he knew what would best please the owner, who had long employed vessels in the slave-trade, and would not be sorry to find that we had run a cargo, and would reward them all liberally. That this would be an excuse to leave the river immediately, whereas otherwise they would have to wait till you recovered or died, and by that time they might half of them be dead themselves. Do you understand me, Sir?"

"Yes, perfectly. Go on, Ingram."

"Well, Sir, the men did not perceive what he was about, and replied that so long as they left the river they did not care how soon, and that it was better that we should take a cargo of slaves at all events, for Olivarez was in command now, and they should do as he ordered them. I made no reply, indeed Olivarez never put the question to me. Well, Sir, the ivory was soon exchanged for slaves, who are now on board, and it is the slaves whom you have smelt and complained of. We received on board 140, and provisions sufficient with what we had, and, having taken in all the water we could, below and on deck, we made sail out of the river, and have since steered for the Brazils."

"But Olivarez has taken a most unwarrantable responsibility," said I; "and one that he shall answer for."

"Stop, Sir," replied Ingram, "you have only heard the first part of the story. When we had been three days at sea, Olivarez, who had been talking to the men, one by one and apart, called them together, and said, it was an opportunity not to be lost, that they had possession of the vessel, and the owner would never have a clue to where she had gone, and that now was the time to take possession of her for themselves, and employ her in the slave-trade on their own account. That, sailing so fast, nothing could overhaul her or board her, and, therefore, they were free from danger. He then proposed that he should command and navigate, and receive one-half of the profits, and that the other half should be divided among the crew—the expense of the provisions, etcetera, being paid out of it previous to their sharing and making a calculation; he showed them that every voyage would be worth about 100 pounds a man after all expenses were paid. The crew consented at once to the terms—all but me; and when he asked me, my answer was, that I would consent to nothing while you were yet alive. I said that, because I was afraid that they would murder me, or throw me overboard."

"Go on, Ingram; go on, and let me hear it all at once."

"'Then you will soon be freed from your difficulty,' said Olivarez.

"'I do not know that, Sir,' I replied, 'for I think Mr Musgrave may get over it.'

"'Indeed,' he returned, 'well, then, so much the worse for him.'

"As he, Olivarez, said this, the whole of the crew, to do them justice, cried out, that there should be no murder, for if there was, they not only would have nothing to do with the affair, but would make it known at the first port to which they came. That you had always been a kind, good officer, and were too brave a man to die in that way."

"'Well, my men,' said Olivarez, 'I never had an idea of the kind, and I promise you, if he lives through it, there shall be no murder; I will put him on shore at the first port we arrive at, but in such a way as to secure our safety—that we must look to.'

"The men said that that was all right, and then they all agreed to join him."

"'And you, Ingram,' said Olivarez, 'what do you say?'

"'What I said before,' I replied; 'that as long as Mr Musgrave lives I will come to no agreement whatever.'

"'Well,' said Olivarez, 'it is but postponing your decision; I know that you will join us. So now, my lads, as we're all agreed, we may as well go to dinner.'"

"The scoundrel shall pay for this," cried I.

"Hush, Sir, hush, I pray; say nothing, but wait patiently and see what turns up. We are not yet at Rio, and when we are, we may be able to do something, but everything depends upon keeping quiet, for if the men become alarmed, they may be persuaded to kill you to save themselves."

"That is very true, Ingram," replied I. "Leave me now for half an hour, I wish to be alone."

You may imagine, my dear Madam, my agitation at hearing this intelligence. I, who had thought that I was within a few days' sail of Liverpool, to be there received by my cherished Amy, to find myself in the hands of pirates, and close to the Brazils with a cargo of slaves; which they, or rather Olivarez, had taken in the vessel to Rio that he might not be discovered; for he might have found a better mart for his live cargo. And then what would be the anxiety of Amy and her father when I was not heard of? It would be supposed that the schooner was upset in a squall, and all hands had perished. Excited and angry as I was, I felt the truth of what Ingram said, and that it was necessary to be quiet. Perhaps I might by that means not only preserve my life, but again find myself in my own country. When Ingram returned, I asked him if Olivarez knew that I was better, and had recovered my reason. He replied that he did, but that he had told him I was so weak that I could hardly recover.

"That is well," said I; "keep him in that belief as long as you can."

He now offered me more gruel, which I took, and I believe that he put an opiate in it, for shortly after I had taken it I again felt drowsy, and was soon fast asleep. I awoke sooner than before, for it was night, and I heard the voice of Olivarez on deck; from what I gathered, land was in sight, and I heard him order the schooner to be hove-to. In the morning Ingram came down in the cabin, bringing me some breakfast, which I ate heartily, for I was recovering fast, and had become quite ravenous.

"Land is in sight," said I.

"Yes, Sir, it is; but we are many miles to the northward of Rio, I understand, for Olivarez knows the coast well. We shall not be in to-day, if we are to-morrow."

"I feel quite strong now," replied I, "and I want to get up."

"Do so, Sir," said he; "but if you hear any one coming down the ladder get into bed again."

With Ingram's assistance I dressed myself, and went into the cabin. I reeled as I walked, but as soon as I felt the cool breeze from the stern-ports, I was revived, and in an hour I could walk quite strong.

"Have you heard any more?" inquired I of Ingram.

"Olivarez asked me this morning how you were. I replied that you were recovering fast."

"'Very well,' said he, 'you will share his fate, whatever it may be, since you have been so careful of him, and have put us in such a dilemma; but I'll contrive to dispose of you both.'

"I made no reply, Sir, as I knew that would only irritate him."

"You did right, Ingram; a few days will decide our fate. I do not think that he dares to murder us."

"Nor do I think he wishes it, if he can be clear of us with safety to himself," replied Ingram.

Two days more passed away, and then Ingram told me that we were a few miles from the town, and should soon be at anchor.

"Go softly," replied I, "and tell me what is going on."

He went up the ladder, but soon came down again, saying, "We are locked in, Sir."

I was very much annoyed at this, but it could not be helped—our only remedy was patience; but I must confess that I was in a state of great anxiety. We heard the anchor let go, and boats came on board, after which all was silent for the night. The next morning we heard them open the hatches, and the slaves were ordered upon deck. The day was passed in landing them. I was ravenously hungry, and asked Ingram whether they intended to starve us. He went up the ladder to call for victuals, when he found on the upper step of the ladder a large vessel full of water and some cooked provisions, which had probably been put there during the night. There was enough to last two or three days. The next day passed and no one came near us, and I had some thoughts of dropping out of the stern-ports and attempting to swim on shore; but Ingram, who had put his head out of them as far as he could, told me that we must be at some distance from the shore, and there were several sharks playing round the stern, as is always the case with vessels laden with slaves.

The next morning, however, put an end to our suspense; for the companion was unlocked, and Olivarez, accompanied by four Portuguese, came down into the cabin, he spoke to them in Portuguese, and they advanced, and, seizing Ingram and me by the collar, led us up the ladder. I would have expostulated, but of course could not make myself understood. Olivarez, however, said:

"Resistance is useless, Mr Musgrave; all you have to do is to go quietly with these men. As soon as the schooner has sailed, you will be released."

"Well," replied I, "it may be so, Olivarez; but mark my words, you will repent this, and I shall see you on a gibbet."

"I trust the wood is not yet out of the ground," replied he; "but I cannot waste any more words with you."

He then spoke to the Portuguese, who appeared to be government officers of some kind, and they led us to the gangway; we went into the boat, and they pulled us to the shore. "Where can they be taking us, Ingram?" said I.

"Heaven knows, Sir, but we shall find out."

I attempted to speak to the officers, but they cried "*Silentio*," which word I fully understood to mean "silence," and, finding that I could not induce them to hear me, I said no more. We landed at a jetty, and were then led through the streets to a large square. On one side of it was a heavy building, to which they directed their steps. The door was opened for us, and we were led in. A paper was produced by our conductors, and was apparently copied into a book, after which they went away, leaving us with the people who had received us, and who, by their appearance, I knew to be gaolers.

"Of what crime am I accused?" inquired I.

No reply was given, but two of the subordinates took us away, unlocked a massive door, and thrust us into a large court-yard, full of men of every colour.

"Well," said I, as the door closed upon us, "we are in gaol at all events; but the question now is, shall we be released as Olivarez had stated?"

"It is hard to say," replied Ingram. "The question is, what gaol is this? Could we find any one who could speak English, we might discover."

Several of those around us had come towards us to examine us, and then left us, when, as we were conversing, a negro came up, and, hearing what we said, addressed us in English.

"Massa want one to speak English—I speak English—some long while on board English vessel."

"Well, then, my good fellow," said I, "can you tell us what this gaol is, and what prisoners are confined here for?"

"Yes, massa, everybody know that, suppose he live at Rio. This gaol for people that go dig diamonds."

"How do you mean?"

"Mean! Massa—people sent here to work in diamond-mines all life long till they die. Keep 'em here till hab plenty to send up all at one time. Then guard take them up the country, and they go dig and wash for diamond. Suppose you find very big diamond, you go free. Suppose not, den you die there."

"Merciful Heavens!" cried I to Ingram, "then we are condemned as slaves to the mines."

"Yes," replied Ingram with a sigh. "Well, it's better than working in the quicksilver-mines. At all events, we shall have fresh air."

"Fresh air, without liberty," cried I, clasping my hands.

"Come, Sir, courage, we do not yet know our fate. Perhaps we may, as Olivarez said, be allowed to go free after the schooner sails."

I shook my head, for I was convinced otherwise.

---

# Chapter Sixteen.

**The Diamond-Mines, and what occurred there—I lose my friend Ingram, and another acquaintance, but they both leave me valuable Legacies.**

After remaining in the court about two hours, it being then near to nightfall, the gaolers came out into the yard, and we were all driven into a large apartment, the walls of which were of such solid materials, and the floor of large flag-stones, as to prevent any possibility of escape. I was never in such a scene of filth and wretchedness. There was not a spot where one could be driven without being defiled in some way or another; and so many human beings—one half of whom were negroes—being crowded into so small a space, with only one barred window, so high up as only to serve as a ventilator, created an atmosphere worse than any slave-vessel's hold. I leaned with my back against the wall, and, I must say, never was so miserable in my life. I thought of Amy, and my sanguine hopes and anticipations of happiness, now all wrecked. I thought of Captain Levee and my brother Philip careering over the seas, free as the wind. I thought of poor Whyna, and the distress she must feel at finding I did not rejoin her. I planned a hundred schemes to make known my situation, but every scheme, as soon as I weighed it, I found was hopeless. Still weak from previous disease, I felt as if I should be suffocated if I remained long in this pestiferous abode, and I wept like a child. Daylight came at last, and soon afterwards the door was opened; we were admitted into the yard, and all hastened to the large tub of water, which was soon emptied. The fighting and scrambling to obtain first possession was really revolting. An hour afterwards some coarse provisions were served out, and then we learnt, to our great delight, that we were immediately to set out for the mines. It would be thought that this could be no great cause for exultation; we were about to go to pass the rest of our lives in bondage; but all misery is comparative, and sooner than have remained another night in that dreadful hole, I would have welcomed any change. About an hour afterwards a guard of dirty-looking soldiers came in; we were all handcuffed to a long chain, at about two feet apart, one on each side, so that we walked in pairs, and as soon as the first chain was full—and I was handcuffed to it—we were ordered out into the square to wait for the others. My superior dress and appearance as an Englishman excited much curiosity; people pointed to me and made remarks, but I had no opportunity of communicating with any of the authorities, nor would it have been of any use if I had had. We remained there more than an hour, as the other chains of prisoners came out one by one; we were five chains in all, about forty on a chain. We were then ordered to move on, walking between a guard of about twenty or thirty soldiers, who marched, on each side of us, with their muskets and bayonets fixed, about three yards from each other. In another hour we were clear of the town, and threading our way through a lane bounded on each side by prickly pears and other shrubs. There was no want of merriment among the party; they talked and laughed with one another and the soldiers who guarded them, and appeared to care little for their fate. As for me, I was broken-hearted with the disgrace and the villainous manner in which I had been thus sacrificed. My heart was full of bitterness, and I could gladly have lain down and died, had I not been still buoyed up with some faint hope that I should have an opportunity of making my position known, and obtain my release. I will pass over the journey, as one day was but the forerunner of the other. We halted at noon, and were supplied with fruit and maize, but we were never unchained, day or night. In a short time I was like all the rest—covered with vermin, and disgusting to myself. It was, I think, between four and five weeks before we arrived at our destination, which was in the district of Tejuco, and the locality of the diamond-mines was called the Sierra de Espinhaço. This sierra, or mountain, was a ridge of inaccessible precipices on each side of a narrow valley, traversed by a small river called the Tequetinhonha, and in this valley, and in the bed of the river, were the diamonds found, for which we were condemned to toil for the remainder of our days. As we entered the ravine, I perceived how impossible it would be to escape, even if a person could find his way back, after having succeeded in his escape. For many miles the road was a narrow path cut on the side of the mountain, a yawning precipice below and inaccessible rocks above, and this narrow way was at every two miles blocked up by a guard-house built upon it, and through the portcullis of which it would be necessary to force a way. And here we were, thousands of miles away from civilised life, in the heart of a country uninhabited except by occasional bands of Indians. At last we filed through the last of the guard-houses, and found ourselves in a wider part of the ravine, which was crowded with buildings of various descriptions. We were led up to the director's house, and our names, persons, and descriptions were taken down by a clerk. When my turn came, and I was asked in Portuguese who I was, I shook my head, and replied "Ingles." An interpreter was called, and I then stated my name and begged the director would hear what I had to say. He shook his head, and, after they had taken my description, desired me to go away.

"Why did you not explain for me?" said I to the interpreter.

"Because he won't hear what you have to say; if he would, every man on the chain would attempt to prove that he was sent here by mistake. You may by-and-by find an opportunity to speak to him, that is, after you have learnt Portuguese, and have been here a year or two; but it will do no good."

During the whole of the journey I had been separated from Ingram, and now, for the first time since we left prison, I had an opportunity of shaking him by the hand. I need not say how glad I was to meet again my companion in misfortune, and our only fear was now, that we should be again separated; but such was not the case. There were regular lodgings or barracks for the slaves, which were certainly not bad but as all escape was considered impossible, any one who chose to raise a little hut for himself out of the bushes which grew on the rocks was permitted so to do. The hours of work were regular; we were allotted out in gangs, which took up a certain square of the river, or river's side; we worked from daylight till near dusk, with only an hour allowed for repose in the heat of the day. There was a superintendent over each gang of twenty, who watched them and made them work. These superintendents were controlled by inspectors, who had the charge of four or five gangs, and who brought unto the director the produce of the day's toil. The work was simple. The sand and alluvial soil were thrown into troughs with small sieve bottoms, out of which escaped all the smaller matter, when it was washed with the water from the river. The stones and larger particles were then carefully examined, and any diamonds found were taken out and delivered to the superintendents, who then made them over to the inspectors, when they came round. The inspectors carried them to their houses, (for they had houses from government,) and in the evening delivered every diamond found to the director. After a short time, I found that the office of superintendent, and also of inspector, was open to any of the slaves who conducted themselves well; and that the whole of those now employed in the offices were slaves for life, as well as ourselves. What puzzled me was, how so many people, for in all we amounted to seven hundred or more, were to be found in food; but I afterwards discovered that the government had farms and herds of cattle at a few miles' distance, cultivated by slaves and Indians expressly for the purpose. Our rations were scanty, but we were permitted to cultivate, as well as we could, any spot we could find on the arid side of the mountain as a garden; and some of them, who had been there for many years, had, in course of time, produced a good soil, and reared plenty of vegetables. To my surprise, I found at least twenty Englishmen among the whole mass of slaves; and one or two of them were inspectors, and several of them superintendents—saying much in favour of my countrymen. Their conversation and their advice tended much to soothe the hardships of my captivity, but I found from them that any hopes of ever leaving the mines were useless, and that our bones must all be laid by the side of the mountain. Of course, Ingram and I were inseparable; we worked in the same gang, and we very soon built a hut for ourselves; and Ingram, who was a light-hearted young man, set to work to make a garden. He moved heavy stones on the sides of the mountain, and scraped up all the mould he could find; sometimes he would get his handkerchief full, but not often; but, as he said, every little helped. He killed lizards for manure, and with them and leaves he made a little dung-heap, which he watered, to assist putrefaction. Everything that would assist, he carefully collected; and by degrees he had sufficient for a patch of four or five yards square. This he planted; and with the refuse made more manure; and in the course of a few months, by incessant activity and assisted by me, he had a very tolerable patch of ground covered with this manure and the alluvial soil washed out by the diamond-seeking, mixed up together. We then obtained seeds, and grew vegetables like the rest, and this proved a great increase to our comforts—that is, our bodily wants; but my mind was far away. Amy Trevannion was never out of my thoughts, and I fell into a deep melancholy. I worked hard at my vocation, and was fortunate enough to find some good diamonds, long before I had been a year at the mines. Having acquired the Portuguese language, I was soon after raised to the office of superintendent. I now no longer worked, but overlooked others, with a cane in my hand to administer punishment to those who neglected their business. I cannot say that I liked the change; I was not so miserable when I was employed, but I did my duty with diligence. Ingram was in my gang, and another Englishman, an old man,—I should think not less than seventy years old. He told me that he belonged to a merchant vessel, and in a drunken brawl a Portuguese had been killed; he and two others had been condemned to the mines, but the others were dead long ago. About a month after my elevation, this old man, who was very feeble, and whom I treated with great kindness on account of his age—exacting no more than I thought he could well perform—fell sick. I reported him as being really ill, and Ingram, who was by no means a bad doctor, told me that he would die. A few hours before his death he sent for me to his hut, and, after thanking me for my kindness to him, he said that he knew he was dying, and that he wished to leave me all his property, (which the slaves are permitted to do,) that is, he left me his garden, which was the best on the Sierra, his hut, which also was a very good one, and then, putting his hand under the leaves which formed his bed, he pulled out a tattered, thumbed book, which he told me was a Bible.

"At first I read," said he, "to pass away time in this melancholy place, but of late I have read it I hope to a better purpose."

I thanked the poor man for his present, and wished him good-bye. A few hours afterwards he was dead, and Ingram and I buried him by the side of the mountain. Shortly afterwards our inspector died, and, to my astonishment, I was put into his place. I could not imagine why I was thus so fortunate in being promoted, but I afterwards found out that, although I had never but casually seen her, I was indebted for my good fortune to a fancy which the director's eldest daughter (for he had his family with him) had taken for me.

This was singular, for I had never spoken to her, and, what is more strange, I never did speak to her, nor did she ever attempt to speak to me, so that it was wholly disinterested on her part. I had now still less to do, and was in constant communication with the director, and one day stated to him how it was that I had been brought there. He told me that he believed me, but could not help me, and after that the subject was never again mentioned between us. Having little to do, I now took up the Bible given me by the old Englishman, as I had time to read it, which I had not before, when I was employed the whole day; but now I had a convenient cottage, as I may call it, of my own I and plenty of leisure and retirement.

I studied the Bible carefully and found much comfort in it. Not that I was content with my lot—that I never could be while I was separated from Amy—but still I found much consolation, and I became, to a certain degree, resigned. I thought of my former life with disgust, and this second reading of the Bible, for the reader may recollect that the first took place when I was first confined in the Tower, was certainly of great advantage to me. I had more time to dwell upon it—more time for reflection and self-examination—and every day I reaped more advantage and became more worthy of the name of Christian. I now prayed fervently, and I think my prayers were heard, as you, my dear Madam, will also think as I continue my narrative. About three months after I had been appointed an inspector, Ingram was taken ill. At first he complained of disordered bowels, but in a few days inflammation came on, which ended in mortification. He was in great agony until the mortification took place, when he obtained comparative relief.

"My dear Mr Musgrave," he said, as I was at his bedside, "in a few hours I shall have escaped from the mines, and be no more in bondage. I shall follow the poor old Englishman, who left you his executor. I am about to do the same. I shall now make my will verbally, as we have no writing materials here, and leave you all I possess."

"Why are you not more serious, Ingram," I said; "at such a moment as this?"

"I am most serious," he replied. "I know that in a few hours I shall be no more, and I trust in the mercy of Him who died for kings and for slaves; but, Musgrave, I have a secret to tell you. Do you recollect the story in the fairy tales of the little white cat whose head was obliged to be cut off, and who then turned into the most beautiful princess in the world? Well, my secret is something like hers."

I thought, by his continuing in this strain, that his head was wandering. I was about to speak to him, when he continued:

"Do you know what has occasioned my death? I will tell you the secret. I was washing for diamonds, when I found one of a size which astonished me. I knew it was of great value, and I did not choose that the King of Portugal should receive such a benefit from my hands. I put it into my mouth to secrete it, hardly knowing what I should do afterwards, but I was thinking how I should act, when one of the superintendents passing (that crabbed old Portuguese belonging to the next gang), and seeing me idle and in deep thought, he struck me with his cane such a smart rap on the shoulders, that he not only made me jump out of my reverie, but the diamond went down my throat. I'm sure if I had tried to swallow it I could not have done so, but the shock forced it down. Well, this has occasioned my death, for it has remained in my stomach and occasioned the stoppage, which has ended in inflammation and mortification. I feel it here even now; give me your finger, don't you feel it? Well, now you understand why I talked of the little white cat. Don't cut off my head, but when I am dead, just put your knife down there and take out the diamond and bury it, for I tell you—and they say dying men see clearer than others—but that I am certain you will be released from these mines, and then the diamond will be a fortune to you, and you will find that being my executor was of some value to you. Now, pray—no scruple—I entreat it as a last favour, promise me that you will do as I wish—pray promise me, or I shall die unhappy."

I could not help promising him to execute his wishes, he appeared so earnest and asked it as a last favour, but I felt very repugnant at the idea. In another hour poor Ingram breathed his last, and I was most melancholy at the loss of so worthy a friend, who had by serving me been subjected to the same slavery as myself. I left the hut and went to my own house, thinking over the strange communication that had been made to me. And why, thought I, should I obtain this diamond? I have no chance of leaving this; yet, who knows, Ingram prophesied in his dying moments that I should—well, at all events, I will keep my promise to the poor fellow. I reported his death to the director, and, about an hour afterwards, went to the hut where he lay. His countenance was placid, and I looked at him for a long while, and queried whether he was not happier than I was or ever could be. But, to comply with his request—I could not bear the idea. I did not want the diamond, and I, who in my early career had thought nothing of cutting and maiming the living man, now shuddered at the idea of making an incision in a dead body. But there was no time to be lost, the burials always took place at sunset, and it was near the hour. I bent a piece of bamboo cane double, like a pair of sugar-tongs, and then putting my finger to the part of his stomach which he had pointed out, I felt that there was a hard substance, and I made an incision with my knife—probing with the blade. I touched the diamond and then, using the piece of cane as a pair of pincers, I contrived, after one or two attempts, to extract it. I threw the diamond without examination into a pan of water which stood by the bed, and, covering up the body, I made a hole in the floor of the hut and buried the knife, which I felt I never could use again.

I looked out of the hut and perceived two of the slaves, who performed that office, coming towards me to take away the body. I desired them to carry it leaving the clothes on, followed them, and saw it deposited in the earth; after which I read prayers over the grave, and could not refrain from shedding many tears to the memory of my faithful associate. I then returned to the hut, and taking the pan of water in my hand went to my abode. I could not bear to touch the diamond, but I dared not leave it where it was; so I poured all the water out of the pan, and then rolled the diamond out on the floor, which was of hardened clay. I saw at once that it was one of great value, weighing, I should think, thirteen or fourteen *grammes*, and of a very pure water. It was in the form of an obtuse octahedron, and on one side was quite smooth and transparent. Having made this examination, I picked up some of the clay with a piece of iron, and, rolling the diamond into the hole, I jammed the clay down over it. "There," said I, "you may remain till doomsday, or till some one finds you; you will be of no use to me;" and I thought of the cock in the fable. My tattered Bible caught my eye, and I said to it, "You are of more value than all the diamonds in the world;" and I only uttered what I felt.

For a long time I mourned for Ingram, and thought nothing of the diamond. Three months more passed away, and I had been eighteen months in the mines, when some visitors made their appearance—no less than one of the principals of the Jesuit order, who had been sent by the king of Portugal out to the Brazils, on a tour of inspection, as it was called, but in fact to examine into the state of affairs, and the way in which the government revenue was collected. There had lately been so much peculation on the part of the various officers, that it was considered necessary to make minute inquiry. A Portuguese nobleman had been sent out the year before, but had died shortly after his arrival, and there was every reason to suppose that he had been poisoned, that the inquiry might be got rid of. Now this Jesuit priest had been sent out, probably because a Portuguese, who thought little of poisoning and stabbing a layman, would not dare to attempt the life of so sacred a character. Having full and extraordinary powers, he had made a short inquiry into the different departments of government, and now come to the mines to ascertain how far the delivery of the diamonds at the treasury agreed with the collection at the mines; for these mines had usually produced from a million to a million and a half of revenue. The director was in a great fuss when he heard of this arrival at the further barrier; although immediately announced to him, he had scarcely an hour to prepare before the superior of the Jesuits arrived with his suite, consisting of about twenty people, and fifty or sixty sumpter mules and riding-horses. We were all called out to receive him, that is, all the inspectors. I went to attend the parade, and awaited with much indifference; but my feelings were soon changed, when in this superior of the Jesuits I beheld the Catholic priest who had visited me in the Tower and obtained my release. The superior bowed to the director and to all around him, and as he then looked at us all, he recognised me immediately.

"You here, my son?" said he.

"Yes, holy father," replied I, "and I thank Heaven that your arrival will enable me to prove my innocence."

"Pray how is this?" said he.

In a few words I narrated my story.

"And you were thrown into prison without being permitted to defend yourself?"

"Even so, good father, and sent to the mines to slave for life."

"Did you not make known your case to the director of the mines?"

"I did, Sir, but he stated that he pitied me, but could not help me."

"Is this the case, Mr Director?" said the Jesuit, severely.

"It is, Sir," replied the director; "I have more than once reported cases of what appeared to me great hardship, if what those condemned have said was true, and have been told that I was too officious, and that there could be no reversal of sentence. I can prove to you, Sir, by my journals and letter-books, how many cases I did formerly attempt to bring before the government; but I at last received such replies, which I can show you, as will prove that there has been no fault of mine."

"Allow me to add, holy father," said I, "that the kindness and consideration of the director have been very great to all those under his charge, and I think it very fortunate that such a person has been appointed to this situation, as he has done everything that has been in his power to alleviate the miseries of bondage."

"I am glad to hear you say so, Mr Elrington. Mr Director, this gentleman is a dear friend of mine; let him instantly be released. My orders are not to be disputed by the viceroy himself."

The superior then embraced me cordially, and told me that I was free, and should return with him to Rio. Imagine, my dear Madam, my joy and gratitude. I fell on my knees before him, and kissed his hands. He gave me his blessing, and raised me up.

"Where is your companion in misfortune?" said he.

"Alas! Sir, he is dead," replied I.

The superior shook his head and turned away, saying, "I will search into this affair to the bottom, depend upon it, when I get back to Rio."

He then desired the director to bring out his books, and his own secretary to follow him, leaving his servants in the court-yard with me and the other inspectors. I received the congratulations of all parties present, and as soon as possible I escaped from them, and returned to my own room, where I knelt and fervently thanked God for my unexpected deliverance; and, having paid my duty to the Most High, I sat down, and fell into a most delightful reverie of anticipations. In the evening, after the superior had dismissed him, the director sent for me, and said:

"Allow me to return you many thanks for your kindness in speaking so favourably of me as you have done. You have, indeed, been of service to me, and I am most grateful."

"I only did you justice, director," replied I.

"Yes, but how few have justice done them in this world!" replied he. "The superior desired me to tell you, that you are to live with the gentlemen of his suite. Of course, you know, it is not etiquette for him to admit anybody to his table. At all events you must allow me one pleasure, which is to supply you with clothes proper to your appearance, which I can easily do without inconvenience to myself."

The director then led me into his room, and opened a wardrobe full of rich suits, selected two of the handsomest, with linen and every other article requisite, a handsome sword and hat, all of which he begged me to accept. Calling one of his servants, he ordered him to put them into a valise, and take them to my apartment.

"Is there anything else that I can do?—speak freely."

"No, director," replied I, "I will accept these things from you, as I cannot procure them here, but when at Rio, I have means to obtain everything that I require. I return you many thanks."

"I will send my servant to arrange your hair," said he; "and I pray you to consider him at your disposal during the few days which the superior may remain here."

"Do you think it will take him so long?"

"Yes," replied the director, "I will tell you in confidence, that he has brought with him the produce of the mines accounted for to the government at home, and on his first inspection has found such defalcation from that which has been transmitted by me to Rio, that I expect there will be serious business. They never imagined at Rio that he would have undertaken such a tedious journey as he has done, and they are in much alarm about it; but I will leave you now, that you may go home and make your toilet. Allow me to congratulate you, with all my heart, at the fortunate termination to your unjust bondage."

Having again thanked him for his kindness, I went to my lodging, where I found his servant waiting for me; and having had my hair arranged in a very tolerable manner, and a little powder thrown in, I put on one of the suits, which fitted me pretty well, requiring but a slight alteration, from being rather full, which the servant soon managed. Thus did I once more appear as a gentleman—contrary to all my expectations—and I then went and joined the suite of the superior, who, when they perceived the difference which dress made in my appearance, congratulated me, and warmly welcomed me to join the meal which had just been prepared for them. On the following day, the superior sent for me, and ordering me to sit down requested that I would enter into full detail of what had happened to me since we last parted. I did so, and my narrative occupied the whole afternoon.

"Your life has been full of vicissitude," replied he; "I trust, however, that your adventures are now over, and that you will be restored to your friends: the service you performed for our cause will never be forgotten."

I ventured to ask him how it was that he was now in the employ of the King of Portugal. He replied:

"I am an Irishman by birth, and educated at Saint Omers. I was first sent to Spain by the order when I was young, and have since been employed all over the world in the advancement of our holy church. Country with our order is of no consequence. We all serve the holy church, and go wherever our services are required. I would you were a Catholic, I could advance you beyond all your hopes; but you are engaged to be married, and that puts an end to the question."

As I thought the holy father must be tired with our long conference, I rose and took my leave.

Three days afterwards I was informed by him that he intended to set off on his return to Rio, and now I thought of the diamond, which I resolved to carry with me. I had no fear of being searched while under this excellent superior's protection, and therefore I went to my lodging, dug up the diamond, and, having washed it, for the first time gave it the examination which it deserved. It certainly was a stone of great value, but of what value I could not exactly say. From what I had learnt from the director, who usually put his idea of the value upon any diamond of size which was brought to him, I considered that 20,000 pounds was the least which could be put upon the stone. I took the precaution not to carry it loose in my pocket, but to sew it within the lining of my clothes. Glad I was, indeed, when the orders to start the next morning were given out. I found that a horse was appointed for me, and, having made up my valise, not forgetting my tattered Bible, I went to my bed thanking God that this was to be the last night that I was to pass in the accursed Sierra de Espinhaço.

At daylight the superior took his leave, mounted his mule, and we set forth, passing the guard-house in the narrow road, which I never expected to pass again. Before noon we were clear of the Sierra, and once more in the open country. The attendants, with a portion of the sumpter mules, went in advance, to prepare for the superior's arrival at the spot where we were to halt.

The weather was excessively sultry, and the glare of the sun was very distressing. At noon we stopped to take our dinner, and the usual siesta after it. The attendants in advance had raised a sort of palanquin for the superior, and everything was ready. The superior alighted, and sat down under the palanquin, which protected him from the rays of the sun; we all sat round at a respectful distance. The heat was so intense, that, to relieve himself, the superior had, when he sat down, thrown off his long black robe, such as is worn by the priests of his order. Dinner was served up, and we had a merry party, notwithstanding the great heat. After our meal, we all shaded ourselves as well as we could, and took our siesta for about two hours, when the superior rose up, and gave the signal for resuming our journey. The horses were soon ready, and the superior's mule being brought up to the palanquin, he rose up, and one of his attendants was lifting up his robe for the superior to resume it, when my eye detected the head of a snake just showing itself out of the side-pocket of the robe in which he carried his breviary and his handkerchief. I knew the snake well, for we often found them in the Sierra de Espinhaço, and some two or three of the slaves had lost their lives by their bite, which was so fatal, that they died in less than five minutes afterwards. The superior had his handkerchief in his hand, and would have undoubtedly put it in his pocket before he mounted his mule, and if so would certainly have been bitten, and lost his life. As the superior was fastening his robe at the throat, I darted forward, seized it, threw it on the ground, and commenced stamping upon it with all my force, much to the surprise of the whole party. Some of them thought me mad, and others, who were horrified at such treatment of the holy garment, called out, "Heretico maldetto!" which, Madam, you must know, means, accursed heretic. Having felt the snake (which is very short, but very thick in the body, with a head like a toad) several times moving under my feet, and then moving no more, I then stepped off the garment, and turning it over I lifted it up by the skirt, so that the dead snake rolled out of the pocket.

"I thank the God whom we all worship, and the Son of God, who died for us all, whether Catholic or Heretic," cried I, "that I have been the means of preserving the holy father."

I had knelt down as I thus prayed, and the superior, perceiving the danger that he had been in, did the same, and silently returned his thanks; at his example all the rest went down on their knees.

"Yes," said the superior; "would to God that instead of reviling each other all denominations of Christians would join in thus bruising the head of the serpent which seeks our spiritual death."

He then rose and said:

"My son, I thank thee for the kind service thou hast performed."

I then explained to the superior the deadly nature of the animal, and my fear that he would have put his handkerchief in the pocket of his robe before I had time to prevent him, and begged him to excuse my seeming abruptness.

"There needs no apology for saving a man's life," replied he, smiling.—"Come, let us go forward."

I hardly need say that we were not quite so long in returning to Rio as we were in going to the mines. We accomplished our journey, without using extreme haste, in about half of the time. On our arrival, we took up our quarters at a magnificent palace, which had been appropriated to the superior during his residence at Rio, and I found myself sumptuously lodged. For some days, during which the superior had frequent interviews with the viceroy, I did not see him, but one day I was summoned to his presence.

"My son," said he, "I have lost no time in investigating your affair, and I find that all you have said is quite correct. To the disgrace of the government here, and the manner in which justice is administered, it appears that this man, Olivarez, on his arrival, went to the secretary of the judge of that court in which such offences are tried, and stated that he had two English mutineers on board, who had attempted to take the vessel, and wounded several of his men dangerously; that he wished, of course, to deliver them up to justice, but that the immediate departure of his vessel would be prevented by so doing, as his crew would be required as evidence; that the delay would be very disadvantageous; and he inquired whether it could not be managed that these men might be punished without the appearance of himself and his men, as he would pay a good sum rather than be detained. The secretary perfectly understood the trick, and, upon the receipt of five hundred cruzados, he accepted the deposition of Olivarez, sworn to by him, as sufficient evidence, and you were consigned to the mines upon this deposition by a warrant from the judge. We have had some trouble to obtain all the facts, but the question has been severely applied, and has elicited them. Now, first, as to the judge and his secretary, they have gone to the gaol, and will take your place in the mines for life. Next as to Olivarez. It appears that, on his arrival, he sold his cargo of slaves very advantageously; that having received the money he gave a small portion to each of his men, and that they went on shore, and, like all English seamen, were soon in a state of intoxication; that Olivarez took such steps with the police, as to have them all thrown into prison when in that state; and, on the following morning, he went to them, persuaded them that they had committed themselves during their intoxication, and that it required a large sum to free them. This he pretended to have paid for them, and, having purchased a cargo for his voyage, he got them all on board, and again ran for the coast of Africa. In three months he returned with another cargo, which he sold. He had found out his mother, and now he expended the money he had made, in purchasing a good property about seven miles from Rio, where he placed his mother and some slaves to take care of it, and cultivate it. He contrived to defraud his crew as much as he could, and before he went to the coast again he married an amiable young person, the daughter of a neighbour. He made a third and a fourth voyage with equal success, but on the third voyage he contrived to get rid of a portion of his English crew, who were now becoming troublesome, by taking some Portuguese sailors out with him, and leaving the English on the coast, as if by mistake. Previous to the fourth voyage, it appears that he satisfied the remainder of the English crew by producing accounts, and sharing out to them several hundred dollars previous to their departure for the coast. He made a slight addition to his Portuguese sailors, not putting too many on board, to avoid suspicion, and when on the coast of Africa, a portion of the English crew died, whether by poison or not is not known, and the others he put on shore, seizing all their property, and the dollars with which he had satisfied them. On his return from his fourth voyage, having now nothing to fear from the partners in his atrocious deed, having realised a large sum, he determined to remain on shore altogether, and live on his property with his mother and wife. He did so, and sent out the schooner under a Portuguese captain and crew, to be employed for him as owner in the slave traffic, and she has made two voyages since, and is expected back again every day. Now, my son, retribution has fallen heavily upon this bad man. Had he been discovered and punished when he first did the deed, it would have been as nothing compared to what it has been now; he then had no property—no ties—in fact, nothing or little to regret; but now, with a wife and child, with a valuable property, living in independence, and increasing that wealth daily—now, when he is at the very summit of his ambition, restored to his own country, respected and considered as being a man of wealth, he has been seized, thrown into a dungeon, put to the question, and now lies in a state of misery, awaiting the sentence of death which has been pronounced against him. Neither has he the consolation of knowing that he leaves those whom he loves in a state of affluence, for all his property, having been gained by making use of your property, necessarily is your property, and not his, and it has been confiscated accordingly for your use and benefit. As soon as everything is collected, it will be paid into your hands. Thus, my son, I have at last attained justice for you."

I was, as you may imagine, my dear Madam, profuse in my acknowledgments, but he stopped me, saying:

"I was sent here to see that justice was done to everybody, if I possibly could—no easy task, when all are amassing money, not caring how they obtain it; but, surely, if any one has peculiar claims upon me, it is you."

The superior then asked me many questions relative to my parentage, and I did not conceal anything from him. I told who I was, and why, at an early age, I had left my father's house. He asked me many questions, and, after about two hours' conversation, he dismissed me, saying:

"You may always depend upon my protection and gratitude."

Before he dismissed me, he told me that he was about to send a despatch-boat to Lisbon, and as I might wish to inform my friends of my safety, if I would write letters, he would insure their being safely delivered to my friends in England. I gladly availed myself of this offer, and indeed would have begged a passage for myself, if it had not been that I considered Olivarez's money to be the property of Mr Trevannion, and was determined to remit it to him before I left Rio. This detained me about six weeks longer, during which interval Olivarez had suffered the penalty due to his crimes, having been strangled in the market place.

The money received was 28,000 cruzados, and not knowing how to dispose of it, I applied to the superior, who gave me orders for it in duplicates upon the treasury at Lisbon, one of which I had very soon an opportunity of sending home to Mr Trevannion, with a duplicate of my first letter, and a second to him and Amy, stating my intention of returning as soon as possible. But this was by a Portuguese frigate, which made a very circuitous route home, and I did not choose to go by that conveyance, as her detention at the different ports was so uncertain. At last I became very impatient for my departure, and anxiously awaited the sailing of some vessel to any port of Europe.

I had reserved 1000 cruzados for my own expenses, which I considered as quite sufficient, but they were gradually wasting away, for I was everywhere received, and in the best company of Rio. At last one day the superior sent for me, and told me that he was about to send an advice-boat to Lisbon, and I might take a passage if I wished; that it was a very small one, but a very fast sailer. I thanked him heartily, accepted the proposal, and went to my room to pack up my clothes. In the afternoon the captain of the xebeque called upon me, and told me that he would start on the following morning if I would be ready. I replied that I should be, put some dollars into his hands, requesting that he would procure for me anything that he considered would be necessary and agreeable, and if the sum I had given him was not enough, I would repay him the remainder as soon as we were out of harbour. I took my leave of the superior, who parted with me with many protestations of regard on his side, and tears of gratitude on mine, and early the next morning I was on board of the xebeque. In light winds she was extremely fast, but she certainly was too small to cross the Atlantic Ocean; nevertheless, as the captain said, she had crossed it several times, and he hoped that she often would again.

The passage, however, that he usually made, was to run up to the northward of the Antilles, and then cross over, making the Bahama Isles, and from thence taking a fresh departure for Lisbon. Our crew consisted of only eight men, besides the captain; but, as the vessel was not more than thirty tons, they were sufficient. We made a good run, until we were in about twenty-four degrees of north latitude, when, as we stretched to the eastward to cross the Atlantic, we met with a most violent gale, which lasted several days, and I fully expected every hour that the vessel would go down, buried as she was by the heavy sea. At last we had no chance but to scud before the wind, which we did for two days before a raging and following sea, that appeared determined upon our destruction. On the second night, as I was on deck, watching the breaking and tossing of the billows, and the swift career of the little bark, which enabled her to avoid them, the water suddenly appeared of one white foam, and, as we rose upon the next sea, we were hurled along on its crest, reeling on the foam until it had passed us, and then we struck heavily upon a rock. Fortunately, it was a soft coral rock, or we had all perished. The next wave lifted us up again, and threw us further on, and, on its receding, the little xebeque laid high and dry, and careened over on her bilge.

The waters rose and fell, and roared and foamed about us, but they lifted us no more, neither did they wash us off the decks as we clung to the rigging; for the stout short mast, upon which the lateen sail was hoisted, had not been carried away. We remained where we were till morning, every one holding on, and not communicating with each other. As the night wore away, so did the gale decrease and the sea subside. The waters now gradually left us; at intervals, when the waves receded, we could walk on shore; but we remained on the vessel till noon, by which time we found our vessel high and dry, having been carried over a coral reef, which appeared to extend one or two miles into the offing.

The men, who had been much buffeted by the waves, and who were exhausted by clinging so long to the rigging, now that they found themselves safe, and were warmed by the heat of the sun, rallied, and began to move about. We had a long consultation as to how we should act. There was no chance of getting the vessel off again, and we did not exactly know where we were; but the captain and I agreed that it must be upon one of the small islands of the Bahama group that we had been cast away, and our conjecture was right. After some consultation, the captain and I called the men together, and told them that it was very probable that we might be some time before we could find the means of getting off the island, and that, therefore, we must all do our best; that we would land and erect a tent with the sails, and obtain provisions; after that we would consider the vessel and her stores as public property, but that every man's private property should be secured to him as if we were still on board of the xebeque; that the captain should retain the command as before, and his orders should be obeyed by everybody, as long as they were reasonable and just.

The men, who were well-behaved, quiet fellows,—and not, like English seamen, given to liquor,—readily agreed, and it was arranged that the following morning we should commence our labours. This was a sad blow to me, who was anticipating a speedy meeting with Amy. I knew how doubtful was the chance of our being seen by any vessel, and that I must remain here for months, if not longer; but I had been schooled, and could now say with fervency, "Thy will, O Lord, and not mine, be done."

We remained on board of the vessel that night, and the next morning the gale had ceased, and the waters, to our astonishment, had receded, so as to leave us at least sixty yards from the sea, which was now almost calm. We first took a survey of the island, to ascertain if there was any water, and, as the island was not more than two miles in circumference, this did not take us long. Fortunately, in the centre we found a deep hole sunk in the soft coral rock by some other people who had been wrecked here, and in the hole the water was, although a little brackish, somewhat palatable. It evidently was the sea-water filtered through the soft rock.

The whole of the island was surrounded with coral reefs, with lanes of deep water running between them, and the fish were sporting in thousands after the storm, but there was not a tree or vestige of vegetation upon the whole island. We soon, however, discovered that it was frequented by turtle, for we found some eggs, fresh-buried, in the sand. Having made this survey, we then went back to the vessel, and with spars and sails rigged a tent upon the highest point of the island, which might be ten or fifteen feet above the level of the sea. The tent was large enough to hold fifty men, if required, so we brought our bedding and chests and all our cooking apparatus on shore, made a fire-place outside the tent with the little caboose we had on board of the vessel, sent a man to obtain water from the hole, and put on some meat to boil for our dinners. In the evening we all went out to turn turtle, and succeeded in turning three, when we decided that we would not capture any more until we had made a turtle-pond to put them in, for we had not more than two months' provisions on board of the vessel, and did not know how long we might be detained. The men behaved very well, and indeed seemed determined to make themselves as comfortable as they could under existing circumstances. The next day we put out some lines in deep water, and caught several large fish, and then we went to find a proper spot for a turtle-pond. We selected a hole in the reef which we thought would answer, as we had only one end of it to fill up, and we commenced breaking away the rock with crowbars, and worked hard the whole of the day, some breaking and others carrying the masses broken off. By degrees they rose to the surface of the water, and in two days more we calculated that the pond would be ready to receive the turtle. We had killed one turtle in the morning, and we now lived upon it altogether, as we wished to save our salt provisions. The captain and I had many consultations as to what we should do, and what attempts we should make to get off from this spot. Build a boat we could not, as we had not a carpenter among us, or the means of making the iron-work necessary. We had some tools, such as are usually used on board of vessels, and several pounds of large nails, but none fit for boat-building. I proposed that we should examine the bottom of the xebeque, and see what damage was done to it. We did so, and found that the garboard strake was broken and two of her timbers, but they were easy to repair; in every other respect she was sound. I then proposed that we should cut down the xebeque to a large boat, which we could easily do by ripping off her planks and decks, and sawing down her timbers to the height we required. It would be a heavy boat, it was true, but we should be able to launch her with rollers, and the draught of water would be so small that we could get her over the reefs, which we could not possibly do the xebeque. The captain approved of the idea, and we agreed that as soon as the turtle-pond was finished we would make the attempt. In two days more we had finished the pond, and had turned thirty turtle, which we put into it. The men, now that they found that they had plenty to eat, began to show signs of laziness, and did not very readily commence the work upon the xebeque. They ate and slept, ate and slept again, on the mattresses spread in the tent. At times they would fish, but it was with difficulty that the captain and I could persuade them to work, and if they did work half an hour, they then threw down their axes and crowbars, and went back to the tent. They had plenty of tobacco, and they smoked half the day, ate turtle, and then slept again. Nevertheless, as the captain and I worked hard, the work progressed; in about ten days after we began the work, we had ripped off her decks and her side-planks as as low as we thought right, and we were now sawing through the timbers, when the quiet of our party was disturbed by what may be considered a very strange quarrel. One of the men asserted in conversation that Saint Antony was born in Padua; one or two of the other seamen denied it, and this difference of opinion, which at first was a mere nothing, from sullenness, I presume, and something being required to excite them, in the course of a day or two ended in a serious feud; the Paduans terming the anti-Paduans heretics and Jews. The epithet of Jew was what irritated so much, and the parties being exactly even, four on each side, on the third day, after an angry altercation, they all rushed out of the tent to decide the affair with their knives. The conflict was very fierce, and took place when the captain and I were at the xebeque, and before we could separate them four of them had fallen; two were killed, and the other two badly wounded. It may appear ridiculous that people should take each other's lives for such a trifle; but, after all, nations declare war against each other, and thousands are killed on both sides, for causes almost as slight. With great difficulty we separated the remaining combatants, and such was their rage and excitement, that every now and then they would attempt to break from us and attack each other again; but at last we disarmed them.

This was a sad business; and it was melancholy to think that companions in misfortune should take each other's lives, instead of feeling grateful to the Almighty for their preservation.

We buried the two men who had fallen, and dressed the wounds of the hurt; but after this quarrel the four others came to their work, and continued steady at it. We had now removed the upper portion of the xebeque, and commenced fixing beams and carlines on the lower part, so as to make a decked boat of it, and in another week we had decked her over. But we had a great deal more to do: we had to reduce the mast and yard to a proper size, to alter the sail and rigging, to make a small rudder, and rollers to launch her upon. All this, with our reduced force, occupied us another month; for the two wounded men, although recovering, could but just crawl about. We turned many more turtle at night, that we might have a sufficient supply. We now looked out for a channel of deep water through the reef, to get our boat out, and made one out to a certain extent, but could not survey further without getting off the reef, and the sharks were so numerous that we dared not venture. However, we took it for granted, as we had found deep water in shore, that we should be sure to do so in the offing; and we now got our boat upon the rollers which we had made, by digging away the sand from beneath her, and a trench to the water's edge. We had been two months on the island when all was ready for launching.

Anxious as I was to return to England, I cannot say that I was unhappy when on this island: there was always a fine sea-breeze, which cooled the air, and enabled us to work without exhaustion. With the exception of the unfortunate quarrel I have referred to, everything went on quietly. After work was over, I resorted as usual to my Bible, and read for hours; and this calmed and allayed any impatient feelings which might at times arise. I felt that I had great cause to be grateful to the Almighty for preserving me as he had done, and that it would be folly and wickedness on my part to repine because I could not obtain all that I wished. I waited, therefore, for His own good time, without murmuring, and in full confidence that all was for the best.

At last we contrived to get our boat into the water, and she floated much lighter than we thought she would have done, considering the weight of wood that was in her. As soon as she was anchored about ten feet from the beach, we made a gangway to her with planks, and commenced getting all our salt provisions, water, and stores, which we had selected as most necessary, on board of her. The stowage of these occupied us two days; we then got the yard up, and bent the sail, and, having fitted oars, we determined that the next day we would embark. As she still swam light, we got on board of her as many turtle as we could conveniently carry, and then, for the last time, went on shore to sleep.

As there was no room for our chests, it was agreed that we each should have a bundle on board, selecting those things which we most required and most valued. This proposal, which was made by the captain, put me in mind of the diamond, which had scarcely once entered my thoughts since I had been on the island. When I took it out of my chest, I thought that I might as well make it more convenient to carry, as there was no saying what might be the result of our new expedition; so, when the other men were all busy about their own effects, or asleep, I first took the precaution to roll it up in a covering of pitch, so that, if taken from me or lost, it might not be known to be a diamond, and then I sewed it up in a piece of leather, which I cut from an old glove, putting a strong leather lanyard to it, so that I might wear it round my neck. Having done this without any one taking notice, and having nothing else to do, I took some fine twine and worked it over, like the mousing of a stay, in a way peculiar to sailors, so that, when finished, it was very much in the shape of a miniature buoy to an anchor, and reminded me of a *fend-off* or fender, such as they use to prevent any injury to the sides of a vessel when coming in contact with another. Having finished my work, I put the leather lanyard round my neck, inside of my shirt, so that my diamond was concealed from sight; I then put up my remaining pieces-of-eight—which were nearly 500, the best of my clothes, (for during my stay at Rio I had very much increased my stock,) and I hardly need say that the old Bible was not left behind.

It was a beautiful calm morning when we embarked, and, lifting the anchor, took to our oars, and pulled out through the deep channel, the captain standing at the bow and conning us through, while I took the helm. The boat pulled well and steered well; we had yet to see what she could do under canvass. After a pull of two hours we were clear of the reef, and out in the open sea. We then laid in the oars, and commenced our preparations for hoisting the sail to a breeze, which then blew from the southward. When all was ready, the men hoisted the sail, but in so doing, a rope being foul, as I was attempting to clear it, I was tripped up, and fell with my right knee on a spike, which entered deep, putting me to excruciating pain, and laming me completely. I was obliged to sit down abaft, for I nearly fainted away. In the mean time the sail was set, and the boat stood well up to it. She proved to be very stiff under canvass, which was a source of great congratulation. My knee became so painful and stiff that I could not move it; I took one of my shirts out of my bundle, tore it up into bandages, and put them on. We had resolved to attempt to make New Providence, the largest of the Bahama group, where we knew that there was a town called Nassau, and from whence we hoped to obtain some conveyance to Europe; but we knew nothing of the port, or the inhabitants, or what trade was carried on with them.

For several hours our little bark went gaily over the water, but towards nightfall the wind shifted, and the weather looked threatening. We hardly knew how to steer, as we did not know the position of the island which we had left, and now the wind heading us, we hauled up on the larboard tack, with our head to the northward and eastward. As the sun went down, the wind increased, and the sea ran fast. Our boat behaved well, till it began to blow very hard, and then it took in so much water, that we were forced to bale.

We had reefed our sail, and made everything as snug as we could, but the sea rising fast, and the boat taking in more water, we considered it prudent to lighten her, which we did by throwing overboard all the turtle. This we did without regret, as we were tired of eating them for so long a while. The day broke, and there appeared every sign of bad weather, and the waves now tossed and foamed too much for such a small craft as we were in. About noon we saw a vessel on a wind to leeward of us, which was a source of great delight to us all, and we bore down to her. We soon made her out to be an hermaphrodite brig, under her close-reefed topsails and trysails. We ran under her counter and hailed. We perceived several men standing abaft, and apparently they suspected us for a rover, for they had muskets and other weapons in their hands. We told them that we had been shipwrecked, and the boat was sinking in the gale, and then we rounded-to under her lee.

There we remained for four or five hours, during which the wind and the sea went down very fast, and the boat no longer took in water; but we had been all too much alarmed with the danger in which we had been, to like to continue our voyage in her, and as we thought that we could now go alongside with safety, we hailed again, and asked permission. After some parleying they threw us a rope, which we made fast to the boat, and lowered our sail, keeping off on a broad sheer, as there still was a great deal of sea. They then entered into conversation with us. I told them all that had happened, and inquired where the brig was bound to.

They replied, to James Town, Virginia. I asked them if they could give us a passage there, as we were afraid to proceed in our boat; or if not, would they see us safe into New Providence.

The captain then came forward. He was a very dark man, dark as a mulatto, with keen small eyes, and a hooked nose. I never beheld a more deformed and repulsive countenance.

He said that he could not go to New Providence, as it was out of his way, and that we might easily get there ourselves if we thought proper.

I replied, that the boat was not sufficiently large and seaworthy, and that we had already nearly gone down, and if another gale should come on, we certainly should founder, and again requested that he would take us on board.

"Have you any money to pay for your passage?" inquired he.

"Why," said I, "common charity and the feelings of a seaman towards sailors in distress should be sufficient to induce you to take us on board, and not leave us to perish; but if you require money," I replied, "we have more than sufficient to satisfy you."

"How much?" screamed out a lad of about fourteen, who was the very image of the captain in miniature.

I did not reply to this question, and the captain then said, "What do you propose to do with the boat?"

"Let her go adrift, to be sure," replied I.

"What have you got on board of her?" said he.

I enumerated, as well as I could recollect, the provisions and stores that we had.

"Well," replied he, "I will wait till it is a little smoother, and then we will clear the boat and take you on board."

He then left the gangway, where he had been standing, and we continued to be towed by the brig.

"I do not like that fellow," said I to the Portuguese captain; "he appears, or pretends, to take us for pirates, but he is more like a pirate himself."

"He looks like the devil himself," replied the captain, "and to ask people in our condition to pay for their passage! He is a monster! However, we all have a few doubloons, thank Heaven."

About an hour afterwards, it being much more moderate, the captain of the brig told us to sheer alongside, and that four of us might come out and the others remain in the boat till she was cleared.

"I think you had better go," said I to the captain, "for with so much motion I never shall be able to get up the side with my bad knee."

We then sheered the boat alongside, and the captain and three of our men got on board, but not without difficulty. I saw them go aft and down below with the captain of the brig, but I never saw them on deck again, much to my surprise, although we were more than half an hour before they again hailed us, and told us to come alongside again. During this half-hour my mind misgave me sadly that all was not right, from not seeing the Portuguese captain, or either of the three men, and I took it into my head that the vessel was a pirate; and I knew if such was the case, we should instantly be rifled, if not murdered. I took the precaution of taking off the bandage from my knee, and, having removed the diamond from my neck, I put it under my ham in the cavity, which held it with ease, and then put the bandage on again over it, as I thought they would hardly take a bandage off a bad knee to see if there was anything concealed beneath it. It was with difficulty that I contrived to get on board the brig, and as soon as I had gained the deck, I was ordered to go down into the cabin: as I went aft, I looked round for the Portuguese captain and the men, but could not see them. I contrived, with difficulty, to get down into the cabin, and as soon as I was there I was seized by the arms and held fast by two of the men, while others bound me with seizings.

As the captain was looking on, I inquired into the cause of this outrage. He replied, that we were a parcel of rascally pirates, who would have taken his vessel if he had not been too deep for us; I told him it was false, and that I could easily prove it, as we still had the despatches on board with which we had been charged, and that I could show good proof that I was the same person that I stated myself to be; that I very much feared that we had fallen into the hands of pirates ourselves, but that I would have justice done as soon as we arrived at James Town, without he intended to murder us all before we arrived. His answer was, that he was too old a bird to be caught with such chaff, and that he would secure us and deliver us up to the authorities as soon as he arrived. I replied, in great anger, that he would then be convinced of his error, if it was an error, on his part;

that his conduct was infamous, and he looked like a scoundrel, and I believed him to be one.

"You call me a scoundrel, do you," said he, levelling a pistol at my head.

"You call us scoundrels, do you," cried the boy I have made mention of, and who was evidently the son of the captain, taking up another pistol in his hand. "Shall I shoot him, father?"

"No, Peleg, not yet; we will pay them all when we get in. Take him away, and put him in irons with the rest," said the captain; and I was immediately dragged forward between decks through a door in the bulkheads, where I found the Portuguese captain and three seamen already in irons.

"This is pretty treatment," said he to me.

"Yes, it is, indeed," replied I; "but I will make him smart for it when we arrive."

"Shall we ever arrive?" said the Portuguese captain, looking at me and compressing his lips.

"I say, my man," said I to the seaman who stood over us with a pistol and a cutlass, "who are you, and what are you? Tell us the truth: are you pirates?"

"I never was yet," replied he, "nor do I mean to be; but our skipper says that you are, and that he knew you as soon as you came alongside. That's all I can say about it."

"Why, if we are pirates, as he says, and he recognises us, he must have been in pirates' company,—that is clear."

"Well, he may have been, for all I know," replied the man. "I don't consider him any very great things; but he is our captain, and we must obey orders."

The man now brought forward the other three men who had been left in the boat. They told us that the boat had been cleared; all the provisions, stores, sails, etcetera, had been taken out of her;—a proof that she had been gutted and then cut adrift;—that all our bundles were down in the captain's cabin, and that the ill-looking urchin, his son, had overhauled them, one after another, and handed to his father all the money that he had found; that they had been searched very carefully; and that they had heard the captain say that we were all to be sent up, one by one, and searched in the same manner;—and so it proved. I was first taken aft to have my pockets rummaged by the little villain, and as soon as I had been led forward and again put into irons, the Portuguese captain and three other seamen were sent for and treated in the same way. We inquired of the men what money they had in their bundles and about their persons. They had each man four doubloons at Rio for wages, and the captain had about forty doubloons. I had five hundred pieces-of-eight: so that, altogether, we had been robbed to the tune of about four hundred pounds sterling, independent of our clothes, which were of some value to us; that is, mine were at all events.

The seamen who guarded us, and who relieved each other every watch, were not at all surly or ill-natured. I asked one of them during the night-watch whether he thought the captain would take our lives.

"No," said he; "we will not allow that. You may be pirates, as he says, although we do not think you are; but if pirates, you shall have fair play; that we have all made up our minds to. No hanging first, and trying afterwards."

I had a long conversation with this man, who appeared very much inclined to be sociable. He told me that the vessel was named the *Transcendant*; that she sailed from Virginia to the West Indies, and that some times she went to England; that the captain of her was also the owner, but where he came from, or what he was, they did not know, except that he was a Virginian,—they believed so, for that he had a tobacco estate there, which was carried on by his eldest son. He called the captain a stingy, miserly fellow, who would sacrifice any man's life to save a shilling, and that there were odd stories about him at James Town.

I was well satisfied with my conversation with this man, as it assured me that our lives would not be taken, and I had no fear of the result upon my arrival at James Town, for, as I have mentioned before, Mr Trevannion had vessels which sailed to that port, and I well recollected the names of the parties to whom the vessel and cargo were consigned.

On the following day the captain of the brig, followed by his ill-favoured son, came forward and looked at us as we sat in irons, upon which I addressed him:

"You have put me in irons, Sir, when I threw myself upon your protection. You have robbed us of our money to the amount of nearly 400 pounds, and you detain our other property. I now again desire that I may be released. I offered to convince you that I was a person of property, but you refused to listen to me. Now, Sir, I will tell you that I am a partner in the house of Trevannion, at Liverpool, and that we have vessels that trade between James Town and that port. Our vessels are consigned to Messrs Fairbrother and Wilcocks, of James Town, and on my arrival I will soon prove that to you; and also not only make you surrender the property you have robbed us of, but I will make you smart pretty handsomely for your treatment of us; that you may depend upon."

"Fairbrother and Wilcocks," muttered he; "confound the fellow. Oh," said he, turning to me, "you got the name of that firm from some ship you have plundered and sunk, I suppose. No, no, that won't do,—old birds are not to be caught with chaff."

"I believe you to have been a pirate yourself, if you are not one now," replied I; "at all events you are a thief and a paltry villain—but our time will come."

"Yes, it will," said the captain of the xebeque; "and remember, you scoundrel, if you can escape and buy off justice, you shall not escape seven Portuguese knives,—mind you that."

"No, no," cried the Portuguese sailors; "stop till we are on shore, and then come on shore if you dare."

"I say, father," said young Hopeful, "this looks like mischief; better hang them, I reckon, than to be stuck like pigs. They look as if they'd do it, don't they?"

I shall never forget the diabolical expression of the captain of the brig after the Portuguese sailors had done speaking. He had a pistol at his belt, which he drew out.

"That's right, shoot 'em, father; dead men tell no tales, as you have always said."

"No, no," said the seaman who was on guard, motioning them back with his cutlass, "there will be no shooting nor hanging either; we are all sworn to that. If so be they be pirates, there's the law of the country to condemn them; and if they be not pirates, why then that's another story."

The captain looked at the seaman as if he could have shot him if he dared. Then turned round hastily and went back to the cabin, followed by his worthy offspring.

For seven days we remained in irons, when we heard land announced by the sailors on deck, and the brig's head was put towards it. At night she was hove-to, and the next morning again stood in, and we perceived that we were in smooth water. Towards night the anchor was let go, and we asked the guard if we had arrived at James Town.

He replied, "No, but we were in a river on the coast, but he did not know what river it was nor did any of the crew, nor could they tell why the captain had anchored there. But they had seen several canoes with Indians cross the river, but that there appeared to be no white settlement that they could discover." The mystery was, however, cleared up on the following morning. A small boat, which could barely hold eight people, was lowered from the stern, and hauled up alongside. We were taken up, one by one, the scoundrel of a captain having first stripped each of us to our trousers, not even allowing us a shirt. We were ordered to get into the boat. As soon as we were all in, and our weight brought the boat down to her gunnel, two oars were handed to us, and then the captain of the brig said:

"Now, you rascally pirates, I might have hanged you all, and I would have done so, for I know you well. I recollect your faces when you plundered the 'Eliza,' when I was off Porto Rico; but if I put you in prison at James Town, I shall have to wait two or three months until the court sits, and I cannot be detained for such scoundrels as you; so now you may pull on shore, and get on how you can. Shove off, directly, or I'll put a bullet through your brains."

"Hold fast," cried I, "and let him fire if he dares. You men belonging to the *Transcendant*, I call you to witness this treatment. Your captain has robbed us of a large sum of money, and now turns us adrift, so as to compel us to land among savages, who may kill us immediately. I appeal to you, will you permit this cruelty and injustice? If you are English, I conceive you will not."

There was some talk and expostulation with the captain of the brig, in consequence of what I said; but while it was going on, the captain's son leaned over the side, and with his knife cut the painter, or rope which held the boat, and as the tide was running on very strong, in less than half a minute we were a long way astern of the brig, and drifting fast up the river.

We got our oars, and attempted to pull for the brig, for we knew that the seamen were taking our parts; but it was in vain; the tide ran several miles an hour, and in another minute or two, with all our exertions, we were nearly a quarter of a mile astern of her, and the boat was so loaded that we hardly dared move lest we should upset it. We had, therefore, no option but to go on shore and take our chance; but when the men were pulling round for the shore, on reflection I thought that we had better not land so soon, as the sailors had told us that they had seen the Indians in their canoes. I therefore recommended that we should allow the boat to drift up the river with the tide, and then drift down again when the tide turned, remaining in the middle of the stream till it was dark, when we would land and make our way into the woods. My advice was followed; we sat still in the boat, just keeping her head to the stream with the oars, and, being without our shirts, the sun scorching and blistering our backs, till past noon, during which time we must have drifted nearly twenty miles up the river, which was as broad as the arm of a sea at the entrance; then the tide turned, and we drifted back again till it was dusk, when it was again slack water. All this while we kept a sharp look-out to see if we could perceive any Indians, but not one was to be seen. I now proposed that we should take our oars and pull out of the river, as if we had only gone up on a survey, for the brig had got under weigh, and had anchored, for want of wind, about four miles off, and the Indians, if there were any, would suppose that we were returning to the ship. We did so, and pulled till it was dark, and were within two miles of the brig, where the flood-tide again made strong, when we turned the boat's head up the river, and pulled with the oars to get up as far as we could before we landed. This we did, suffering much from hunger and thirst, as well as being confined so long in one position. As my knee was quite well, I now took off the bandage, and hung my diamond round my neck as before. I could not help feeling a satisfaction, when I thought that the thief of a captain little imagined what a mine of wealth he was losing when he turned me adrift. It was about midnight when the tide ceased to flow, and we then agreed to land, and the question then was, whether we should separate or keep together. After some discussion, we agreed to separate in twos, and the Portuguese captain and I agreed to keep each other company. We first pushed the boat into the stream, that she might drift away, and then, shaking each other by the hand and bidding adieu, we all started in different directions. For some time the captain and I threaded the woods in silence, when we were stopped by a stream of deep water, with such high banks, that in the dark we did not know how to cross it. We walked by the side of it for some time to discover a passage, and in so doing we at last found ourselves again on the banks of the river, and our boat lying close to us, having grounded not far from where we had shoved her off. We tasted the water in the creek, and found it quite fresh: we had several times tried it on the river, and found it quite salt from the tide running in. We drank plentifully, and sat down to recover ourselves, for although we had not walked more than half an hour, the pushing through the brush-wood was very fatiguing.

"I think," said I, "that this boat will certainly betray us, and would it not be better to take possession of it again? It will hold two comfortably, and I think we shall get on as well, if not better, in a boat than in the woods without compass and without guide."

"I agree with you," said the captain; "but what shall we do?"

"Let us retrace our steps; let us pull again, with the ebb-tide, for the mouth of the river, and then coast it along shore; we may arrive at some settlement, if we do not starve by the way."

"I agree with you," he said, "it will be the best plan; we must conceal ourselves in the day, and coast along at night."

We waded into the river, got into the boat, and again pulled out. The boat being light now pulled well, and we made good speed; and at daylight we were clear of the river, and close to a small island near the mouth of it. Upon this we agreed to land, to try if we could procure food, for we were much exhausted, and also to conceal ourselves from the natives. We ran our little boat on shore, and concealed her among some bushes which grew down at the water's edge. We looked well round, but could see nothing, and we then walked out in search of food; we found some wild plums, which we eagerly devoured; and going down again to the beach, where there were some rocks, we found shell-fish, of which we broke the shells between two stones, and made a meal of. After our hunger was satisfied, we lay down under the shelter of the boat, and fell fast asleep. We were so tired that we did not wake up till it was nearly dark, when we agreed to start again, and pull along the coast to the northward. We were just launching our boat, when we perceived a canoe about three miles off, steering for the mouth of the river to the island. This stopped us, and we remained in our hiding-place. The canoe approached, steering directly for the spot where we lay concealed, and we imagined that they had discovered us. Such, however, proved not to be the case, for they ran on shore about fifty yards from us, and, hauling up the canoe, they got out and walked away on land. There were four men, but it was now too dark to distinguish any more. We remained quiet for a quarter of an hour, when I proposed that we should embark.

"Have you ever managed a canoe?" said the Portuguese captain to me.

"I have been in one in Africa very often," I said, "but they are dug-outs, as we call them."

"So have I, and I do not think there is so difference between them and these canoes. Can you paddle?"

"Yes," I replied.

"So can I," he said. "Now observe, the best thing we can do is to take possession of that canoe; and then we shall get on better, for our boat will always attract notice, whereas a canoe will not; besides, it will prevent these Indians, if they are come to look for us, which I suspect they have, from following us."

"I think you are right," I said; "but how shall we manage?"

"In this way. You shall shove off our boat and walk by its side, dragging it up to where the canoe lies; I will go to the canoe, launch it, and then we will make off with both till we are too far out to be taken; then, when we have got into the canoe, we will turn our boat adrift."

I agreed to the proposals. We launched our boat very quietly, and I walked in the water up to my knees, drawing it after me till I arrived opposite to the canoe. The Portuguese crept on his hands and knees till he had gained the canoe, pushed her off, and joined me. We made her fast to the tow-rope of our own boat, then got into the boat, and pulled away from the island.

We had not gained more than a hundred yards when the whiz of an arrow met our ears. The Indians had discovered us, it was evident. Two or three more arrows came flying by us, but we had now got well out, and they fell harmless. We continued to pull till we were half a mile from the island, and then we laid on our oars. The stars shone bright; there was a young moon, so as to enable us to see pretty well. We found the paddles of the canoe lying on the cross-pieces. We had nothing to take from the boat but our tow-rope and the two small oars; these we put into the canoe, and then, getting in ourselves, we let the boat go adrift. We put her head to the northward, between the island and the main, and paddled away as fast as we could.

The captain was a much better hand than I was, and he therefore took the office of steersman. The water was as smooth as glass, and we made rapid progress, and did not discontinue our exertions, except now and then resting for a few moments, till the morning dawned, when we could hardly distinguish the island we had left, and found ourselves about five miles from the mainland. We had now time to examine the contents of the canoe, and had much reason to be gratified with our acquisition. It had three bear-skins at the bottom, several pounds of yams, cooked and uncooked, two calabashes full of water, bows and arrows, three spears, a tomahawk, three fishing-lines and hooks, and some little gourds full of black, white, and red paint;

and, what we prized more than all, some flints and a large rusty nail, with rotten wood to serve as tinder.

"We are fortunate," said the captain; "now, before we pull in for the shore we must paint ourselves like Indians; at all events, you must black yourself, as you have no shirt, and I must do the same, although I do not require it so much as you do."

"Let us have something to eat and drink first," replied I, "and we will proceed to our toilet afterwards."

---

# Chapter Seventeen.

## My adventures with the Indians, with what happened to the Portuguese Captain, my companion.

Having eaten some venison, and drunk out of the calabash, the captain painted me black, with here and there a line of red and white on the face and shoulders. I performed the same duty towards him, and we then resumed our paddles, and pushed in a slanting direction for the shore. The tide now ran down against us, and we could hardly stem it, and finding ourselves opposite a beach clear of trees for a quarter of a mile, we agreed to run on shore to look for a large stone. We soon found one which answered our purpose, and, paddling off again to three or four hundred yards, we made the stone fast to the bow-rope of our boat, and anchored the canoe with it. Having succeeded in this, we got out the fishing-lines, and, with a piece of raw meat as a bait, we soon had several fish in the canoe; after which we put on no more baits, but pretended to fish till the tide slacked, when we lifted our anchor and recommenced our paddling to the northward.

At night we landed on a rock, close to the beach, having well reconnoitred before it was dark, to see if there were any canoes or Indians to be seen on the shore; and thus we continued for five days, during which we passed the mouths of one or two rivers, and had gained, as we supposed, more that 150 miles along the coast, but how much to the northward we could not tell, as we followed the windings of the shore. We were twice obliged to land to obtain water, but we always did so in the daytime, having taken the precaution to black the whole of our bodies and take off our trousers before we landed. Our deer's flesh was all gone, and we continued to live on fish, cooking as much as we could at one time. The collecting fire-wood was the great risk which we ran; for we were then obliged to land where there was wood. It was on the sixth day that we were first in danger. As we rounded a point, we fell in with another canoe with six or seven people in it. They were not more than 800 yards off when we first saw them. The Indians stood up in the canoe, looked at us very earnestly, and then, perceiving that we were not of their tribe, I presume, pulled towards us. We immediately turned and pulled away. They had been fishing, and two of them were pulling up the lines, while the others paddled, which gave us a little advantage; but they had three paddles and we had only two. They shouted and paddled with all their might, but they gained little, as they were seven in the canoe, five men and two women, and deep in consequence. As they gained slowly upon us, notwithstanding all our exertions, the Portuguese said to me, "They have no weapons in the boat, I should think; if they had, they would use them, for we are within bow-shot. Can you use a bow and arrow?"

"I could once," replied I, "use it very fairly;" for when I was captive with Whyna, she would often practise the bow and arrow with me, and I became somewhat expert before I left her.

"Well, then," said he, "let me paddle on, and do you put an arrow in the bow and threaten them, at all events."

I did so, and stood up, taking aim as if about to shoot, at which they ceased paddling, and after talking a little they turned the head of their canoe round, and made for the shore. We proceeded, as may be imagined, with all diligence. I laid down my bow and arrows and resumed my paddle, and in an hour we could no longer see our late pursuers. We continued our voyage, and for three days met with no further adventures, when about noon, on the fourth day, the sky became overcast, and there was every prospect of rough weather. Before night the wind and sea rose, and it was no longer possible for us to keep along the coast, which already was covered with breakers.

We had therefore no remedy but to make for the shore and haul up the canoe, for we could not perceive any inlet which might shelter us. It was quite dark when we dashed the canoe through the breakers and landed. We hauled her up some distance, as there was every appearance of worse weather, and sheltered ourselves under the lee of a high rock. The wind now blew fiercely, and rain descended in torrents. We tried to light a fire to warm ourselves, but could not succeed, so we lay down on one bear-skin, and covered ourselves with the others, waiting impatiently for daylight. When the day dawned the weather was worse than ever. We now looked out for a better place of concealment for ourselves and our canoe, and found one at about fifty yards' distance: between two high rocks there was a narrow cleft or passage, which was large enough for us and for the canoe, and this hid us both from the storm and from the sea. Into this cleft we hauled our canoe and withdrew ourselves, making a meal off some fish we roasted on the embers. We remained there for two days, when the weather moderated, but the sea was still too rough for us to launch the canoe; so we decided upon remaining one day more, although our provisions were all gone and our calabashes quite empty. On the third day, to our great surprise and alarm, we heard the report of a musket not far from us. From this we knew that we could not be very far from the English settlements, for it was only the Indians near to the settlements who had obtained muskets. But whether it was an Indian or a white man who fired we could not, of course, tell. I recollected that, in the last advices we had had from James Town, our factors had stated that there was a cruel war carried on between the Indians and the settlers, and that the Indians had ravaged the plantations; but that was two years ago, and how it might be now it was impossible to tell. A second report of a musket still nearer induced me to creep along by the side of the rock, and look out to see if any one was near. To my great alarm, I perceived five Indians with muskets not a hundred yards off. I drew back, as I hoped, unperceived, but the eye of an Indian was too keen. They had discovered me; and whilst I was relating to the Portuguese captain what I had seen, they were suddenly upon us. We had no time to make resistance, even if we were inclined so to do; we therefore sat still. They came up and looked at us. The wet had washed off a great portion of the paint upon my back and shoulders. One of the Indians touched me on the shoulder, and said, "Ugh!— white man paint like Indian." They then examined the canoe and its contents, and, having spoken a few words to each other, apparently relating to the canoe, they put a thong of leather round each of our arms, and, making a motion for us to follow them, they led us away.

"We've done our best, and could do no more," said the Portuguese; "I feel that it's all over with me now, and I shall soon sleep in the bosom of Jesus."

My heart was too full to make any reply. The Indians led on, and I followed in silence.

We passed through the woods, which appeared to be interminable, till the night closed in, and then the Indians halted, and while one remained as guard over us the others collected wood for a fire. They had some provisions, but offered none to us. After an hour they lay down to sleep round the fire, placing me and the Portuguese captain next to the fire, and lying outside of us. They were soon fast asleep, or appeared to be, when I said to the captain, "Have you your knife? For if they remain asleep, let us wait an hour or so, and if you can cut the leather thong which the Indian holds in his hand, and then watch your opportunity, I will do the same, and we may escape."

"I have my knife, but my Indian is not asleep," replied he; "I will wait till he is."

"What signal shall we make if we succeed?" said I.

"When you are ready, lift your arm up,—I shall understand,—and if I am ready I will do the same. Agreed; and now let us be quiet, for depend upon it our conversation has roused them all."

We then composed ourselves, as if to sleep, and remained in that way for more than an hour, by which time we were convinced that our captors were slumbering. I then drew out my knife, for the Indians had not attempted to rifle us, and cut the thong which was round my arm, without awaking the Indian who had the other end in his hand. I remained quiet for a quarter of an hour, when the Portuguese lifted up his arm as a signal that he was free. I listened attentively, and, being certain that the Indians were asleep, I lifted up my arm also.

The Portuguese then rose up carefully, and without noise, stepping past the bodies of the Indians, till he was clear of the circle. I did the same, and pointed to the muskets, which lay on the grass by the Indians. He took one up and I another and we retreated to a short distance.

"We must have the other muskets," said I; "stay where you are."

I advanced cautiously and took up the other three muskets, and was retreating with them, when one of the Indians turned round as if awaking. I ran past, the Portuguese, and making a sign for him to follow me we retreated a few yards into the wood, where we could watch the Indians without being seen ourselves. The Portuguese motioned to be off but I detained him, and I was right. The Indian roused up and sat upon his haunches; perceiving that we had escaped, he waked up the others. They started on their feet, and looking round found that the muskets were all gone; and then they held a consultation. At last they appeared to have made up their minds to follow, and, if possible, recapture us, for they went back in the direction of the sea.

"Now, then, we must hide three of the muskets," said I, in a whisper, "and keep the others to defend ourselves."

We examined and found that they were all loaded, and the Portuguese then said to me, "There are five of them. If they meet with us, and we discharge two muskets and we do not kill, we shall be at their mercy. If we do kill, still there will be three against two; we had better carry all the muskets. Do you take two, and I will take three."

As I thought he was right, I consented, and we now went the same path towards the sea which the Indians had done before us in pursuit of us. We walked fast, as we knew the Indians would do the same, and they had the start of us, so that we were not likely to come up with them. It was severe work, but we did not slacken our pace, and before dawn the sea was quite visible through the branches of the trees, for we had arrived at the outskirts of the wood.

As soon as we had gained the beach, which was 500 yards wide, we looked round to see if we could perceive the Indians, but we could observe nobody.

"Let us, while it is yet dark, go round so as to get on the opposite side of the rocks where we were concealed," said the Portuguese. "If they are there, we shall take them by surprise."

Keeping just within the wood, we walked half a mile to the southward, and then emerged just as the day was breaking, and made for the rocks. As soon as we arrived, we examined very cautiously before we entered the cleft, but there was nobody there, and the canoe was safe.

"They are not here," said I; "where can they be?"

"They cannot be far off," said the Portuguese; "I suspect they are hidden somewhere, and intend to surprise us while we are launching our canoe, and when our muskets will be out of our hands."

"I agree with you; let us now wait at some little distance from the rocks till broad daylight,—we shall then be secure from surprise."

We did so, and when the sun rose we looked well round, but could see nobody. We entered the cleft, and were about to lay down the muskets, and lay hold of the canoe, when I perceived a small piece of rock to drop down. This caused me immediately to suspect the truth, and I cried to the Portuguese to come back with me. He did so, and I told him that I was certain that the Indians had climbed the rock, and were lying down on the top of it, ready to pounce upon us.

"Depend upon it they must be there," said he, when I mentioned the falling piece of rock; "let us walk round and see if we can discover them."

We did so, but they were too well concealed.

"But what must be done now?" said he. "It is useless our attempting to clamber to the top of the rock, for no one could do it with a musket in his hand."

"No," replied I, "that is certain; and if we attempt to bring the canoe out of the cleft, they may drop down upon us."

"I think," said he, "that if we were to go in and take the tow-rope in our hands, which is several yards long, we might haul out the canoe by it, and when once it is clear of the cleft they cannot move without our seeing them."

"We will try, at all events," replied I. "Do you stay on the watch while I get hold of the tow-rope and bring it out."

The Indians did not expect this manoeuvre, it was clear. Still keeping the muskets in our possession, the butts on the sand, and the muzzles resting on our shoulders, we laid hold of the tow-rope, and by great exertion hauled the canoe several yards away from between the two rocks. We then paused for breath after a minute or two, with our eyes fixed upon the top of the rock to see if they moved, and then we hauled it at least a hundred yards further on, when for the first time I perceived that the bow and arrows were not in the canoe, and that they must have been taken by the Indians.

"Then we must haul again," said the Portuguese, when I stated this to him, "till we are out of bow-shot. Let us put the muskets into the canoe, and drag it as fast as we can."

We did so, and gained another hundred yards before we stopped, when an arrow was discharged from the summit of the rock, and buried itself in the sand close to my feet.

"Haul again," said the Portuguese, "we are not out of shot yet."

Again we exerted ourselves, and gained another hundred yards, during which two more arrows were discharged, and one of them went through the left arm of my comrade; but as it was through the fleshy part, and did not touch the bone, it did not disable him. A third arrow was sent after us, but did not reach us, and we knew that we were out of distance.

"Cut the shaft of the arrow, and draw it through the arm," said the Portuguese.

"Not now," said I; "they will perceive me doing so, and will think that you are disabled. That may induce them to rush upon us, thinking they have only one man to deal with."

"Well, it's no great matter," replied he; "we must now drag our canoe down to the water and launch her, if they will let us. We have outwitted them so far."

We now turned the head of the canoe towards the sea, and slowly dragged her down; our eyes, as may be supposed, constantly kept upon the rock, to see if the Indians would move, but they did not. They perhaps felt that they had no chance with us, having all the fire-arms and an open beach in our favour. We launched our canoe without further interruption on their part, and in a few minutes, taking care to be out of arrow distance, we passed the rock with our head to the northward. When about two miles off, we perceived the Indians to descend from the rock and walk away into the woods.

"Let us praise God for this miraculous escape," said I to the Portuguese.

"I do; and the holy patron saint who has preserved me," replied the Portuguese captain; "but I am still heavy at heart. I feel that we have escaped only to come into more strange and fresh calamity. I shall never get back to Lisbon,—that I feel convinced of."

I tried all I could to encourage him, but it was of no avail, he told me that the presentiment was too strong, and could not be overcome by any argument. Indeed, he appeared to have allowed the idea so to have taken possession of his mind, that his reason became enervated; and, having heard how the Indians burnt their prisoners, he talked about martyrdom at the stake, and rising up to heaven in great glory, there to be received by the whole body of saints and legions of angels.

"What is the use of our thus labouring at the paddle?" said he; "why not at once let us go ashore and receive the crown of martyrdom? I am ready; for I long for the hour, and shall rejoice."

I said all I could to keep him quiet, but it was useless; and such was his insanity, that he gradually neared the shore by steering against me with his paddle, so that I could not prevent it. I had drawn the shaft of the arrow through his arm, and he appeared to feel no pain. I expostulated with him at his keeping the canoe so near the shore, but he smiled and gave no reply.

We had the stream against us and made but little way, and it vexed me very much to hear him talk so loud as he did, as the Indians must have heard him, and I thought would follow us along the coast; but he ransacked the whole book of martyrs, telling me how one had his body sawn in two, another was pinched to death; this one burnt, that tortured; every variety of death he entered upon during the whole of that day without ceasing.

I ascribed much of this to the pain arising from the wounded arm, notwithstanding which he paddled with as much vigour as ever. As the night came on I entreated him to hold his tongue, but it was in vain, and I felt assured that his reason was quite gone. He continued to talk loud and rave without intermission, and I now considered our fate as sealed. We had no water in the boat or provisions of any kind, and I proposed that we should heave-to and catch some fish, telling him that if he talked we should scare them away.

This made him quiet for a time, but as soon as we had hooked four or five fish, he again commenced his history of the glorious martyrs. I prayed him to be silent, for a short time at least, and he was so for about four or five minutes, when he would break out into some ejaculation, which I immediately stopped. At last he could talk no more for want of water; his lips were glued together, and so were mine. Nevertheless, I continued paddling for two hours more, when I found by the canoe grounding that he had steered her on the beach. There was no help for it. We landed and went in search of water, which we found about half of a mile from where our canoe was beached.

We drank heartily, filled the calabash, and were returning to the canoe, when he again commenced talking as loud as ever. I was in great anger, but I put my hand before his mouth, beseeching him in a whisper to be quiet. As we were doing this, we were suddenly sprung upon and seized by several Indians, and in a minute were bound hands and feet.

"I knew it," cried the Portuguese; "I knew it would be so. Well, I am prepared; are not you, my good friend?"

I made no reply. I felt that in his madness he had sacrificed his own life and mine also; but it was the will of Heaven. The Indians left two to guard us, and went down to the canoe, returning with their muskets. I soon perceived that they were the same whom we had escaped from the night before, and the one who had spoken a little English when we were first captured, now came to me and said, "White man paint like Indian, steal gun—ugh."

When the Indians had returned from the canoe, our feet were unbound, and we were again led away by the leather thong which was fast to our arms. The Portuguese now began to find his tongue again, and talked incessantly, the Indians not checking him; from which it was evident that they were on their own domains. After four hours' walking they kindled a fire, and went to repose as before: but this time they took our knives from us, and bound our legs so tight that they gave us much pain. I did not expostulate as I knew it was useless. My companion, as the thong entered into his flesh, seemed pleased, saying, "Now my martyrdom is commencing."

Alas! Poor man—but I will not anticipate. We travelled three days, during which we were supplied with a small portion of parched Indian corn every day, just sufficient for our sustenance, and no more. On the fourth morning the Indians, after an hour's travelling, set up some shrill and barbarous cries which I afterwards discovered was their war-whoop. These cries were replied to by others at a distance, and in about a quarter of an hour afterwards we found ourselves close to a number of wigwams, as they are termed, (the Indian houses,) and soon surrounded by a large party of men, women, and children, who greeted us with taunts and menaces.

We were led into a larger wigwam than the others, where we found several Indians of grave aspect assembled, and a man who could speak English was ordered in as interpreter, he asked us where we came from in the canoe. I replied, that we came from the south, but we had been wrecked in a big ship, and had taken the canoe, which we found on the beach. They asked no more questions. We were led out, and in about an hour afterwards the Indians who had spoken English to us when we were captured, came up with two others and painted us black, saying, "The white men like paint. Black paint good."

I did not know till afterwards that this painting black was a sign that we were condemned to death, but so it was. They took off our trousers, the only garment we had on, and left us naked. To my surprise, they did not take the diamond which was sewed up in leather from off my neck; but, as I learnt subsequently, the Indians are much given to conjurors and charms, wearing many round their own necks and about their persons, and they respect the charms that their enemies wear, indeed are afraid of them, lest they should be harmed by having them in their possession. We remained in a wigwam during that day, with guards over us. The following day we were led out and cast loose, and we found all the Indians, women and children, ranged in two lines, each holding in their hands a club or stick, or rod of some description or another.

We were led to the end of the row, and looked about us in amazement. They made signs to us which we did not understand, and while we were remaining in doubt as to what was to be our fate, an old woman, who had been menacing and grinning at me for some time, and who was the most hideous animal that I ever beheld in the shape of a woman, thrust a straw into my eye, giving me most excruciating agony. I was so carried away by rage and pain, that I saluted her with a kick in the stomach, which laid her doubled up on the ground, expecting to be scalped for so doing the next moment.

On the contrary, the Indians laughed, while some of the other women dragged her away.

At last the interpreter came, and from him we learnt that we had to run the gauntlet, and that, as soon as we gained the large lodge where we had been examined by the old Indians on the day previous, we were safe, and that we must run for that as fast as we could. The Portuguese, who was still as mad as ever, was then pushed on; he would not run, but walked glorying in the blows, which showered down upon him like hail; and, moreover, he prevented me from running for some time, till I got past him. I had been cruelly punished, and was mad with pain, when I perceived a tall, gaunt Indian waiting for me with a heavy club. Careless of life or consequences, I rushed past him, and as I passed I threw out my fist with such impetus, that, hitting him under the right ear, he fell senseless, and it appears that he never rose again, for the blow killed him; after which I at last gained the council-house, and was soon afterwards followed by my companion, who was streaming with blood. We were then led away, and tied by our necks to two stakes about twenty yards apart, and there we remained for the night.

The Portuguese passed the night in singing; I passed it in silence and prayer. I felt convinced that we were to die, and I feared that it would be by fire or torture, for I had heard something of the manners and customs of these Indians. I made my peace with God as well as a poor sinner could, prayed for mercy through Jesus Christ, sighed my adieu to Amy, and made up my mind to die.

Early the next morning the Indians brought fire-wood, and placed it in bundles round the stakes, at a distance of about fourteen yards from the centre. They then went to the Portuguese, tied his hands behind him, and exchanged the rope by which he had been fastened for a much stronger one, one end of which they fastened to his wrists behind him, and the other to the stake. As they left me as I was before, it was plain that the Portuguese was to suffer first. They then set fire to the piles of wood which were round the stake, which were too far from him to burn him, and I could not imagine what they intended to do, but you may conceive that I was in a state of awful suspense and anxiety, as I was well convinced that his fate, whatever it might be, would be my own.

During these appalling preparations, the Portuguese appeared as if he really enjoyed the scene.

"Now, my good friend," said he to me, "you shall see how I can suffer for the true faith. Even a heretic like you shall be converted by my example, and I shall ascend to heaven with you in my arms. Come on, ye fiends; come on, ye heathens, and see how a Christian can suffer."

Much as I felt for him and for myself, I could not lament that his reason had left him, as I thought his sufferings would be less; but his exclamations were soon drowned by a loud yell from the Indians, who all rushed upon my unfortunate companion.

For a moment or two they were crowded so thick round him that I could not perceive what they were doing, but after that they separated, and I beheld him bleeding profusely, his ears and nose having been cut off and a broken iron ramrod passed through both cheeks. And now a scene took place, at the remembrance of which, even now, my blood curdles. Some caught up the burning sticks and applied them to his flesh, others stuck him full of small splints, the ends of which they lighted. The Indian warriors shot at him with muskets loaded with powder only, so as to burn him terribly on every part of the body. The women took up handfuls of lighted ashes and showered them down on him, so that the ground he trod upon was a mass of burning embers, and he walked upon fire.

Red-hot irons were now brought forward, and his body seared in all parts, his tormentors seeking out where they could give him the most pain. At last one applied the hot iron to his eyes, and burnt them out. Imagine my feelings at this horrid scene—imagine the knowledge that this was to be also my fate in a short time, but what is more strange to tell, imagine, Madam, my companion not only deriding his torturers, but not flinching from the torture; on the contrary, praising God for his goodness in thus allowing him to be a martyr for the true faith, offering his body to their inflictions, and shouting manfully; but such was the behaviour of my insane friend, and this behaviour appeared to give great satisfaction to the Indians.

For nearly two hours did this torture continue, his body was black and bloody all over, and the smell of the burning flesh was horrible; but by this time it appeared as if he was much exhausted, and, indeed, appeared to be almost insensible to pain. He walked round the stake as before upon the burning coals, but appeared not to know when further torture was applied to him or not. He now sang hymns in Portuguese in a low voice, for he was much exhausted. Soon afterwards he staggered and fell down with his face upon the burning embers; but even the flesh of his face grilling, as it were, appeared to have no effect upon him. An Indian then went up to him, and with his knife cut a circle round his head, and tore off the whole scalp, flesh and hair together, and when he had done this the old woman whom I had saluted with a kick before I ran the gauntlet, and who had his ears hanging on her neck to a string, lifted up a handful of burning coals, and put them upon his bleeding head.

This seemed to rouse him. He lifted up his head, but his features were no longer to be distinguished, as his face was burnt to a black coal, and he said, "Take me, ye holy saints,—Angels, receive me," and, to my great astonishment, he again rose on his legs, and tottered round and round for a few minutes. At last he sank down, with his back against the stake, and one of the Indians cleaved his brain with his tomahawk; and thus ended the life and the misery of my unfortunate companion—and it was now my turn.

"Well," thought I, "it is but two hours of suffering, and then I shall be beyond their malice. May God have mercy upon my soul."

The same preparations were now made for me. I was fastened with the stout rope, and my arms tied behind me, the wood was fired, and one of the chiefs was haranguing the Indians. He finished, the low yell was given, when the old woman whom I had before mentioned, ran up to me, and, saying something which I could not understand, put her hand upon me.

When she did this the other Indians, who were about to rush on me, drew back with signs of disappointment on many of their wild countenances. The chiefs then went into the council-house, leaving me tied where I was, and the wood burning around me, the mass of Indians standing about as if waiting the decision of the chiefs. After a time three Indians, one of whom was the interpreter, came up to me, and, kicking aside the burning poles, cast me loose.

I asked the interpreter what he was about to do. He replied, "You kill Indian here, (pointing to his own ear,) you kill him dead. Squaw lose husband—want another—take you—stead of him."

They led me to the council-house before the chiefs. The old woman whom I had kicked was there. It was her husband that I had killed by the blow behind the ear, and she had claimed me in his stead, and, according to the custom of the country, her claim was allowed, and I was made over to her, and received into the tribe. Strange custom for a woman to marry the murderer of her husband, but still such it was, and thus did I find myself freed from the stake when I least expected it. The principal chief made me a speech, which was interpreted, in which he told me that I was now the husband of Manou, and was one of their own tribe; that I must be strong in war, and must hunt and procure venison for my family.

They then washed off the black paint, and after a few more speeches and ceremonies I was handed over to the hideous old hag, whose neck was still decorated with the two ears of my companion. To say that I would have preferred the torture would be saying too much, but that I loathed the creature to excess was certain. However, I said nothing, but allowed her to take me by the hand and lead me to her wigwam. As soon as we were in she brought me some venison, which I ate greedily, for I had had nothing for thirty-six hours. She then offered me the leggings, as they call them, which the Indians wear, and the other portions of the Indian dress, which probably belonged to her late husband. I put them on, as I was glad to cover my nakedness, and, worn out with walking and exertion, I first thanked God for my miraculous preservation, and then lay down and fell into a deep sleep.

It was not until the next day that I awoke, and I then perceived the old woman rubbing oil upon the deep cuts made in my wrists and shoulders by the leather thongs. She again set meat before me, and I ate heartily, but I looked upon her with abhorrence, and when she attempted to fondle me I turned away and spit with disgust, at which she retired, grumbling. I now had leisure to reflect. I passed over with a shudder the scenes that had passed, and again returned thanks to God for my deliverance. I called to mind how often I had been preserved and delivered. From my bondage in Africa, from my imprisonment in the Tower, from my hopeless slavery in the mines, from our wreck on the island, and now, after passing through such dangers, from an almost certain cruel death by torture! Truly did I feel how grateful I ought to be for that Providence which had often preserved me, and that my only reliance in future must be in its gracious protection.

But here I was, married to a woman I detested, and living with barbarians; and I said to myself, "That kind Heaven which has already done so much for me will, in its own good time, also release me from this thraldom. In the mean while let me not murmur, but be thankful." My squaw, as they call their wives among the Indians, now came up to me and offered to paint me, and I thought it advisable that she should, as I felt that the sooner I conformed myself to their customs the more chance I had of making my escape, which I was resolved to do the first opportunity.

As soon as she had completed my toilet I walked out of the wigwam, that I might look about me and be seen. The Indians, who were sauntering about, met me with a friendly "Ugh," which appeared a favourite monosyllable with them. At last I met with the interpreter, and began to converse with him. I asked what nation I was now belonging to, and he said the Massowomicks. I asked how large their country was, and he told me much which I could not understand, except that it appeared to me a very powerful nation.

I was very careful of mentioning the English, or anything about their settlement, although I was anxious to know where it was; but I asked him whether they were at war with any other nation. He said, "No, they had been at war with other tribes, but that they had all made peace that they might join against the white man, who had taken their land."

"I am an Indian now," said I.

"Yes, and you will forget the white man," said he. "You have now red blood in your veins. You marry Indian wife, you all the same as one Indian."

I said, "War Indian beat his wife, suppose she talk too much?"

"Plenty talk, plenty beat," said he.

"Suppose my wife talk too much and I beat her, what Indian people say?"

"Say good. Suppose wife too old, you take two wife, one more young."

I was very much pleased with this conversation; not that I had the slightest idea of profiting by his information by taking another wife, but I felt such a disgust at my present one, and had already seen what a fury she could be, that I was resolved, if necessary, to show her that I was master, for I felt certain that if I did not, she would soon attempt to master me and so it turned out.

On the third day she took down a bow and arrows and made a sign to me to go out, and, I presumed, bring back food; and as there was nothing in the house I thought the request reasonable. I therefore went out of the wigwam and found that many of the young men were going out on a hunting-party, and that I was to join them. We set off and travelled for six hours before we came to the hunting-ground, and as the deer passed me I thought of Whyna and my hunting excursions with her. I was, however, fortunate, and killed two deer, much to the surprise of the Indians, who thought a white man could not use a bow and arrows, and I rose very much in their estimation in consequence. The deer was cut up, and we hung upon branches what we could not carry.

We did not go home that night, but feasted over a large fire. The next morning we all carried home our loads, and mine was as large as any of the others, if not larger; neither did I flag on the way, for I was naturally very strong and active, and had lately been inured to fatigue. When we arrived, the squaws and men among the others were despatched for the remainder of the venison. I now went out every day by myself and practised with my bow, till I had become more expert, for I wanted practice. I had no musket, but I had a tomahawk and a long knife. I began to pick up a few words of the language, and by means of the interpreter I gained them very fast. Before I had been three months with the Indians I had acquired their confidence and respect. They found that I was expert, and able to gain my own livelihood, and I may add that before I had been three months I had also mastered my wife. When she found that I would not submit to her caresses, she was very indignant and very violent, but I immediately knocked her down, and beat her unmercifully. This brought her to her senses, and after that I treated her as my slave with great rigour, and as she was a notorious scold the Indians liked me all the better for it.

You may think that this was not fair treatment towards a woman who had saved my life; but she only saved it for her own purposes, and would have worn my ears, as well as my companion's, if I had not killed her husband. The fact is, I had no alternative; I must have either treated her kindly and submitted to her nauseous endearments, or have kept her at a respectful distance by severity, and I hardly need say that I preferred the latter. So far as her choice of a husband was concerned, she made a bad one, for she received nothing but blows and bad usage. I had one day driven my wife out of the wigwam in consequence of her presuming to "talk too much," as the Indian said, when the interpreter told me that one of the chiefs was willing that I should marry his daughter, polygamy being one of their customs.

I was very much annoyed at this, for I knew the young girl very well: she was very graceful and very pretty; and I felt that my fidelity to Amy would be in great danger if the marriage was to take place; and if proposed, I dared not refuse so great a distinction.

I replied that I was fortunate, but that I feared my present wife would make her very unhappy, as she wanted to be the chief woman of the wigwam, and when I was away I could not tell what the old woman might do to her, and the conversation was dropped.

This little Indian had, before this, shown me as much favour as an Indian girl ever ventures to show, sufficient, at all events, to satisfy me that I was not disagreeable to her, and what the interpreter had said made me very uncomfortable. However, I consoled myself with the recollection that if I were compelled to marry this girl, it would be an involuntary infidelity on my part, and on that account might well be excused; for the hope of again rejoining Amy never left me at any time.

One day I went out in search of deer, and was led away from my companions after a buck which I had wounded and attempted to overtake. They saw me in chase of my quarry, and left me in pursuit. I followed for several hours, continually coming up with it and as continually losing it again. At last, I heard the report of a musket close to where the deer was last seen by me, and I thought that some Indian had shot it. I walked forward, however, very cautiously, and perceived a white man standing by the animal, which lay at his feet. I started back, for I did not know whether I had fallen in with a friend or a foe; but as I knew that he had not had time to reload his musket, I hallooed to him, concealing myself at the same time behind a tree.

"Is that you, Evans?" said the man in reply.

"No," said I, "it is an Englishman."

"Well, show yourself, then," said he.

"I am dressed as an Indian," replied I; "I was taken by the Indians."

"Well, come along," said the man, who was attired as a seafaring man.

I came from behind the tree, and when he saw me he snatched up his musket.

"Don't be afraid," said I.

"Afraid!" said he; "I should like to see what I am afraid of; but I'll be on my guard."

"That's right," I replied.

I then told him that I had been taken by the Indians, and they saved my life because one of their women chose me as her husband, and that I was anxious to escape from them.

"Well," said he, "I am on board of a schooner at anchor down below in the river. There are a few of us come on shore to get some venison, and I have lost my comrades; but I had no idea that the Indians were down here so close to the English settlements."

"How close are we, then?" said I; "for I know not where I am. This is certainly not our usual hunting-ground, for I have been led many miles from it, in pursuit of the animal you have just shot."

"Well, I thought so; for I have been on shore here more than once, and I have never met with an Indian. You ask how far you are from the settlement; that I can hardly tell you, because the settlers have spread out so far; but you are about forty or fifty miles from James Town."

"And what river, then, is your schooner at anchor in?"

"I don't know the name," replied the man; "I'm not sure that it has a name. We come here for wood and water, because it is quiet, not inhabited, and no questions asked."

"What are you, then?" inquired I.

"Why, to tell you the truth, we are what are called 'Jolly Rovers;' and if you have a mind to come on board, we can find a berth for you, I dare say."

"Many thanks," replied I; "but I am not sufficiently fond of the sea, and I should be of no use," (for by this term of Jolly Rover I knew that they were pirates).

"That's as you please," replied he; "no harm's done."

"No," replied I; "and I thank you for your kind offer, but I cannot live long on board of a vessel. Will you now tell me which is the right track to the English plantations?"

"Why," said he, "they bear right out in that direction; and I dare say, if you travel five or six leagues, you will fall aboard of some plantation or another—right in that quarter; follow your nose, old fellow, and you can't go wrong."

"Many thanks," I replied; "am I likely to meet your companions?— they may take me for an Indian."

"Not in that direction," replied he; "they were astern of me a long way."

"Farewell, then, and many thanks," I replied.

"Good-bye, old fellow; and the sooner you rub off that paint, the sooner you'll look like a Christian," said the careless rover, as I walked away.

"No bad advice," I thought, for I was now determined to make for the English settlements as fast as I could, "and I will do so when I once see an English habitation, but not before; I may fall in with Indians yet."

I then set off as fast as I could, and being now inured to running for a long time without stopping, I left the rover a long way behind me in a very short time. I continued my speed till it was dark, when I heard the barking of a dog, which I knew was English, for the Indian dogs do not bark. I then proceeded cautiously and in the direction where I heard the dog bark, and arrived in a quarter of an hour to a cleared ground, with a rail fence round it.

"Thank God!" I cried, "that I am at last among my own countrymen."

I considered, however, that it would not be prudent to show myself, especially in my Indian paint, at such a time of night, and I therefore sat down under the lee-side of a large tree, and remained there till morning. I then looked about for water, and having found a running stream I washed off my paint, and appeared what I really was, a white man in an Indian dress. I then went up again to the clearing, and looked for the habitation, which I discovered on the top of a hill, about four hundred yards off. The trees were cleared away for about three hundred yards all round it. It was built of heavy logs, let into one another, with one window only, and that very small. The door was still shut. I walked up to it, and tapped at the door.

"Who's there?" replied a hoarse voice.

"An Englishman, and a stranger," I replied. "I have just escaped from the Indians."

"We'll see what you are in a very short time," replied the voice. "James, get me my gun."

In a minute the door opened, and I beheld a woman more than six feet high, of gaunt appearance and large dimensions: I thought that I had never seen such a masculine creature before. It was her voice which I had heard. Two men were seated by the fire-place.

"Who are you?" said she, with the musket ready for the present.

I told her in a few words.

"Show me the palm of your hand—turn it up at once."

I did so, without the least idea of the reason for the demand; but I afterwards discovered that it was to ascertain whether I was one of those who had been transported to the settlement, as they all had the letter R branded on them.

"Oh, you're not a gaol-bird, then, I see: you may come in; but you'll give me that bow and arrows if you please."

"Certainly," replied I, "if you wish it."

"Why, there's nothing like making sure in this world; and although you look a very peaceable, good-looking sort of personage, notwithstanding your Indian set-out, still I've known just as amiable people as you, in appearance, very mischievous at times. Now come in, and let us hear what you have to say for yourself. Jeykell, get some more wood."

One man went out to obey her orders; the other sat by the fire with his musket between his knees. I sat down by the fire, at the request of the woman, who had seated herself by the side of the man, and then, on her repeating her question, I gave her a narrative of my adventures, from the time that I left Rio.

"Well," says she, "we seldom hear stories like them; it's all the world like a book; and pray what's that thing (pointing to the diamond in its case) you have hanging to your neck there? You have left that out in your history."

"That's a charm given me by my Indian wife, to preserve me from disasters from wild animals; no panther, wolf, or bear will ever attack me."

"Well," said she, "if so be it has that power, all I can say is, it's not a bad charm to wear in these parts, for there are animals enough in the woods in summer, and round the house all night in winter; but I don't believe a bit in the charm, and that's the truth; however, if it does no good, it can't do no harm, so you may keep it on, and welcome."

"May I ask how far it is to James Town?" said I. "What, going to James Town already? I suppose you expect to be there to-night?"

"Not exactly, my good woman," replied I. "I must trespass upon your kindness to give me something to eat, for I am hungry."

"Good woman! Bah! And pray how dare you call me good woman? Call me mistress, if you want anything."

"I beg your pardon," said I. "Well, then, mistress; will you give me something to eat?"

"Yes, I will. James, fetch the meal-cake and a bit of salt pork, and give him to eat, while I call the cows from the bush."

The mistress, as I shall in future call her, then put down her musket and left the cabin. During her absence I entered into conversation with the man called James, for the other had gone out. To my inquiry how far it was to James Town, he replied that he really did not know; that he was sent out a convict, and sold for ten years to the husband of the mistress, who had died two years ago; that this man had a small vessel, in which he went to James Town by water, and that he had returned with him in his vessel; that the distance by water he considered about one hundred and fifty miles, but by land it was not half that distance; that he did not know the way, nor did he believe that there was any road as yet made to James Town, as this plantation was quite by itself, and a long way from any other. He understood that the nearest plantation was twenty miles off, and he knew there was no road to it, as no one ever went or came except by water.

"But," said I, "are not the settlers at war with the Indian tribes that surround them?"

"Yes; and have been now for three or four years; and the Indians have done great mischief to the plantations, and killed a great many people, but the settlers have punished them severely."

"Then how is it that this plantation, which is so solitary, has not been attacked?"

"Because the mistress's husband was a great friend of the Indians, and, it is said, used to bring them cargoes of muskets and ammunition from James Town, contrary to all law and regulation. But if he was friendly with them, the mistress is not; for she has quarrelled with the principal chief, and I should not be surprised if we were attacked some day, and all scalped."

"And what does the mistress say to that?"

"Oh, she don't care; she'd fight a hundred Indians, or white men either. I never saw such a creature—she's afraid of nothing."

"Who is the other man I saw here?"

"Oh, he's another like myself. There were three of us, but one was drowned by falling overboard from the sloop."

"Well, but my good fellow, how shall I get to James Town?"

"I'm sure I can't tell; but my idea is that you will never get there unless mistress chooses."

"Why, surely she won't detain me by force?"

"Won't she?—you don't know her. Why she'd stop an army," replied the man. "I don't think that she will let you go—I don't know; but that's my opinion. She wants another hand."

"What, do you mean to say that she'll make me work?"

"I mean to say that, according to the laws of the settlement, she has a right to detain you. Any person found roving here, who cannot give a satisfactory account of himself, may be detained till something is heard about him; for he may be a runaway convict, or a runaway apprentice, which is much the same, after all. Now, she may say that your account of yourself is not satisfactory, and therefore she detained you; and if you won't work, she won't give you to eat; so there you are."

"Well, we will see if she is able."

"Able! If you mean strong enough, why she'd take you up with one hand; and she is as resolute and severe as she is strong. I had rather have to deal with three men, and that's the truth."

"What's the truth, James?" cried the mistress, coming in at the door. "Let's hear the truth from your lips, it will be something new."

"I said that I was sent here for finding a pocket-book, mistress; that's all."

"Yes; but you did not tell him where you found it—at the bottom of a gentleman's coat-pocket, you know. You can only tell the truth by halves yet, I see."

Wishing to ascertain how far the man's suspicions were correct, I said to her:

"I have good friends in James Town: if I were once there I could procure money and anything else to any amount that I required."

"Well," says she, "you may have; but I'm afraid that the post don't go out to-day. One would think, after all your wanderings and difficulties, that you'd be glad to be quiet a little, and remain here; so we'll talk about James Town some time about next spring."

"Indeed, mistress, I hope you will not detain me here. I can pay you handsomely, on my arrival at James Town, for your kind treatment and any trouble you may take for me."

"Pay me! What do I want with money?—there's no shops here with ribbons, and calicoes, and muslins; and if there were, I'm not a fine madam. Money! Why I've no child to leave what I have to—no husband to spend it for me. I have bags and bags of dollars, young man, which my husband heaped up, and they are of as much use to me as they are now to him."

"I am glad that you are so rich, mistress, and more glad that your money is so little cared for and so little wanted; but if you do not want money, I do very much want to get back to my friends, who think I am dead, and mourn for me."

"Well, if they have mourned, their sorrow is over by this time, and therefore your staying here will not distress them more. I may as well tell you at once that you shall not go; so make up your mind to be contented, and you'll fare none the worse for it."

This was said in so decided a tone, that, bearing in mind what I had heard from the convict servant, I thought it advisable to push the question no further for the present, making up my mind that I would wait a short time, and then make my escape, if she still persisted in detaining me by force; but this I could not venture upon until I was in possession of fire-arms, and I could not obtain them while she had any suspicion. I therefore replied—"Well, since you are determined I shall not go, I have nothing more to say, except that I will wait your pleasure, and, in the mean time, let me make myself as useful as I can, for I don't want to eat the bread of idleness."

"You're a very sensible young man," replied she; "and now you shall have a shirt to put on, which will improve your appearance a great deal."

She then went into the inner room, which I presumed was her bed-room, as there were but two rooms in the cabin. As she went out, I could not help wondering at her. On examination, I felt assured that she was more than six feet high, and her shoulders as broad and her arms as nervous as a man's of that stature. Her chest was very expanded, but bosom she had none. In fact, she was a man in woman's clothing, and I began to doubt her sex. Her features were not bad, had they been of smaller dimensions, but her nose was too large, although it was straight; her eyes were grand, but they were surmounted with such coarse eyebrows; her mouth was well shaped, and her teeth were good and regular, but it was the mouth of an ogress; her walk was commanding and firm; every action denoted energy and muscle; and certainly, from the conversation I have already made known, her mind was quite as masculine as her body—she was a splendid monster. In a minute she returned, bringing me a good check shirt and a pair of duck trousers, which I thankfully accepted.

"I've plenty more for those who please me," said she, carelessly; "when you've put them on, come out to me, and I'll show you the plantation."

In a minute or two I joined her, and she led me round the tobacco-fields, then to the maize or Indian corn grounds, pointing out and explaining everything. She also showed me the cows, store pigs, and poultry. Wishing to please her, I asked many questions, and pretended to take an interest in all I saw. This pleased her much, and once or twice she smiled—but such a smile! After an hour's ramble we returned, and found the two servants very busy, one husking maize, and the other in the shed where the tobacco was dried. I asked some questions of her about the tobacco—how many casks or bales she made a year? She replied that she made it in bales, and sold it by weight.

"It must be heavy carriage from here to James Town?" said I.

"Yes, indeed, if it went that way it never would arrive, I imagine," replied she; "but I have a sloop in the river below, which carries it round."

"When is the time it is harvested and fit to be carried round?" inquired I.

"It is now turning fast," said she; "all that you see hanging in the drying sheds has been already drawn; in three or four weeks it will be housed, and then we begin to pack: in about two months from this the sloop will take it round."

"But is it not expensive keeping a sloop on purpose, with men to have her in charge?" inquired I, to hear what she would say.

"The sloop lies at anchor, without a soul on board," said she. "No one ever comes up this river. I believe Captain Smith, who made the settlement, did so once. There is another river, about twenty miles further down, which is occasionally frequented by buccaneers, I am told—indeed, I know it, for my husband had more to do with them than perhaps was good for his soul, but this little river is never visited."

"Then your servants take her round?"

"Yes; I leave one in charge, and take two with me."

"But you have but two."

"Not till you came—one died; but now I have three," and she smiled at me again.

If I had not been so afraid of affronting her, I certainly would have said to her, "Do anything, I beg, but smile."

I said no more on that point. She called Jeykell, who was in the tobacco-shed, and desired him to kill a couple of chickens, and bring them in. We then entered the cabin, and she observed—"I don't doubt but you are tired with so much fatigue; you look so; go and sleep on one of their beds; you shall have one for yourself by night."

I was not sorry to do as she proposed, for I was tired out. I lay down, and I did not wake till she called me and told me that dinner was ready. I was quite ready for that also, and I sat down with her, but the two convict servants did not. She ate in proportion to her size, and that is saying enough. After dinner she left me, and went with her two men on her farming avocations, and I was for a long while cogitating on what had passed. I perceived that I was completely in her power, and that it was only by obtaining her good-will that I had any chance of getting away, and I made up my mind to act accordingly. I found a comfortable bed, of the husks of Indian corn, prepared for me at night, in an ante-room where the two servant-men slept. It was a luxury that I had not enjoyed for a long while. For several days I remained very quiet, and apparently very contented. My mistress gave me no hard work, chiefly sending me on messages or taking me out with her. She made the distinction between me and the convicts that I always took my meals with her and they did not. In short, I was treated as a friend and visitor more than anything else, and had I not been so anxious about going to England, I certainly had no reason to complain except of my detention, and this, it was evident, it was not in her power to prevent, as, until the sloop went away with the tobacco, she had no means of sending me away. One day, however, as I was walking past the tobacco-shed, I heard my name mentioned by the two convicts, and stopping I heard James say:

"Depend upon it, that's what she's after, Jeykell; and he is to be our master, whether he likes it or not."

"Well, I shouldn't wonder," replied the other; "she does make pure love to him, that's certain."

"Very true; everything's fierce with her—even love—and so he'll find it if he don't fancy her."

"Yes, indeed:— well, I'd rather serve another ten years than she should fall in love with me."

"And if I had my choice, whether to be her husband or to swing, I should take the cord in preference."

"Well, I pity him from my heart; for he is a good youth and a fair-spoken and a handsome, too; and I'm sure that he has no idea of his unfortunate situation."

"No idea, indeed," said I to myself, as I walked away. "Merciful Heaven! Is it possible!" And when I thought over her conduct, and what had passed between us, I perceived not only that the convicts were right in their supposition, but that I had, by wishing to make myself agreeable to her, even assisted in bringing affairs to this crisis.

That very day she had said to me: "I was very young when I married, only fourteen, and I lived with my husband nine years. He is dead more than a year now."

When she said that, which she did at dinner, while she was clawing the flesh off a wild turkey, there was something so ridiculous in that feminine confession, coming from such a masculine mouth, that I felt very much inclined to laugh, but I replied:

"You are a young widow, and ought to think of another husband."

Again, when she said, "If ever I marry again, it shall not be a man who has been burnt on the hand. No, no, my husband shall be able to open both hands and show them."

I replied, "You are right there. I would never disgrace myself by marrying a convict."

When I thought of these and many other conversations which had passed between us, I had no doubt, in my own mind, but that the convicts were correct in their suppositions, and I was disgusted at my own blindness.

"At all events," said I to myself, after a long cogitation, "if she wants to marry me, she must go to James Town for a parson, and if I once get there, I will contrive, as soon as extra constables are sworn in, to break off the match." But, seriously, I was in an awkward plight. There was something in that woman that was awful, and I could imagine her revenge to be most deadly. I thought the old Indian squaw to be bad enough, but this new mistress was a thousand times worse. What a hard fate, I thought, was mine, that I should be thus forced to marry against my will, and be separated from her whom I adored. I was a long while turning over the matter in my mind, and at last I resolved that I would make no alteration in my behaviour, but behave to her as before, and that if the affair was precipitated by my mistress, that I would be off to the woods, and take my chance of wild beasts and wild Indians, rather than consent to her wishes. I then went into the cabin, where I found her alone.

"Alexander," said she (she would know my Christian name, and called me by it), "they say widows court the men, and that they are privileged to do so," (I turned pale, for I little thought that there was to be an explanation so soon;) "at all events, whether they are or not, I know that a woman in my position cannot well expect a young man in yours to venture without encouragement. Now, Alexander, I have long perceived your feelings and your wishes, and I have only to say that mine are such as yours," (oh, I wish they were, thought I), "and therefore you have but to ask and to have."

I was mute with fear and despair, and could not find a reply to make to her.

"Why do you not answer, Alexander? Do you think me too forward?"

"No," stammered I; "you are very kind, but this is so unexpected—so unlooked for—so unhoped for—I am so overcome."

Observe, Madam, how strangely the sexes were changed. I was the woman in this instance.

"I should like to consult my friends."

"Consult your fiddlesticks," replied she, quickly. "Who have you got to consult? I hope, Alexander," said she, setting her broad teeth together, "that you are not trifling with me?"

"Indeed, I never should think of trifling with your mistress," replied I. "I feel much obliged to you for showing such a preference for me."

"I think, Alexander, that you ought; so now then, if you please, give me your answer," replied she.

"Had I been prepared for your kindness, I would have done so at once, but I have many serious questions to put to myself, and, if you please, we will renew the subject to-morrow morning. I will then tell you candidly how I am situated; and if after that you do not withdraw your proposal, I shall be most happy to be yours as soon as we can go to James Town to be married."

"If," replied she, "you mean to insinuate, Alexander, that you have a wife in England, that is of no consequence in this settlement; for those who live here are free from all English marriages; and as for going to James Town, that is quite unnecessary. If the people in the settlement were to wait for a parson when they married, they would never be married at all. All that is necessary is, that we shall draw up an agreement of marriage on paper, sign it, and have it witnessed. However, as I perceive that you are flurried, I will wait till to-morrow morning for your decision."

My mistress then rose from her stool, and went into her chamber, shutting to the door with more emphasis than was at all agreeable to my nerves. I walked out into the open air to recover myself, and to reflect upon what course I should take in this awkward and dangerous dilemma. Marrying was out of the question—but how to avoid it? It was almost like being stopped by a highwayman. He says, "Your money or your life." My mistress's demand was, "Marriage or your life." There was but one hope, which was to escape that very night, and take my chance in the woods, and so I resolved to do.

I did not go in till dark; my mistress was in her own room; the two convicts were sitting by the fire. I took my seat by them, but did not speak, except in a whisper, telling them that their mistress was not well, and that we had better go to bed, and not talk. They stared at me at the idea of the mistress being ill; they had never known her to complain of anything since they resided with her; but the hint was sufficient. They went to bed, and so did I with my clothes on, watching the crevices of the door of her room to see if her lamp was out. In about half an hour the little thin beams through the chinks of her door disappeared, and then I knew that she had gone to bed. I watched two hours more before I ventured to stir. The convicts were both snoring loud, and effectually drowned any slight noise I might make in moving about. I went to the locker, secured all the cold meat for provision, took down one of the muskets and ammunition-belts, and, having put the latter over my shoulders, I then took the musket in my hand and crept softly to the door of the cabin. Here was the only difficulty; once out, but five yards off, and I was clear. I removed the heavy wooden bar, without noise, and had now only to draw the bolt. I put my finger to it, and was sliding it gently and successfully back, when my throat was seized, and I was hurled back on the floor of the cabin. I was so stunned by the violence of the fall, that for a short time I was insensible. When I recovered, I felt a great weight upon my chest, and opening my eyes found my mistress sitting upon me, and giving orders to the convicts, one of whom had already lighted the lamp.

"For mercy's sake, get off my chest," said I, in a faint voice.

"Yes, I will, but not yet," replied my mistress. "Now, James, hand them to me."

James handed some chains to his mistress, who, turning round as she sat on my body, made the manacle at the end of the chain fast round my ankle. This went with a snap-spring, which could not be opened without a key belonging to it. At last she rose off my body, and I could breathe free. She then called to the convicts, saying:

"Go both of you into the tobacco-shed, and wait there till I call you out. If I find you one foot nearer to us, I'll flay you alive."

The servants ran off as fast as they could. When they were gone, my mistress said:

"So you were about to escape, were you? You would avoid the chances of matrimony, and now you have other chances which you little dreamt of."

"I thought it was the wisest thing that I could do," replied I. "Since I must be plain, I am sacredly betrothed to another person, and I could not even for you break my faith. I meant to have told you so to-morrow morning, but I was afraid it would annoy you, and therefore I wished to go away without giving you any answer."

"Well, Sir, I offered to be your wife, which would have made you my lord and master. You refuse it, and now I make you my slave. I give you your option; you shall either consent to be my husband, or you shall remain as you are, and toil hard; but any time that you think better of it, and are willing to embrace my offer, you will be free, and I will be as a wife in subjection."

"So you say," replied I; "but suppose I was to make you angry after I married you, you would do to me as you have done now. I may, perhaps, one day get free from this chain, but, once married to you, I am a slave for ever."

"You may think otherwise before long," replied she; "in the mean time, you may walk out and cool yourself."

She then returned to her room, and I rose, having determined to walk out and cool myself, as she proposed; but when I was on my legs, I found that to the other end of the chain, which was very heavy and about two yards long, was riveted an iron ball of about thirty pounds weight, so that I could not walk without carrying this heavy weight in my hands, for it could not be dragged. I lifted up the iron ball, and went out of the house. I was no longer afraid of her. I was in too great a rage to fear anything. As I calmed, I considered my case, and found it to be hopeless; as I thought of Amy, and the many months of hope deferred, I wept bitterly; and I had no consolation, for the reader may recollect that I lost my Bible when I was sent on shore, naked almost, by the rascally captain of the Transcendant.

I had now been twenty months away from Liverpool, and I felt as if my chance of seeing her that I loved was indeed hopeless. I might remain chained in such a solitude for years, or I might expire under her barbarous treatment, for I fully knew what I had to expect. However, I was resolved. I prayed fervently for support and succour in my time of trouble, and became more composed. I remained out the whole of the night, and watched the rising sun. The two convicts came out to their work, and shrugged their shoulders as they passed me, but they dared not speak to me.

My mistress at last came out. She commenced with abuse, but I gave no answer. She tried soothing, but I was mute. At last she became frantic in her passion, hurled me away from her, and after being dreadfully beaten I fell to the ground. She put her foot upon my neck, and she stood there, looking like a fury. She loaded me with epithets, and then of a sudden went down on her knees by me, and begged my pardon, calling me her dear Alexander—her life—entreating me to accede to her wishes. Never was there such a tigress in love before, I really believe.

"Hear me," replied I; "as long as I am chained, I never will give any answer upon the present subject, that I swear."

She rose from my side, and walked away.

It is impossible, my dear Madam, for me to describe what I suffered from this woman for more than six weeks, during which she kept me chained in this way—at one time entreating me, the next moment kicking me, and throwing me down. I had no peace—my life became a burden to me, and I often entreated her, in mercy, to put an end to my sufferings. I also had my paroxysms of rage, and then would spurn her, spit at her, and do everything I could, and say all that I could imagine, to show my hatred and contempt. At other times I was sullen, and that always annoyed her. She would bear my reproaches patiently—bear any thing, so long as I would talk; but if I remained obstinately silent, then, in a short time, her fury would break forth. I pitied her, notwithstanding her ill-treatment, for the woman did love me (after her own fashion) most intensely.

It was on the seventh week of my confinement on the chain, that one morning very early, as I was lying in the tobacco-shed, for she had turned me out of the cabin, I perceived among the trees, which were about three hundred yards from the cabin, two Indians, in what is called their war-paint, which is a sign that they were on a hostile excursion. I remained perfectly quiet, and well concealed, that I might watch them. The convicts had more than once told me that the Indians would attack us, in consequence of an insult which my mistress had offered to their chief, with whom her husband had been so friendly; and when they stated what had passed, I agreed with them that they would not fail to resent the insult as soon as they could. I had therefore always been on the look-out, but had never seen any Indians before. My mistress, to whom I had, in our days of sweet converse, spoken about them, always laughed at the idea of their attacking her, and said that they might come if they liked. She had made every preparation for them, as she had loop-holes stuffed up with moss just below the roof of the cabin, from which you could fire down upon them till they were within four yards of the cabin, and other loop-holes, from which you might shoot them when close to; the window and door were impregnable, and, provided that we were once in the cabin, there was no doubt but that a serious, if not effectual, resistance might be made. That the Indians were reconnoitring the cabin was evident, and that they did not do so for nothing was equally certain. After a while, during which I made out six of them, they fell back in the wood, and disappeared. The dog at that moment came out to me, and it was probably the sight of the dog which made them retreat, as they feared that he would have given notice of their being so close to us. I waited till the convicts came out, and then I went into the cabin, and said:

"You drove me out of the house last night, and I come to return good for evil. As I lay in the tobacco-shed, I saw six Indians in the wood, to the east of the cabin, reconnoitring, and I have no doubt but that you will be attacked this night, so I give you notice."

"And you hope that, by this fear of their attack, you will be set free, is it not?"

"It is perfectly indifferent to me whether I am or not. I have often asked you to put an end to my misery, and as you have not done it, I shall bless those Indians for the friendly act; a blow of a tomahawk will release me, if you will not."

"Well, then, let them come with their tomahawks," replied she, "and I will protect you from them, for no one shall release you but myself."

"As you please," replied I; "I have done my duty in telling you what I have seen, and you may take precautions or not; for myself I care nothing."

So saying, I lifted up my ball of iron and went away out of the door. I remained out of doors the whole of the day, and therefore did not know whether my mistress took any precautions or not, but I told the two convicts what I had seen, and advised them not to go far from the cabin, as they would run great danger.

They inquired of me where I had seen the Indians and I pointed out the spot in the wood, after which they went away. I was certain that the attack would be on this night, as there was no moon till three hours before daybreak; and as it was very dark it would probably take place in the early part of the night. I had made up my mind what I would do, which was not in any way to defend the cabin while chained, but, when I was freed, I would fight to the last, so that I might be killed where I stood, and not be taken alive and tortured.

I did not go out from home all that day, and, to my surprise, I was not molested by my mistress. At dark she called the convicts, but they did not answer; she came out to look for them, and asked me whether I had seen them.

I told her that I had not seen them for two hours, and I had thought that they were in the house.

"Did you tell them about the Indians?"

"Yes, I did," I replied, "and stated my opinion that they would attack us this night, and I advised them not to go far from the cabin, or they might be cut off."

"Then the cowardly sneaks have run off to the woods, and left us to defend ourselves how we can."

"I shall not defend myself," replied I. "I shall stay here where I am. I wait for death, and will not avoid it."

"Come into the house," said she, abruptly.

"No," replied I, "I will not."

"You will not," said she, and, catching up the chain and ball in one hand, with her other arm she caught me round the waist, and carried me into the house.

"Well," replied I, "it is only deferring it a little longer; they will force their way in it at last, and I will die here."

"Wait until they arrive," replied my mistress. "But do you mean to say that you will not defend the house?"

"Certainly not, as long as I am chained as a slave," replied I.

My mistress made no reply, but busied herself with barring the door and window. She then placed the table and stools so that she might stand upon them and fire out of the upper loop-holes; pulled the moss out of the loop-holes; took down the muskets—of which there were six—from their rests; examined the priming of those which were loaded, and loaded those which were not. She then got out a supply of powder and ball, which she put ready on the table, brought the axes out, that they might be at hand, examined the water-jars to ascertain whether the convicts had filled them as she had ordered, and then, when all was prepared for defence, she removed the lamp into the inner room, leaving the one we were in so dark, that the Indians could not, by looking through the chinks or loop-holes, discover where the occupants of the cabin might be. All these arrangements she made with the greatest coolness, and I could not help admiring her courage and self-possession.

"Is there any more to be done, Alexander?" said she, in a mild voice.

"Where is the dog?" replied I.

"Tied up in the tobacco-shed," said she.

"Then there is no more to be done," replied I; "the dog will give you notice of their coming, as they will first occupy the tobacco-shed as an advanced post."

"Alexander, will you promise not to escape if I set you free?"

"Certainly not," replied I. "You set me free for your own purposes, because you wish me to help to defend your property; and then, forsooth, when the Indians are beat off, you will chain me again."

"No, no; that was not my feeling, as I sit here alive," replied she; "but I was thinking that, if forced to retreat from the cabin, you would never be able to escape, and I never could save you; but they should hack me to pieces first."

"Answer me one question," said I. "In a time of peril like this, would you, as a conscientious person, think that you were justified in retaining in such fetters even a convict who had robbed you? And if you feel that you would not, on what grounds do you act in this way to a man whom you profess to love?—I leave it to your conscience."

She remained silent for some time: when the dog barked, and she started up.

"I believe I am mad, or a fool," said she, sweeping back her hair from her forehead.

She then took the key of the manacle out of her dress, and released me.

"Alexander—"

"Silence!" said I, putting my hand to her mouth, "this is no time to be heard speaking. Silence!" repeated I in a whisper, "I hear them, they are round the house."

I stood upon one of the stools and looked through a loop-hole. It was very dark, but as the Indians stood on the hill, there was clear sky behind them as low down as their waists, and I could perceive their motions, as they appeared to be receiving orders from their chief; and they advanced to the door of the cabin with axes and tomahawks. My mistress had mounted on the table at the same time that I had got on the stool. We now got down again without speaking, and, each taking a musket, we kneeled down at the lower loop-holes which I have described. On second thoughts I mounted the stool, whispering to her, "Don't fire till I do."

The Indians came to the door and tapped, one asking in English to be let in. No reply was given, and they commenced their attack upon the door with their axes. As soon as this aggression took place, I took good aim at their chief, as I presumed him to be, who was now standing alone on the hill. I fired. He fell immediately.

As I leaped from the stool my mistress discharged her musket, and we both caught up others and returned to the loop-holes below. By this time the blows of the axes were incessant, and made the cabin-door tremble and the dust to fly down in showers from the roof; but the door was of double oak with iron braces, and not easily to be cut through; and the bars which held it were of great size and strength.

It was some time before we could get another shot at an Indian, but at last I succeeded, and as his comrades were taking the body away my mistress shot another. After this the blows of the axes ceased, and they evidently had retreated. I then went into the inner room and extinguished the lamp, that they might not be able to see us—for the lamp gave a faint light. We returned to the table, and loaded the muskets in the dark.

As I put my musket on the table, my mistress said, "Will they come again?"

"Yes;" replied I, "I think they will; but if you wish to talk, we had better retreat to the fire-place: there we shall be safe from any shot."

We retreated to the fire-place, and sat down on the ashes; it just held us both, and my mistress took this opportunity of embracing me, saying—"Dear Alexander, if I had a thousand lives, I would sacrifice them for you."

"We have but one," replied I, "and that one I will devote for your defence; I can do no more."

"Who did you fire at?" said she.

"The chief, as I believe, who was on the hill giving orders. He fell; and I think that he fell dead."

"Then depend upon it they will retreat," said she.

"I think not; they will be revenged, if they possibly can; and we must expect a hard fight for it."

"Why, what can they do? They never can break through the door, and when daylight comes we can shoot them by dozens."

"Depend upon it," said I, "they will try to burn us out. The wind is high, which is all in their favour, and I suspect they are now gone to collect fire-wood."

"And if they do fire the cabin, what shall we do? I never thought of that."

"We must remain in it as long as we can, and then sally out and fight to the last; but everything depends on circumstances. Be guided by me, and I will save you if I can."

"Be guided by you!"

"Yes! Recollect I am not in chains now, and that although you have the courage of a man, still you have not been so accustomed to warfare as I have been. I have long been accustomed to command, to plan, and to execute, in times of peril like this."

"You have great strength and courage; I little thought what a lion I had chained up," replied she. "Well, I love you all the better for it, and I will be guided by you, for I perceive already that you have the best head of the two. Hark! What is that?"

"It is what I said," replied I; "they are laying fire-wood against the logs of the cabin on the windward side—(this was on the side opposite to the door). Now we must try if we cannot pick off some more of them," said I, rising and taking a musket. "Bring the stools over to this side, for we must fire from the upper loop-holes."

We remained at our posts for some time without seeing an Indian. They had gone back to the wood for more combustibles. At last we perceived them coming back with the wood. I should imagine there were at least twenty of them.

"Now, take good aim," said I.

We both fired almost at the same moment, and three Indians fell.

"Get down, and give me another musket," said I to my mistress.

She handed me one, and, taking another for herself, resumed her station. We fired several times; sometimes with and sometimes without success; for the Indians went away twice for fire-wood before they had collected what they considered sufficient. By this time it was piled up to the eaves of the cabin, and our loop-holes were shut up; we therefore went over to the other side, where the door was, to see if there were any Indians there, but could not see one. We had been on the look-out for about five minutes, when the crackling of the wood, and the smoke forcing itself though the crevices between the logs, told us that the fire had been applied, and the wind soon fanned it up so that the flame poured through every chink and loop-hole, and lighted up the cabin.

"We must retreat to the fire-place," said I. "Come quickly, or we shall be shot."

"Why so?" said she, as she did as I requested.

"They will peep through the loop-holes on the side of the cabin where the door is and see us plainly, until the cabin is filled with smoke, which it soon will be."

"But tell me what we are to do now, for I feel if this smoke increases we shall not be able to speak to one another."

This she said about five minutes after we had remained standing in the fire-place, with our heads up the chimney.

"Perhaps it will be as well," replied I, "that I do speak so. This fierce wind drives the smoke to leeward in volumes, but the great burst of smoke will be when the roof is well on fire. It is now burning fiercely on the windward side, but we must wait till the lee-side has caught, and then the volume of smoke will be greater. The great point is to hit the precise time of opening the door, and escaping shrouded in a volume of smoke. If too soon, they will perceive us, and we shall be shot down; if too late, the roof will fall upon us, and we shall be smothered or burnt. We had better now, I think, leave this, and be all ready. Our best weapon, if we had to fight our way, will be an axe. Let us each take one; and, by now going near to the door, and putting our mouths to one of the loop-holes, we shall breathe freer, and unbar the door at the right time. Do you agree with me?"

"You are right," said she; "you are a *man*, and I am a *woman*."

We left the fire-place, and, having felt for and found the axes, we went near the door, and put our mouths to the loop-holes below; and the smoke passing above them enabled us to breathe freer. I looked out and perceived that, with the exception of about six yards to leeward of the cabin, there was a dense volume of smoke rolling along the ground for a long distance; and that if we could only once gain it without being perceived, we should probably be saved. I therefore unbarred the door, drew the bolt, and held it in my hand, all ready for a start. The cabin was now in flames in every part as well as the roof. I touched my mistress, and then took her hand in mine, watching at the loop-hole. At last, when the heat was almost unbearable, an eddy of the wind drove back the smoke close to the lee-side of the cabin, and all was dark. I jumped up, opened the door, and dragged my mistress after me; we walked out into the black mass completely hid from our enemies, and then running hand-in-hand as fast as we could to leeward in the centre of the smoke, we found ourselves at least one hundred yards from the cabin without the Indians having any idea that we were not still inside. As we retreated, the density of the smoke became less, and I then told her to run for her life, as the Indians would discover that the door of the cabin was open and that we had escaped—and so it proved. We were still a hundred yards from the wood when a yell was given which proved that they had discovered our escape and were in pursuit. We gained the wood; I turned round a moment to look behind me, and perceived at least forty or fifty Indians in full pursuit of us—the foremost about two hundred yards distant.

"Now we must run for it, mistress," said I, "and we must no longer take hands. We shall have to thread the wood. Away! We have no time to lose."

So saying, I snatched my hand from her and sprang forward; she following me as fast as she could, more fearful, evidently, of my making my escape from her than of her own escape from the Indians. As soon as I was a hundred yards in the wood, I turned short to the right, and fled with all my speed in that direction, because I hoped by this means to deceive the Indians, and it was easier to run where the wood was not so thick. My mistress followed me close; she would have hallooed to me, but she had not breath after the first half-mile. I found out that I was more fleet than she was. Whether encumbered with her clothes, or perhaps not so much used to exercise, I heard her panting after me. I could easily have left her, but my fear was that she would have called to me, and if she had, the Indians would have heard her, and have known the direction I had taken, and, when once on my trail, they would, as soon as daylight came, have followed me by it to any distance; I therefore slackened my speed so as just to enable my mistress to keep up with me at about ten yards' distance; when we had run about three miles I felt certain that she could not proceed much further: speak she could not, and as I ran without once looking behind me, she could make no sign. I continued at a less rapid pace for about a mile further. I did this to enable her to keep up with me, and to recover my own breath as much as possible previous to a start. The voices of the Indians had long been out of hearing, and it was clear that they had not discovered the direction which we had taken. I knew, therefore, that they could not hear her now if she did cry out as loud as she could, and I gradually increased my speed, till I could no longer hear her panting behind me; I then went off at my full speed, and after a few minutes I heard her voice at some distance faintly calling out my name. "Yes," thought I, "but I have not forgotten the ball and chain; and if you thought that you had let loose a lion while we were in the cabin, you shall find that you have loosed a deer in the woods." I then stopped for a few moments to recover my breath; I did not, however, wait long; I was afraid that my mistress might recover her breath as well as myself, and I again set off as fast as I could. The idea of torture from the Indians, or again being kept confined by my mistress, gave me endurance which I thought myself incapable of. Before morning I calculated that I had run at least twenty miles, if not more.

With the perspiration running down me in streams, and hardly able to drag one leg before the other, I at last, just about daybreak, gave it up, when I threw myself on the ground, and dropped out of my hand my axe, which I had carried the whole way. I lay there for more than half an hour, tormented with thirst, but quite unable to move. At last I recovered; and, as I well knew that the Indians would divide in parties of three or four, and hunt every part of the woods, and by daylight probably discover my track, I rose and prepared to resume my toil, when, looking round me, I perceived that I was exactly on the spot where I had followed the deer, and had fallen in with the Jolly Rover, as he termed himself, who had pointed out the way to the plantations. I turned and saw the river below, and as he had told me that the Indians never came there, I resolved to go to the river, where, at least,

I should find shell-fish and water. I did so; and in half an hour arrived at the skirts of the wood, and found that the river was about four hundred yards from me and clear of trees at the mouth for some distance. I went down to the river, which ran swiftly cut, and I drank till I was ready to burst. I then rose on my feet, and walked along its banks towards the mouth, thinking what I should do. To get to James Town appeared to me to be an impossibility, unless by water, and I was not likely to meet with any other vessel here but a pirate. Should I, then, go aboard of a pirate? It appeared to me to be my only resource, and that I should be happy if I could find one.

By this time I had arrived at the mouth of the river, and, looking out to seaward, I saw a schooner at anchor. She was about three miles off. That she was a pirate vessel, I presumed. Should I go on board of her or not? And if so, how was I to get on board? All her boats were up; and I surmised that she had just left the river with the intention of sailing as soon as there was any wind, for now it was calm. The river ran out swiftly, and I thought I should be able to swim the distance with the assistance I should obtain from the current, which swept down right for her, and she was riding to its strength.

I was demurring. I had been perhaps two hours on the beach, waiting to see if she might send a boat on shore, when, as I stood at the river-side, still hesitating, I happened to turn round and perceived three Indians coming down upon me as fast as they could. I hesitated no longer, but plunged into the stream, and was swept out two hundred yards before they arrived at the beach. I made for the schooner; and the current ran out so fast, that in half an hour I was close to her. I swam for her cable, which I clung to, and then shouted loudly. This induced some of the crew to look over the bows, and they handed me a bowling knot, into which I fixed myself, and was hauled on board.

I was dragged aft to give an account of myself, and I stated in few words that I had been pursued by the Indians, and swam off to save my life.

"Hav'n't we met before?" said a rough voice.

I looked, and saw the Jolly Rover whom I had fallen in with on shore. I said, "Yes; I was escaping from the Indians when I met you, and you showed me the direction of the plantations."

"All's right," said he. "It's a true bill; and were those Indians after you that we saw on the beach just now?"

"Yes," I replied; and then I stated how it was that they had attacked our cabin, and how we had escaped.

"That was well done, and so you swam off three miles. Fire and water won't hurt you; that's clear. You're just the man for us. What thing-um-bob is this that you have hung round your neck?" said he, taking up the leathern bag with the diamond in it.

"That," replied I—a sudden thought having struck me—"is my caul; I was born with a caul, and I have always worn it, as it saves a man from drowning."

"No wonder that you swam three miles, then," replied the man.

You must know, Madam, that some people are born with a membrane over the face, which is termed a caul, and there has been a vulgar error that such people can never be drowned, especially if they wear this caul about their person in after-life. Sailors are superstitious in many things, but particularly in this, and my caul was therefore as much-respected by them as it hung round my neck, as it was by the Indians when they thought it was what they call "magic" or "medicine."

"Well," said the Jolly Rover, "as you had so much fire, so much water, and so much running, I think you won't be sorry to have a biscuit and glass of grog, and then turn in; to-morrow we will talk to you."

I went down below, very glad to accept the offer, and as I was regaling myself, who should come up to me but two of the Portuguese who had been wrecked in the xebeque, and put on shore with me in the little boat by the captain of the Transcendant. I was very glad to see them. They told me that, after great hardship and suffering, they had arrived famished at the banks of this river, and had been taken on board by the pirates, and had remained with them ever since; that they were very anxious to get away, but never had an opportunity. I begged them not to say who I was, but merely that I was once a shipmate of theirs. They promised, and being very tired, I then lay down and fell asleep. I was so worn out, that I did not wake till the next morning, when I found that we were under all sail running down to the southward. I saw the Jolly Rover, as I had termed him, on deck, (his real or assumed name, I don't know which, I found out to be Toplift,) sitting on a gun abaft. He called me to him. I said:

"Are you the captain?"

"Yes," he replied, "for want of a better. I told you months ago what we were, so it's no use repeating it. Do you intend to join us?"

"Then," replied I, "I will be very candid with you. I have been driven, as it were, on board of your vessel, but certainly without knowing exactly what she was. Now, captain, I have to ask you one question:—Would you, if you could go on shore in England, with plenty of money at your command, and plenty of good friends,—would you be here?"

"No; certainly not," replied he.

"Well; I am in that position. If once in England, I have money enough to live upon, and plenty of friends; I therefore naturally want to get back to England, and not to run the risk of my neck on board of this vessel."

"That's very true," replied he, "but there are other considerations; my men won't have a man on board who will not swear fidelity, and if you will not, I cannot protect you,—they will throw you overboard. We don't carry passengers."

"That's very true, also; and I will swear fidelity so far as this, that you never shall be betrayed by me, and I never will appear as a witness against one of you; it were most ungrateful if I did. While I am on board, I will do any duty you please to put me to, for I cannot expect to eat my bread for nothing."

"And suppose we come to action?"

"There's the difficulty," replied I; "against an English ship I never will fight."

"But if we are opposed to any other nation, and there is a chance of our being overpowered?"

"Why, then, if you are overpowered, as I shall be flung along with the rest, I think I must do all I can to save my own life; but, overpowered or not, I will not fire a shot or draw a cutlass against my own countrymen."

"Well, I cannot deny but that's all very fair."

"I think," replied I, "it is as much as you can expect; especially as I never will share any prize-money."

"Well; I will talk to the men, and hear what they say; but, now, answer me one question—Are you not a seaman?"

"I will answer the truth to everything; I am a seaman, and I have commanded a privateer. I have served many years in privateers, and have seen a great deal of hard fighting."

"So I thought," replied he; "and now answer me another question,—Was it not you that played that trick to that French privateer captain at Bordeaux?"

"Yes it was," replied I; "but how came you to know that?"

"Because I was the mate of a merchant vessel that had been captured, and I saw you three or four times as you passed the vessel I was on board of; for, being put in quarantine, we were not sent to prison till the pratique was given. I thought that I knew you again."

"I have no concealment to make."

"No: but I will tell you candidly, my men, if they knew all this, would not allow you to leave the vessel. Indeed, you might be captain if you pleased, for I do not suit them. Our captain—for I was his officer—was killed about six months ago; and I really am not fit for the office—I am too tender-hearted."

"Well; you don't look so," replied I, laughing.

"Can't judge of outsides," replied he; "but it's a fact. They say that they will be all condemned if taken, from my not destroying the crews of the vessels we take; that they will be so many witnesses against them; and I cannot make up my mind to cold-blooded murder. I am bad enough; I rob on the high seas; I kill on the high seas—for we must kill when we fight; but I cannot commit deliberate murder either at sea or on shore, and so I tell them. If any one else could navigate the vessel, I should be superseded immediately."

"I am glad to hear you say what you have, captain; it makes me less dissatisfied at finding myself here. Well; I have said all I can, and I must trust to you to manage with your ship's company."

"It will be a difficult job," said he, musing.

"Tell them," replied I, "that I was once a captain of a vessel like this (after all, there is not so much difference between a pirate and a privateer as you may think)—and that I will not be under the command of any one."

"If they hear that, they will give you the command of this vessel."

"I will refuse to take it; and give my reasons."

"Well; I'll tell them that: I leave you to settle with them how you can; but," added he, in a low tone, "there are some desperate villains among them."

"That I take for granted," replied I; "so now I leave you to speak to them."

Toplift did so. He told them that I was a pirate captain, who had lost his vessel and been thrown on shore, but I refused to join any ship except as captain of her; that I would not serve as first officer, and would obey no one. He told them that he knew me before, and he narrated the business at Bordeaux when I commanded a privateer, extolling me, as I afterwards found, beyond all measure.

The crew, having heard what he had to say, went forward, and, after consultation, came to Toplift and said that I must take the oath.

Toplift replied that he had desired me so to do, and that I had answered that I would not. "But," said he, "you had better speak to him yourselves. Call all hands aft and hear what he has to say."

This was done, and I was sent for.

"I have told them what you said, Sir. I don't know your name."

"I have no name," replied I, proudly, "except 'Captain,'—that's my name."

The fact is, Madam, I was determined to carry it out bravely; knowing that it is the best way to deal with such people as I now had in hand.

"Well, then, Captain, I have told the men that you will not take the oath."

"Take the oath!" replied I, with scorn; "no; I administer the oath to others. I make them take it. I make them swear fidelity to me. Such has been my conduct, and I shall not depart from it."

"Well, but, Captain Toplift, you don't mean to say that he is to remain on board with us and not take the oath," said a surly-looking ruffian. "In spite of you, he shall take the oath, Captain Toplift."

"Captain Toplift," said I, calmly, "do you allow one of your crew to use such language as this? Had I been captain of this ship, I would have blown his brains out as he stood. You don't know how to deal with these rascals. I do."

Captain Toplift, who appeared much pleased at being supported in this way by me—(strange that a single individual, whom they might have thrown overboard in a minute, should have gained such an ascendency, but so it was)—and who perceived that the men fell back, as if taken by surprise, then said, "Captain, you have taught me a good lesson, which I will take advantage of. Seize that fellow and put him in irons."

"Hah!" cried the man, seeing that no man touched him; "who is to bell the cat! Hah!" and drew his cutlass.

"I will, then," said I to Captain Toplift, "if you desire it;" and stepping forward I went up to the man, saying, "Come, come, my good fellow, this won't do here; I am used to deal with such chaps as you, and I can manage worse than you, a good deal."

I advanced till I was within the stroke of his cutlass before he was aware of it, and, seizing him by the waist, I threw him flat on his back and put my foot on his neck.

"Now," cried I, in an authoritative voice, "put this man in irons immediately—refuse who dares. Here, you Sirs, lay hold of this fellow," continued I, looking to the Portuguese; who accordingly came forward and led him away, assisted by others, who now joined them.

"Are there any more mutineers here?" inquired I; "if so let them step forward."

No one stirred.

"My lads," said I, "it is very true that I have refused to take the oath, for the oath is not given to those who command, but to those who obey; but at the same time I am not one to betray you. You know who I am; and is it likely?"

"No, no," replied the men.

"Sir," asked one of them, who had been most forward and insolent, "will you be our captain?—say but the word,—you are the sort of man we want."

"You have a captain already," replied I, "and in a few weeks I shall command a vessel of my own; I cannot, therefore, accept your offer; but while I am on board I will do all in my power to assist Captain Toplift in any way, and you can desire no more. And now, my men, as an old hand, I have but this advice to give you, which is—to return to your duty; for everything in a vessel of this description depends upon obedience; and to you, Captain Toplift, I have also advice to give, which is—to shoot the first man who behaves as that scoundrel did who is now in irons. Boatswain! Pipe down."

I hardly knew whether this latter order would be obeyed by the boatswain, or, if obeyed by the boatswain, whether it would be obeyed by the men; but, to my great satisfaction, it was; and the men retired peaceably.

"Well, Captain Toplift," said I, "I have done you no harm, and myself some good."

"You have indeed," replied he; "come down into the cabin." When we were in the cabin he said, "You have unarmed and subdued the most mutinous rascal in the vessel, and you have strengthened my authority. They fully believe you are what you assert from your behaviour, and I feel, with you at my side, I shall get on better with these fellows than I have done. But now, to keep up the idea, you must, of course, mess in the cabin with me, and I can offer you clothes, not my own, but those of the former captain, which will suit your shape and make."

I readily agreed with him; and, having equipped myself in the clothes he offered me, which were handsome, I soon afterwards went on deck with him, and received the greatest respect from the men as I passed them. A cot was slung for me in the cabin, and I lived altogether with Captain Toplift, who was a good-hearted, rough sort of a man, certainly wholly unfit for the command of a vessel manned by such a set of miscreants, and employed on such a service. He told me that he had been taken three years before by a pirate vessel, and finding that he could navigate, they had detained him by force, and that at last he had become accustomed to his position.

"We all must live," said he, "and I had no other means of livelihood left me; but it's sorely against my conscience, and that's the truth. However, I am used to it now, and that reconciles you to anything, except murder in cold blood, and that I never will consent to."

On my inquiring where they were about to cruise, he said, on the Spanish Main.

"But," said I, "it is peace with the Spaniards just now."

"I hardly knew," said he, "it was peace. Not that peace makes any difference to us, for we take everything; but you refer to myself, I know, and I tell you frankly that I have preferred this cruise merely that we may not fall in with English vessels, which we are not likely to do there. I wish I was out of her with all my heart and soul."

"No doubt of it, Captain Toplift, I think you are sincere. Suppose you put into one of the inlets of Jamaica, they won't know where we are; let us take a boat on shore and leave her. I will provide for you, and you shall gain your living in an honest way."

"God bless you, Sir," said he; "I will try what I can do. We must talk the matter over, for they may suspect something, and then it would be all over with us."

We continued to run down till we were in the latitude of the Virgin Isles, and then we altered her course for Jamaica. The first and second mates generally received information of Captain Toplift as to his movements and intentions, which they communicated to the crew. If the crew disapproved of them, they said so, and they were considered to have some voice in the matter.

Now, although no navigators, these men knew enough of a chart and a course to find that there must be some reason for its being altered as it was, instead of running down by the Spanish Main, and they inquired why the cruise was altered.

Captain Toplift replied that he had taken my advice, and that I had assured him that at the back of the island of Jamaica we should certainly fall in with some rich Spanish vessels, if we lay there quiet in some nook or another for a short time, as this was their time for coming up from the south to the Havannah, where they rendezvoused for a convoy.

This reply appeared very satisfactory to the crew, for they were all cheerful and obedient, and we ran down to Jamaica, and when we were close in shore we shortened sail and hove-to. We remained three or four days in the offing, that we might not cause any suspicion by our leaving too soon. Captain Toplift then told the mates that I proposed anchoring in some secret bay or inlet, as we were certain to see the Spanish ships if we could send any one ashore on the hills to look out for them. This was agreed to, and we made sail and ran along the coast, looking out for some convenient anchorage.

As we were so doing, a vessel hove in sight, and we immediately made all sail in chase. As she did not attempt to avoid us, we hauled off as she came near, to see what she might be. She then hoisted a yellow flag at her peak (for she was an hermaphrodite brig); this puzzled us not a little, and we edged down towards her, for she was very rakish-looking, except in her sails.

As we neared, finding, I suppose, that we did not answer her signals, and we were not the vessel she expected us to be, she suddenly altered her course before the wind, setting all the sail that she possibly could. We immediately crowded canvass in chase, and came up with her fast. As we ran, the mate and I looked at her through the glass, and I made her out to be the Transcendant, the captain of which had treated us so cruelly when we were in the boat, and who had robbed us of our money and clothes. I called the Portuguese and desired them to look at the vessel through the glass, and give me their opinion. They directly said that it was the vessel I supposed.

"Let us only catch the rascal," said I, "and we will pay him in his own coin;" and I immediately gave directions for the better trimming of the sails, so anxious was I to come up with him.

The men of the schooner were much pleased at the anxiety I displayed to come up with the chase, and by the alacrity with which they obeyed me I saw how anxious they were that I should be their captain. In two hours we were within gun-shot, and sent one of our bow-chasers after him. Perceiving that it was useless to run, the fellow hove-to, and as we came alongside he was all ready with his boat to come on board. He did so, and at first I kept out of sight to hear what he would say. He was followed up the side by his amiable son. Captain Toplift received him on deck, and he looked around him, saying, "I believe I am right. I was afraid I had made more mistakes than one. I believe you are in the free trade?"

"Yes," replied Toplift, "we are."

"Yes, I thought so, captain, but I expected to meet another schooner which is very like to yours, and is also in the trade. I made my signal to her, as, when she has anything to get rid of, why I take it off her hands. Perhaps you may have something of the kind which is not exactly safe to show,—church-plate and the like. I pay ready money—that's my plan."

As it afterwards appeared, Madam, this scoundrel had been in the free trade, or pirating, himself for many years, but he had taken an opportunity of walking off with a large sum of money belonging to the pirate crew, and with this money he had purchased his property in Virginia and the brig which he now commanded. Although he did not follow up the free trade any more, he had made arrangements with a pirate captain whom he met at Port Royal to meet them at the back of the island and receive such articles as the pirate might want to turn into cash, by which he, of course, took care to secure large profits.

This he had done several times, and as he sold his cargo at Port Royal for dollars, he had always cash to pay for what the pirate wished to get rid of. But he had now run into the lion's jaws, for not only were I and the Portuguese on board to denounce him as a robber, but, what was still more unfortunate for him, three of the pirate's crew, whom had he swindled out of their property, were also on board of us, and recognised him immediately.

As Captain Toplift knew how I had been treated by him, he thought it was time he should be confronted with me, and to his question as to whether there was anything to dispose of, he replied to him, "You must put that question to the captain. There he is."

The fellow turned to me; he looked at me, stared, and was mute, when his cub of a boy cried out, "As sure as a gun it's he, father, and no mistake."

"Oh, you imp of Satan, you know me, do you?" replied I. "Yes, it is he. Send all the men aft."

The men came fast enough. They were only waiting till I had spoken to them to come and give information against him.

"Now, my lads," said I, "this is a scoundrel who fell in with some of us when we were in distress, after we had lost our vessel. Instead of behaving as one seaman does to another, he robbed us of all we had, and turned us adrift naked to be killed by the Indians. Of all, I and the two Portuguese you took on board about four months back are the only three left: the others perished. The one who was with me was burnt to death by the Indians, and I narrowly escaped. I leave you to decide what this scoundrel merits."

"But there is more against him, captain," said the men, and then four of them stepped out and declared that he had run away with the money belonging to the crew of which they were a part, and that the sum he had stolen amounted to 25,000 dollars.

"What have you to say for yourself?" said I to him.

"That I've been a cursed fool to be caught as I have been."

"What will they do, father?"

"Hang us, I suppose," replied he.

"Captain Toplift," said I, "I do not command this vessel, and I shall therefore leave you to decide upon the fate of this miscreant;" and, having said that, I was going below to the cabin, when the captain of the Transcendant's son ran to me, and said, "I want to speak to you, Sir, when you are alone."

"What are you after, Peleg?" cried his father.

"I'm going to save your life, father, if I can," replied he.

"You'll be clever if you do that, boy," said the man, sneeringly.

I allowed the boy to follow me down into the cabin, and then asked him what he had to say.

"I have that to tell you which is of more value than the lives of a hundred boys like me."

"Boys like you? Why I thought it was to save your father's life that you came down, Sir?"

"Pooh!" said he, "let him hang; he was born for a halter. I am come to save my own life. I only said that to gammon him."

"You're a hopeful youth," said I; "and pray what is that you can tell me that will save your own neck from the halter?"

"That which will save your own, most likely," replied the boy, "and tit-for-tat's all fair."

"Well, let's hear it then," replied I.

"No, not unless you promise. I can swing, if need be, as well as father, but I'd rather not, 'cause I know where all his money is hidden."

"I can't make any promise," replied I.

"Then I can't tell," replied he, "so I may e'en go on deck and tell father that I cannot manage it;" and as he said the latter part of this speech, the undaunted little villain actually laughed at the idea of gammoning his father, as he termed it.

Train up a child in the way he should go, and he will not depart from it, is mostly true; but it is more certain that if you train a child up in the way that he should not go, he will be a more true disciple. Could there be a more decided proof of the above than the behaviour of this young villain? But his father had made him so, and thus was he rewarded.

"Stop," said I, for I had reflected whether, after all, there were any grounds for hanging the boy, and come to a conclusion that a jury would have probably acquitted him. "Stop," said I; "you say that what you can tell is of the greatest consequence."

"And becomes of more consequence every minute that passes," replied he. "I will tell you everything, and let you into father's secrets. I peach upon father altogether."

"Well, then," replied I, "if what you have to disclose proves important, I will do all I can to save your life, and I have no doubt that I shall be able so to do."

"No more have I," replied he, "or I would not have come to you. Now then, father came to the back of the island to do a little business with a pirate schooner, as he said just now; and he has very often done it before, as he said just now; but father did not tell you all. When we were in Port Royal, father went to the captain of a king's vessel who is there, having been sent to put down the pirates if possible, and he offered this captain of the king's ship, for a certain sum, to put our friends that we exchange with into his hands."

"What, betray his friend the pirate?"

"Yes, father agreed that he would come round as he has done this day, and would contrive to chaffer and bargain with him and keep him so late in the bay that the king's ship should come upon him all of a sudden and take him, and this was father's intention, only you have pinned him. The king's ship will be round that point in two hours or thereabouts, so if you are found here you will be taken and handed as sure as I ain't hanged yet. Now ain't this important news, and worth all I asked for it?"

"It certainly is, if it is true, boy."

"Oh, I'll prove it, for I always goes with father, and he trusts me with everything. I saw the paper signed. The king's ship is called the Vestal, and the captain who signed the paper signed it Philip Musgrave."

"Indeed," said I, turning away, for I did not wish the boy to perceive my emotion at this announcement. I recovered myself as soon as I could, and said to him, "Boy, I will keep my promise. Do you stay below, and I will go on deck and plead for your life."

"Mayn't I go on deck for a bit?" said he.

"What to wish your father good-bye? No, no, you had better spare yourself and him that painful meeting."

"No, I don't want to wish him good-bye,—I'll wait till it's over, only I never did see a man hanged, and I have a curiosity to have just a peep."

"Out, you little monster," cried I, running up on deck, for the information I had received was too important not to be immediately taken advantage of.

"Well, captain, has the boy saved his father's life?"

"No," replied I, in a loud voice.

"Then, up he goes," said the men, for the halter had been round his neck and run out to the yard-arm for some time, and the men had manned the rope, only awaiting my return on deck. In a second, the captain of the Transcendant was swinging in the air, and certainly if ever a scoundrel merited his fate it was that man. Shortly afterwards I turned round, and there was the young hopeful looking at his father's body swinging to and fro with the motion of the vessel.

I looked in vain for a tear in his eye; there was not a symptom of emotion. Seeing me look sternly at him, he hastened down below again.

"My lads," said I to the men, who were all on deck, "I have received intelligence of that importance that I recommend that we should cut that vessel adrift, and make sail without a moment's loss of time."

"What, not plunder?" cried the men, looking at the Transcendant.

"No, not think of it, if you are wise."

At this reply all of the men exclaimed that "that would not do"—"that plunder they would"—that "I was not the captain of the vessel,"—and many more expressions, showing how soon a man may lose popularity on board of a pirate vessel.

"I gave my opinion, my men, and if you will hear why I said so—"

"No, no, out boats," cried they all, and simultaneously ran to lower down the boats, for it was now calm, that they might tow the schooner alongside of the Transcendant.

"You might as well talk to the wind as talk to them when there is plunder to be obtained," said Toplift to me in a low tone.

"Come down with me," said I, "and I will tell you what I have heard."

"Ain't they going to plunder the brig?" said Master Peleg, when we came down; "I know where father's dollars are," and up he ran on deck.

I made a short remark upon the depravity of the boy, and then informed Captain Toplift of what he had told me.

"If you had told them, they would not have paid attention to you. The boat's crew who came with the captain have told them that there is money on board, and all authority is now at an end."

"Well," replied I, "I believe that the boy has told the truth."

"And what do you mean to do?"

"Remain below quietly, if I am allowed," replied I.

"But I cannot," said he; "they would throw me overboard."

"Make as bad a fight of it as you can," replied I.

"That I will," said Captain Toplift, "and with so superior a force opposed, we cannot stand long. But I must tell you where you must be."

"Where?" replied I.

"At the entrance of the magazine, for as sure as we stand here they will blow up the vessel rather than be taken. Not all of them, but two or three I know are determined so to do, and resolute enough to do it. My pistols are there. You have only to open this door, and you are in the magazine passage. See," said he, opening the door, "there is the scuttle where they hand the powder up."

"I will be on the watch, depend upon it; and, Captain Toplift, if the schooner is taken, and I am alive, you may have no fear for yourself."

"Now let us go on deck again."

"I will follow you," replied I.

"I am alone at last, thank Heaven!" said I to myself. "What a position am I in, and how much will be in suspense before twenty-four hours are over! My own brother here, not ten miles perhaps from me, commanding the vessel which will attack this on which I am on board. That they will take us I have no doubt; but what risk do I run—of death by shot, or by their blowing up the vessel in spite of me, or of no quarter being given. Well, I wish it were decided. At all events, I am long supposed dead, and I shall not be recognised among the heaps of the bodies."

I then went to the locker and took out my duck frock and trousers, determining that I would, if I were killed, be killed in those clothes, and be thrown overboard as a common seaman. I then went on deck, for I heard the grating of the sides of the two vessels, and knew that they were in contact.

All was uproar and confusion on board of the Transcendant, but there was nobody on board the schooner except Toplift and myself. I cannot say that I never saw such a scene, for I had seen quite as bad on board of a privateer. The common seamen, as well as the soldiers, when let loose to plunder, are like maniacs. In half an hour they had broken open everything, cut the crew to pieces, and found out the hoard of dollars, which was shown them by young Peleg, who tried for his share, but for so doing received a chop with a cutlass, which cut off his right ear, and wounded him severely on the shoulder; but his right arm was not disabled, and while the man that out him down was bending over a heap of dollars, which took both hands to lift them, the boy ran his knife deep into the man's side, who fell mortally wounded. The rush for the dollars thus at the mercy of the rest was so great, that Peleg was not minded, and he crept away and came on board the schoog. We saw that he was bleeding profusely, but we asked no questions, and he went down the ladder forward.

"What has that young villain been after?" said Toplift.

"I presume he has been quarrelling for plunder, and considered that he had a greater right to his father's money than anybody else."

Among other plunder the people had not forgotten to look for liquor, and an hour had not passed before three-fourths of the men were more or less intoxicated. They had found plenty of good clothes, and were strutting about with gold-laced waistcoats and embroidered coats over their dirty frocks. The uproar increased every minute, when Toplift, who had been looking out with the glass, exclaimed, "There she is, by all that's sacred!"

I caught the glass out of his hand, and found it was the king's ship. She was a large flush vessel, apparently of eighteen or twenty guns, just opening from the point, and not seven miles from us. We were still becalmed, and she was bringing the wind down with her, so that to escape appeared impossible.

"Now, what shall we do?" said Captain Toplift; "shall we allow her to come down upon us and say nothing to the men, or shall we point out the danger and persuade them to come on board and prepare?"

"You must do as you please," replied I, "I am indifferent which. It will be dark in another hour, and she will not be down by that time. I would rather avoid fighting, and get away from the schooner quietly if I could, but that I fear is impossible now."

"Well, I must go on board of the brig and let them know, for if they find it out themselves they will throw us overboard."

Captain Toplift then went on board of the brig, and railing to the men who were still sober, told them that there was a king's ship coming down upon them not seven miles off. This had the effect of putting an end to the confusion and noise of a great portion of the men, who hastened on board of the schooner, but others, who were intoxicated, were with difficulty persuaded to return.

At last they were all got on board, and the schooner, clear from the brig, was made ready for action; but Toplift was obliged to make some alteration in the stationing of the men, as those who were to hand up the powder were all of them tipsy. By the time that the schooner was ready, and the breeze had come down to her, the corvette was not more than three miles from us; but it was quite dark, for there is no twilight in those parts. We consulted what course we should take to avoid her, if possible, and agreed that we would stand in shore and pass her if we possibly could. We knew that, if seen, we were then certain to be obliged to fight; but if not seen, we might escape.

We then shifted the helm and bore up across her bows, but we had not steered in this direction more than a quarter of an hour, when the Transcendant was perceived to be on fire, having been fired by the drunken men before they left her, and soon afterwards she burst out into flames that threw a strong light to a great distance, discovering the corvette to us at two miles' distance, and of course exposing us to the corvette, who immediately altered her course for us. We had therefore only to fight, and the crew, being most of them in liquor, declared that they would fight till the schooner sunk under them. In a quarter of an hour, the corvette being close to us, and standing stem on, we opened our fire, raking her masts and yards, and then I went down below. I had changed my clothes for the duck trousers and shirt which I had swum on board in, and I now remained quietly in the cabin. A few minutes afterwards the corvette opened her fire, and the shot did great execution. The cries of the wounded and the shouts of the tipsy men were mingled together, but the crew of the schooner fired with great rapidity, and sustained the unequal conflict most gallantly.

After a time some men darted down into the cabin. I was then at the door which led to the magazine passage, and busied myself handing up the powder, as it secured me from observation, and it was supposed that I was one of the crew sent down for that duty.

The men roared out, "Where is the captain? We want him to fight the ship. Toplift is an old fool, and don't know what he is about."

I made no reply, but with my back towards them continued to hand up the powder, and, having changed my dress, they did not recognise me, so they rushed upon deck again.

The corvette was now alongside of the schooner, pouring in her broadsides with fatal execution, the shot passing in every direction through her, so that there was as much danger below as on deck, and it was evident that the schooner could not oppose them much longer. Still they continued to fire with great resolution, being now sobered into more steadiness than at first. But by this time more than half the men were killed and wounded, and our guns were encumbered with the wreck and bodies. I heard them, at the very time that a crashing broadside was poured in by the corvette, cry out, "Avast firing for a moment and clear the decks."

They did so, and, having thrown the bodies overboard and cut away the spars and rigging which had fallen, so as to enable them to work their guns, during which time three broadsides were poured in, they remanned their guns, and fought with as much spirit as before. I could not help admiring the courage of the scoundrels, for nothing could exceed it; but resistance was useless, further than they preferred dying at their guns to being hanged on the gibbet.

But the shouts of the pirates and the reports of the guns gradually decreased. The men were swept away by the enemy's fire, and the guns were one by one disabled. The schooner's sides were torn out, and the water poured in so fast that it was rising to the magazine. I heard a cry of boarders, and the striking of the two vessels together, and then there was a rush down below, when a man came aft to the magazine passage. It was the fellow whom I had struck down on the quarter-deck and had put into irons.

"Come along," said he, to the others; "we'll send the corvette and ourselves all to the devil together. Out of the way there."

"Stand back," said I.

"Stand back," replied he, pointing his pistol down to the magazine.

I threw up his arm, and the pistol went off, striking the beams above.

"Blast you," cried he, "whoever you are; but I've another," and he attempted to draw it out of his belt; but before he could effect it I blew out his brains with the pistol which I had ready cocked in my hand.

His companions started back, and I pointed my second pistol at them, saying, "The man who comes forward this way dies."

As I said this the crew of the corvette, who had cleared the decks, charged down below, and the pirates ran away and secreted themselves. Perceiving them coming forward, I said to them, "Put a guard over the magazine; they have attempted to blow up the vessel already."

"Who are you?" said an officer.

"A prisoner," replied I.

"Well, then, lead him on deck, and stay here, two of you; shut down the magazine scuttle and keep guard."

"Thank Heaven," thought I, "that this affair is over," as a seaman led me by the collar on deck, and handed me to others, who took me on board of the corvette.

We were all put down below that remained out of the schooner's crew, about eighteen or nineteen, not more, and I was glad to find Captain Toplift, although badly wounded with a splinter, was among the number. We remained there huddled together with a guard of ten men over us for more than an hour, when we heard, from the conversation on deck, that the schooner had sunk. After that the guns of the corvette were secured, and the men had an allowance of liquor served out to them, the watch was called, and all was quiet during the remainder of the night. For some time I was in a state of excitement from the events of the last twenty-four hours crowding so rapidly, but by degrees I became calm. I asked one of the guard who was the captain of the corvette.

"What's that to you, you gallows-bird?" replied he. "A civil question might receive a civil reply," answered I.

"So it might with any one else; but if you don't want the hilt of my cutlass down your throat, you will hold your tongue."

But I did not require to repeat the question, as I heard one of the officers on deck say, "It's Captain Musgrave's orders."

This satisfied me, and I lay down with the rest of the prisoners, waiting for daybreak, when I trusted my troubles would soon be over. They were all sound asleep. Strange that men who knew that they would be hanged in a few days, if not the next morning, should sleep so sound—but so it was—while I, who had every reason to believe that my sufferings were over, could not sleep one wink. I was, however, fully satisfied with my own castle-buildings during the night, and more satisfied when it was again broad daylight. After the men had had their breakfast, an order came down for all the prisoners to be brought on deck. We were led up under guard, and made to stand all in a row. I looked round for my brother, but he was not on deck. It was the first-lieutenant who was there, with several other officers, and the clerk, with pen and ink, to take down the names of the prisoners.

"Who was the captain of this vessel?" said the first-lieutenant.

"I was, Sir," replied Toplift; "but much against my will."

"Oh, of course; every man was on board of her against his will. What is your name? Put him down, Mr Pearson. Any other officers alive?"

"No, Sir," replied Toplift.

The name of every man was then asked and put down, and it so happened that I was the last; for, anxious to see my brother, I had walked up the foremost, and they had commenced their interrogation at the other end of the line.

"What is your name?"

"I do not belong to the schooner," replied I.

"Of course not: you dropped on board her from the clouds."

"No, Sir, I did not; I swam on board of her to save my life."

"Then you went out of the frying-pan into the fire, I reckon, my good fellow, for your life is forfeited now."

"I rather think not, Sir," replied I. "On the contrary, I feel it is quite safe."

"Give us none of your jaw, my good fellow, but give us your name."

"Certainly, Sir, if you require it. My name is Alexander Musgrave, Sir," replied I; "I am the elder brother of your captain, Philip Musgrave, and I will thank you to go into his cabin and inform him that I am here."

The first-lieutenant and officers started back in astonishment, and so did Captain Toplift and the pirates. The first-lieutenant hardly knew whether to consider it as a pretence on my part or not, and was undecided how to act, when Captain Toplift said, "I do not know whether the gentleman is as he says, but this is certain, and all the men can prove it as well as myself, that he did swim on board, as he said, to escape from the Indians, and that he has never joined the crew. They offered to make him captain in my stead, and he positively refused it."

"Yes," said all the pirates; "that's true enough."

"Well, Sir," replied the first-lieutenant, "I will certainly carry your message."

"To make all certain," replied I, "I will write my name on a slip of paper for you to take in to the captain. He knows my signature."

I did so, and the first-lieutenant took the paper, and went into the cabin. In a minute he returned, and requested me to follow him. I did so, and in another minute I was in the arms of my brother. For some time we neither of us could speak. At last Philip said, "That you are alive and well let me thank Heaven. I have considered you as dead, and so have others; and to find you on board of a pirate—on board of a vessel which I have been riddling with shot, any one of which might have caused your death! Thank God I was ignorant that you were on board, or I never could have done my duty. I will not ask how you came on board of this vessel, for that must be the end of your narrative, which I must have from the time that you first left Rio, and afterwards in detail the whole from the time that you left the Coast."

"Then they received my letters from Rio?"

"Yes, after imagining you were dead, they were rejoiced by those letters; but I will not anticipate my story, nor will I now ask for yours; it is sufficient at present that you are alive, my dear Alexander, and once more in my arms."

"Let me ask one question," replied I.

"I know what it will be. She was in good health, but suffering much in mind from having no account of you. Her father and others have reasoned with her, and painted the impossibility of your being in existence, as the xebeque you sailed in had never been heard of. She still adheres to the opinion that you are alive, and will not abandon the hope of seeing you again; but hope deferred has paled her cheek even more pale than it usually is, and she evidently suffers much, for her life is wrapped in yours. Now, having told you this, you must come into my state-room, and allow me to enable you to appear as my brother ought to do. I do not think that there is any difference in our size now although there was when we last parted."

"Many thanks, Philip, but before I adonise my outward man I should wish to satisfy my inward cravings; and, to tell you the truth, I'm so hungry from not having broken my fast for nearly twenty-four hours, that if you could order something to eat while you are looking out the clothes, I should feel in no small degree grateful."

Philip rang the bell and ordered the steward to bring something to eat and drink, and after eating I occupied a quarter of an hour more in getting rid of the pirate smoke and dirt, and putting on one of his uniforms, for he had no other clothes on board, when I came out looking not at all like a pirate.

"Now, then," said Philip, "before we have our *tête-à-tête*, come out with me, and let me introduce you to the officers as my brother."

I went out with him, and was formally introduced. The first-lieutenant apologised for his rough speech, but I told him that there was no occasion for any apology, as I had no doubt that I looked very much like a pirate at the time.

"More than you do now, Sir, at all events," replied he.

"By the bye, brother," said I, "there is one man among the prisoners who, although compelled to act as captain by the men, is no pirate. His conduct I will explain to you. May I request him to be kindly treated? His name is Toplift—and also two Portuguese, my former companions."

"Certainly," replied Philip, "your word is sufficient. Let those persons be released and taken care of," said he to the first-lieutenant. "We will wait for the particulars by-and-by."

I remained on deck about ten minutes, and then returned to the cabin with my brother.

"What is this which you have left on my dressing-table?" said Philip, surveying the leather bag which contained the diamond.

"That, Philip," said I, "is a portion of my narrative, and eventually may prove a very important one. I don't think that I can afford to make you a present of it, but I shall see."

"It does not look very valuable," replied he.

"At all events, do me the favour to lock it up carefully," replied I.

"Well, if you are in earnest I will," he said, and having put it in a drawer and locked it up, he said, "Now, Alexander, let me have your history."

I commenced, and told him all that the reader is now acquainted with. Dinner broke off my narrative, and as soon as it was over I resumed it. When I had finished, he expressed his astonishment, and asked many questions. Among others he said, "And that little wretch Peleg, the captain of the Transcendant's son, is he on board?"

"I have not seen him," replied I, "and therefore presume that he was not able to move, and went down in the schooner." Which was the case.

"You have indeed told me a strange tale," said Philip, "and you have had some extraordinary escapes. You must have a charmed life, and you appear to have been preserved to prove that Amy's persuasion of your being still alive was just and well-founded; and now it is my turn to talk, and yours to listen. When I left you as lieutenant of Captain Levee's schooner, we very shortly afterwards had an action with a Spanish vessel of very superior force, for she mounted thirty guns. Having no chance with her, from her superior weight of metal, we threw ourselves on her bow and boarded. The Spaniards did not relish this kind of close fighting, and gave us immediate possession of their deck. Captain Levee, when he brought in his prize, was appointed to a frigate of thirty-six guns, and I followed him as his first-lieutenant. We had another combat with a vessel of equal force, in which we were the victors, and I was sent in the prize. Captain Levee wrote very kindly in my behalf and I was made a captain, and given the command of a small brig. But let me first finish with Captain Levee. He captured a galleon, which gave him a large fortune, and he then gave up the command of his ship, and went on shore, telling me in a letter that he had hitherto squandered away all his money, but now that he had got so much, he intended to keep it. He has done so, for he has purchased a large landed property, is married, and, I believe, is very happy."

"He deserves it," replied I; "and long may he be so."

"Well, to continue. I was sent out on this station, and, having information that the vessel which you are now on board of was at anchor in a bay close to the Havannah, I ran in and reconnoitred. She hoisted Spanish colours, and I did the same. It fell calm, and I lay about four miles outside. I was mistaken for another Spanish vessel, and the captain of this vessel, or, to speak correctly, the Spanish captain of the Spanish brig, came out to see me, and did not discover his mistake till he was on board. I detained him and his boat's crew. It continued calm till the evening, when the breeze sprung up, and I put the head of the brig right for the bay, as if I were going to anchor. The breeze being light, it was dark before I got in and alongside this vessel. They were completely surprised, for they imagined that their captain was dining with his old friend, and, having no idea that we were anything but Spanish, had not the least preparation for resistance. We had possession of her decks before they could seize their arms, and I brought her out without any one knowing that she had been captured. On my arrival, the admiral gave me the command of her, which I have held for nine months; but she is very defective, and I was ordered home, and should have sailed, had it not been that that scoundrel, the captain of the Transcendant, gave me the information which induced me to come round to the back of the island. Little did I think what happiness awaited me. So much for myself. Do not think me an egotist for speaking of myself, I am only clearing away the less important information to arrive at that which most interests you. The Amy arrived safe with her valuable cargo. The captain reported that he had remained at the rendezvous until blown off by a sort of hurricane, and that, finding himself a long way off, he considered, when the gale had ceased, that he was not justified in remaining with so valuable a cargo, but was bound to make the best of his way to Liverpool. He was right, and his conduct was approved of by Mr Trevannion, who looked for your arrival every hour. At last a week passed away and you did not make your appearance, and great alarm was entertained for your safety. The weeks grew into months, and it was supposed that you had been upset in the same hurricane which had driven the Amy so far off from her rendezvous. The poor girl Whyna was, as you may suppose, kindly received by Mr Trevannion and his daughter, and soon gained their affection; but she pined for your return, and when she was told that you were dead she never recovered it. The climate certainly did not agree with her, and she contracted a very bad cough during the winter, but I believe from my heart that it was your loss which affected her the most severely. After she had been about eighteen months in England, she fell into a consumption and died."

"Poor Whyna!" said I, with a sigh.

"Alexander," said Philip, "perhaps it was all for the best, for that poor girl loved you sincerely, and, supposing that she was now still alive and living with Miss Trevannion, and on your return your marriage should (which, of course, unless Heaven decrees otherwise, it will) take place, that poor creature would have been very unhappy; and although the idea of her being a rival to Miss Trevannion is something which may appear absurd to us, yet she had the same feelings, and must have endured the same pangs, as any other woman, let her colour be what it may. I think, therefore, that her removal was a blessing and a happy dispensation. I saw Mr Trevannion and his daughter but once previous to their receiving your letters from Rio, acquainting them with your misfortunes and happy deliverance from slavery. They were both very dejected, and Mr Trevannion talked of retiring from business, and living upon his property near Liverpool. As I corresponded regularly with Amy, I learnt that he had done so, and had just wound up his affairs when your letters arrived from Rio with an order on the Portuguese Exchequer for a considerable sum. I hardly need say that the joy occasioned by this intelligence was great. Amy recovered her good looks, and her father bitterly lamented his having retired from business, as he had wished to have made the whole over to you. The money you remitted from Rio he considered as your own, and he also set apart your share of the business from the time that you were admitted as a partner. He was not aware that you could carry a diamond of such immense value about your person, exposed to the view of every one; among Indians, settlers, and pirates. That my delight was equal to theirs you will, I am sure, give me credit to believe; and although I was obliged to sail for the West Indies, every day I anticipated receiving a letter informing me of your arrival in England. Judge then my distress at first receiving letters stating that you had not been heard of for three months after your leaving Rio, and expressions of fear that some accident had happened, and then month after month many more and more desponding letters, in which Mr Trevannion plainly stated that the xebeque must have foundered; and only Amy clinging to the hope that you were still alive. I acknowledge that I considered you dead, and you may therefore imagine my surprise and delight when your signature on the slip of paper proved that you were not only in existence, but on board of the same vessel with me."

Such was the narrative of my brother Philip in return for mine, and it was late at night when we parted. Oh! How sincerely did I pray that night, thanking heaven for all its mercies, and entreating that the cup might not be again dashed from my lips. When I arose next morning I found that Philip was on deck, and I followed him.

"We shall soon be in Port Royal with this wind," said he, "and I hope to find the admiral still there."

I had some conversation with the officers, and then went below to see Toplift. He was in his hammock, for he had much fever and suffered from his wound, but the surgeon said that he would do well.

"Toplift," said I, "you must keep your mind at ease, for my brother has promised me that you shall not be tried with the others, and has no doubt that when he explains the whole to the admiral you will be thanked for your service."

"Thanked!" said Toplift, "if I am not hanged, I shall be fortunate enough."

"No fear of that," replied I, "so keep your mind easy and get well as fast as you can."

"Well then, Sir, you have saved my life, at all events, for had you not come on board, no one would have ever spoken for me, or believed that I was not a pirate in heart like all the others, except the two Portuguese."

"If necessary, they will be evidence in your favour, but I do not think any evidence will be required except mine, and that will be sufficient with the admiral. I promised you that you should never want the means of getting your livelihood, and I repeat that promise now."

"Thank you, Sir," replied he, and I then left him and went up to the cabin to breakfast.

The following day we were at anchor at Port Royal; my brother reported what had occurred, and the admiral sent for all the pirate prisoners except Toplift, whose case was so fully represented by me and my brother, that he was permitted to go at large, and to take a passage home to England free of expense if he wished it. It is hardly necessary to say that Toplift accepted this offer, and remained in the vessel with me. The two Portuguese were also liberated. Three days after our arrival we sailed for England, and after a quick run of between five and six weeks, we anchored at Spithead. My brother could not leave his ship, and I therefore requested him to write to Liverpool, stating that he had intelligence of me, and that I was alive; that I had been wrecked and had fallen into the hands of the Indians near the English settlements in Virginia, and that I had escaped and was, he believed, at James Town.

I considered it wise to make a communication like this at first, as too sudden an announcement might be dangerous to one in so weak a state of health as Philip stated my Amy to be from the letter he had received from her father. I remained with him at Portsmouth until the reply came. Mr Trevannion wrote and told Philip that his communication had, as it were, raised his daughter from the grave— as she had fallen into a state of profound melancholy, which nothing could remove—that he had very cautiously introduced the subject, and by degrees told her what was reported, and eventually, when he found that she was more composed, that he had put Philip's letter into her hand.

He concluded that he trusted that I would arrive, and soon, for if any accident was now to happen to me it would be the death of his daughter, who had not strength enough left to bear another reverse.

At my request Philip then wrote that he had received a letter from a brother officer stating that I was well and safe on board, and that they would be in England a few days after the receipt of the letter.

Leaving directions to Philip how to proceed, I now went off to London, and, having fitted myself out with every requisite of dress and toilet, I called upon a celebrated Jew diamond merchant and showed him my diamond, requesting that he would weigh it and then estimate its value. He was much astonished at the sight of such a stone, as well he might be, and after weighing it and examining it he pronounced it worth 47,000 pounds, provided a purchaser could be found for an article of such value.

I told him that I was not a merchant, and could not be travelling about to show the diamond to crowned heads; but if he would give me a liberal price for it, I would abate a great deal, that he might dispose of it to his own advantage, he requested that he might call upon me with two of his friends, that they might see the diamond and consult with him; and then he would give me an answer. We fixed the time for twelve o'clock on the following day, and I took my leave.

The next day he called at the time appointed, accompanied by two gentlemen of his own persuasion. They weighed the stone again very carefully, examined it in the light of a powerful lamp to ascertain its water, and to see if there were any flaws in it, calculated the reduction of weight which would take place in cutting it, and, after a consultation, I was offered 38,000 pounds. I considered this an offer that I ought not to refuse, and I closed with them. The next day the affair was settled. I received money and bills on government to the amount, and wrote to Philip telling him what had taken place. Strange that from two slaves in the mines I should have received such valuable legacies; from poor Ingram a diamond worth so much money, and from the other Englishman a tattered Bible which made me a sincere Christian—a legacy in comparison of which the diamond was as dross.

Philip replied to my letter congratulating me on the sale of the diamond, and informing me that to his letter he had received a reply containing so satisfactory an account of Amy's restored health, that he had written to tell them that I had arrived safe in England, and would be very soon with them. He recommended my going immediately, as the anxiety and suspense would be very injurious to Amy's health. I therefore made every arrangement for my departure, purchased horses, and procured four stout serving-men, well armed, to accompany me, and wrote a letter, which I sent by an express courier, stating the exact day which I expected to arrive at Mr Trevannion's country-seat.

I waited in London two days to wind up all my affairs, and to give time for the express to arrive before me, as I intended to travel very fast. My stay in London was the occasion of an important discovery. I was at the coffee-house at Saint Paul's, and was talking with one of Captain Levee's officers, with whom I had picked up an acquaintance, when, on his calling me by the name of Musgrave, a pinched-up sort of looking personage, in a black suit, who was standing at the bay-window, turned round, and coming up to me said, "Sir, as a stranger I must apologise, but hearing your friend call you by the name of Musgrave, may I venture to ask if you are any relative to Sir Richard Musgrave, Baronet, who lived in Cumberland?"

"Lived, did you say, Sir? Is he then dead?"

"Yes, Sir; he has been dead these last seven months, and we are looking out for his heir and cannot find him."

"I knew the family very well," replied I, "for I am connected with it. His eldest son, Richard, of course, must be his heir, as all the estates are entailed."

"His eldest son, Richard, Sir, is dead. We have authenticated documents to prove that; and, moreover, his second son, Charles, is also dead. He came home very ill and died, not at his father's house, but at the house of one of his tenants on the estate. It is his third son, Alexander Musgrave, whom we seek, and seek in vain. He is now the heir to the baronetcy and estates, but we have lost all clue to him. We understand that a Captain Philip Musgrave is just arrived from the West Indies. He is, we presume, the fourth son. But until we can find out what has become of Alexander Musgrave, and whether he is dead or alive, we cannot act. I have written this day to Captain Musgrave, requesting any information he can give, but have received no answer. I presume, Sir, it is useless to inquire of you?"

"Not exactly, Sir, for I am the Alexander Musgrave you seek."

"Indeed, Sir, but what proof have you of your identity to offer to us?"

"The evidence of my brother, Captain Philip Musgrave, in whose ship I have just arrived from the West Indies; that his answer to your letter will be satisfactory enough, I have no doubt. Here is a letter from him to me, in which you see he addresses me 'dear Alexander,' and concludes with 'your affectionate brother, Philip Musgrave.'"

"This is indeed satisfactory, Sir," replied the gentleman, "and I have only to receive an answer from your brother to make all right and clear. Allow me, Sir, to congratulate you upon your accession to the title and property. I presume you will have no objection, as soon as the necessary proofs are obtained, to accompany me down to Cumberland, where I doubt not, you will be recognised by many."

"Of that, Sir, I have not the slightest doubt," replied I, "but I cannot go down with you to Cumberland at present. I leave London for Liverpool the day after to-morrow on important business, and cannot disappoint the parties."

"Well, Sir, it must indeed be an important business which will prevent you from taking possession of a title and 4000 pounds per annum," replied he; "but here is my address, and I hope I shall hear from you as soon as possible, as I shall remain in town till I can bring the heir down with me."

The man now looked as if he doubted me. He could not imagine that I could neglect the taking possession of the estate for any other business, and it did appear singular, so I said to him, "Sir, I have been long out of England, and am affianced to a young lady who lives near Liverpool. She has been waiting to hear from me for some time, and I have sent an express to say that I will be with her on such a day. I cannot disappoint her, and I tell you more, that, without I possess her, the possession of the title and estates will give me very little pleasure."

"Sir," replied he, making a bow, "I honour your sentiments, and she must be a worthy lady who can inspire such feelings. I only hope that you will not remain too long at Liverpool, as London is expensive, and I am anxious to return to Cumberland."

I then wished the gentleman farewell, and went home to my lodgings. I had given him my address in case he wanted to see me before my departure.

The next day I received a letter from Philip enclosing the one written to him by this gentleman, whose name was Campbell, and who was a lawyer. Philip told me what reply he had made to him, and congratulated me on my accession to the title and estates. Almost an hour afterwards Mr Campbell called upon me with Philip's letter, which he declared to be highly satisfactory, and sufficient in any court of justice.

"But," said he, "I would wish to ask you a few particulars."

"And I also would wish to make a few inquiries, Mr Campbell. I have heard your name in my youth, although I cannot recollect ever having seen you."

"I was the confidential adviser of your father at one time, Sir," replied he, "but latterly all intercourse had ceased; it was not until he was on his death-bed, and fully repented the foolish step which he had taken, and the injustice he had been guilty of, that he sent for me,—much to the annoyance of Lady Musgrave, who would have prevented me from coming into the house even when I arrived, had it not been for the servants, who disobeyed her."

"And my sisters, Sir, Janet and Mabel?"

"Are both well, and have grown up very fine girls. Your father destroyed the deed by which Lady Musgrave was to have had a large jointure upon the estate, and she is now entirely dependent upon you for what she may receive. When do you expect to be able to come up from Liverpool?"

"I can hardly say, but of course as soon as I can."

"Well, Sir, my own affairs will require my presence in the metropolis for a month. In the mean time, although I should have preferred to have gone down with you to Faristone Hall, and have at once put you in possession, yet affairs may remain as they are (for everything is under seal, and Lady Musgrave has been compelled to remove) till it suits your convenience. I shall, however, write to let them know that you have been found and will soon come down and take possession."

Mr Campbell then asked me a few questions, to which I replied satisfactorily, and then for the first time he saluted me with my title, saying, "Sir Alexander, I will now take my leave."

The next morning I set off on my journey, and travelled with as much speed as the horses would permit. I arrived on the fifth day at Mr Trevannion's seat, about nine miles from Liverpool. As I rode up the avenue of chestnut trees, I perceived a female form looking out from an upper window, which soon afterwards made a precipitate retreat. I alighted, and was received at the door in the embrace of Mr Trevannion, who welcomed me with tears, and taking me by the hand he led me into an apartment where I found my adored Amy, who threw herself into my arms and wept as if her heart would break; but her sobs were the sobs of joy, and when she did raise her head and look at me, it was with eyes beaming with pleasure, and with smiles upon her beautiful lips. I clasped her to my bosom, and felt that I was more than repaid for all I had suffered, and my heart was throbbing with gratitude and love.

It was some time before we could sufficiently compose ourselves to enter into lengthened conversation, and then Amy inquired what had occurred to me to occasion such lengthened absence. We sat down on a sofa, and with Amy on one side of me and her father on the other I entered into my narrative.

"And so you have been married since we last heard from you?" said Amy, smiling, when I had finished my history.

"Yes," replied I, "I have been; but I hope I shall treat my second wife a little better than I did my first."

"I hope so too," replied Amy; "but I have great fear that your Virginian mistress may come over and claim you."

"I do not think that likely. From the Indians having followed me to the beach, they must have fallen in with her."

"And what do you think became of her?"

"Of course I cannot exactly say; but I presume she died gallantly, and fought with her axe to the last."

That evening I had a long conversation with Mr Trevannion. He told me what he had done with the money, which he considered as mine, and I put into his care the sum I had received for the diamond. I then spoke to him about our marriage, and requested that it might not be postponed.

"My dear Musgrave," said he, "my daughter's happiness so depends upon her union with you, that I can only say I am willing that it should take place to-morrow. For yourself you know that I have the highest esteem, and that you must be convinced of when I have consented to the match without even making inquiry as to your family and connexions. Now, however, is the time that I should wish to have some information about them."

"My dear Sir, if you will only make inquiries, you will find that the family of Musgrave is one of the most highly connected in the north, and that the head of it is, or was, a Sir Richard Musgrave, Baronet, of Faristone Hall, in Cumberland. I am a near relative of his, as I can satisfactorily prove."

"That is sufficient," replied Mr Trevannion. "I shall leave you to plead your cause with Amy to-morrow; so now, good night."

The following day I told Amy that, since my arrival in England, I had heard of the death of my father, and that it was necessary that I should go to the north, as family affairs required my presence.

"Are you serious?" replied she.

"Never more so in my life. My presence is absolutely necessary, and I made arrangements with the legal adviser of our family that I would be there in less than a month."

"It is a long journey," said Mr Trevannion, "and how long do you stay?"

"That I cannot possibly say," replied I; "but not longer than I can help."

"I do not think that I shall let you go," said Amy; "you are not to be trusted out of sight. You are so born for adventure that you will not be heard of again for another two years."

"Such is my misfortune, I grant," replied I; "but, Amy, you look pale and thin; change of air would do you much service. Suppose you and your father were to come with me. Indeed, Mr Trevannion, I am in earnest. At this delightful time of the year nothing would prove so beneficial to her health; and, Amy, then, you know, that I shall not be out of your sight."

"I should like the tour very much," replied she, "but—"

"I know what you would say. You do not like the idea of travelling with me as Amy Trevannion. You are right. Then let me propose that you travel with me as Amy Musgrave."

"I second that proposal," said Mr Trevannion.

"Consent, Amy; let our marriage be quite private. I know you will prefer that it should be so, and so will your father. You will then travel with me as my wife, and we never shall part again."

Amy did not reply till her father said, "Amy, it is my wish that it should be so. Recollect it will be the last time that you have to obey your father, so do not annoy me by a refusal."

"I will not, my dear father," replied Amy, kissing him. "Your last command I obey with pleasure. And oh! If I have sometimes been a wilful girl, forgive me everything at this moment."

"My dear child, I have nothing to forgive. May God bless you; and, Mr Musgrave," said he, putting her hand in mine, "if she proves as good a wife as she has been a daughter, you now receive a treasure," and I felt that the old man stated what was true.

It was arranged that the marriage should take place on that day week, and that it should be quite private. There was no parade of bridal clothes; in fact, no one was invited, and it was, at my request, quite a secret marriage. A clergyman had been engaged to perform the ceremony, and, on the day appointed, I received the hand of my Amy in the drawing-room, and in the presence only of Humphrey and two other confidential servants.

After the ceremony was over, the clergyman requested me to come with him into the adjoining room, and said, "it was necessary that he should give a certificate of the marriage, which must be inserted in the parish register." He had called me aside for that purpose, that I might give him my exact name, profession, etcetera.

"My name is Alexander Musgrave, as you have heard when you married us."

"Yes, I know that, but I must be particular. Have you no other name? Is that the name that you have been and will be in future known by?"

"Not exactly," replied I; "I have been known by that name, but in future shall not be."

"Then what am I to say?"

"You must say, Sir Alexander Musgrave, Baronet, of Faristone Hall, Cumberland."

"Good," said he, "that is what I required; and the lady your wife, has she any other name but Amy?"

"None, I believe."

The clergyman then wrote out the marriage certificate and signed it, taking a copy for registry, and we returned into the drawing-room.

"Here is the certificate of marriage, Madam," said he; "it ought to be in the care of the lady, and therefore, my lady, I hand it over to you."

"My lady is much obliged to you for your kindness," replied Amy, for she thought that the clergymen was only facetious.

She held the certificate in her hand folded as it had been given her for some time. At last curiosity, or, perhaps, having nothing else to do, induced her to open it and read it. I was at this time talking with the clergyman, and presenting him with a handsome douceur for his trouble; but, perceiving her to open the certificate, I watched her countenance. She read and started. I turned away as if not observing her. She then went up to her father and desired him to read it.

The old gentleman took out his glasses, and it was amusing to see the way in which he looked at his daughter with his spectacles falling off his nose. He then came up, and pointing to the certificate said, "Pray how am I in future to address my daughter?"

"As Amy, I trust, Sir, unless you wish to scold her, and then you must call her Lady Musgrave. I am, my dear Sir, as the certificate states, Sir Alexander Musgrave, of Faristone, with a handsome property descended to me. I did not know it till I arrived in London; and if I concealed it from you till now, it was only that; my Amy should have the satisfaction of proving to me that she wedded me in pure disinterestedness of affection."

"It was very, very kind of you, Alexander, to do as you have done, and I thank you sincerely for it."

"And now, my dear Amy, you understand why I wished you to come with me to Cumberland, that you may take possession of your future abode, and assume that position in society which you will so much grace. I trust, Sir," continued I, "that you will not part from us, and that one roof will always cover us, as long as Heaven thinks fit to spare our lives."

"May God bless you both," replied Mr Trevannion, "I cannot part with you, and must follow."

About half an hour after this, I requested Amy and Mr Trevannion to sit by me, as I had now another narrative to give them, which was an explanation why and how it was that they found me in the position that they had done; in short, what were the causes that induced me, and afterwards my brother Philip, to quit our parental roof, and to come to the resolution of fighting our own way in the world. It was as follows:

"Sir Richard Musgrave, my father, married a young lady of high connexion, a Miss Arabella Johnson, and with her lived, I have every reason to believe, a very happy life for nearly twenty-five years, when it pleased God to summon her away. I have a good recollection of my mother; for although I lived with my brother at a private tutor's, about six miles off, I was continually at home, and she did not die till I was nearly sixteen; and I can only say that a more elegant, amiable, and truly virtuous woman, as I believe, never existed. By this marriage my father had four sons and two daughters; Richard, the eldest; Charles, the second; myself, the third; and Philip, the fourth; and my sisters, who came last, were named Janet and Mabel. At the time of my mother's death, my eldest brother was serving with the army, which he had entered from a love of the profession, although, as heir to the baronetcy and estates, which are a clear 4000 pounds per annum, he of course had no occasion for a profession. My second brother, Charles, being of an adventurous turn, had gone out to the East Indies in a high position, as servant to the Company. I was still at home, as well as Philip, who is four years my junior, and my sisters were of course at home. I pass over my regrets at my mother's death, and will now speak more of my father. He was a good-tempered, weak man, easily led, and although, during my mother's lifetime, he was so well led that it was of little consequence, the case proved very different at her death. For a year my father remained quiet in the house, content with superintending his improvements on his property, and he had lately become infirm, and had given up the hounds and rural sports in general. The dairy was one of his principal hobbies; and it so happened that a young girl, the daughter of a labourer, was one of the females employed in that part of the establishment. She was certainly remarkably good-looking; her features were very small, and she did not show that robust frame which people in her class of life generally do. She was about seventeen years old, slight in figure, and certainly a person that you would not pass without making some commendatory remark upon her good looks and modest appearance. She was not, however, what she appeared; she was beyond measure cunning and astute, and, as it proved, inordinately ambitious. My father, who was naturally of an amorous disposition, was attracted by her, and very soon was constantly in the dairy, and his attentions were so marked, that the other servants used to call her 'my lady.' A few months after my father had shown a preference for this girl, he was seized with his first attack of gout. It did not last him long, and in six weeks he was about again, and resumed his attentions to her. Philip and I, who were at our tutor's, when we came home, heard from others what was going on, and very foolishly played the girl many tricks, and annoyed her as much as we could. After we returned, my father had another fit of gout, and when he was confined to his room, he desired this girl to be sent for to attend upon him. I cannot say what took place, but this is certain, that my father's unfortunate passion became so great, and I presume the girl's ambition rose in proportion, that about six months afterwards this daughter of a menial was raised to the dignity of Lady Musgrave—she being at that time about eighteen, and my father verging on seventy.

"When this ill-assorted and disgraceful connexion was known, the gentry and aristocracy of the country refused any longer to visit my father, and all communication was broken off. In a short time the ascendency which this artful girl gained over the old man was most wonderful. He lived but in her sight, and knew no will but hers. Her father and family were removed to a good house in the neighbourhood, and gave themselves all the airs of gentlepeople. The good old steward was dismissed, and her father established in his room, although the man could not read or write, and was wholly unfit for the office. The expense which she launched out into, by his permission, was excessive. New liveries, new coaches, diamonds, and dresses fit for the court—indeed, every kind of luxury that could be conceived, and much greater than my father could afford. She now showed herself in her true colours; vindictive and tyrannical to excess, she dismissed all the old servants, and oppressed all those to whom she owed a grudge; yet my poor father could see nothing but perfection in her. It was not till four months after the marriage that Philip and I came home, and our new step-mother had not forgotten our treatment of her. She treated us with great harshness, refused our taking meals at my father's table, and ordered us the coarsest fare; and when we complained to my father, denied everything that we said. As we found that we could not induce our father to listen to us or to believe us, we tried all we could, and retaliated and annoyed her as much, if not more, than she annoyed us, by talking of her mean origin and her former occupation; we defied her, and, in so doing, we ruined ourselves; for, after a useless struggle on my father's part, he gave way to her imperious commands, and sending for me told me that I had become such a reprobate that I was no longer a son of his. He threw me a purse, telling me that it was all I might expect from him, and that I was instantly to leave the house, and never show my face in it any more. I replied, with more spirit than respect, that it was high time that the son of a gentleman and lady should leave the house, when such low-born creatures were installed in it as the mistress. My father, in a rage, flung his crutch at my head, and I left the room.

"As I went out I met her in the passage; she had evidently been listening to what had passed, and she was full of exultation.

"'It is your turn now, you she-devil,' said I, in my rage; 'but wait till my father dies. You shall go a-milking again.'

"I do not mean to defend my conduct, but I was then not seventeen, and that must be my excuse. I little thought, when I said so, that it would be from my hands that she would have to receive bounty; but so it is, as Mr Campbell informs me that my father destroyed, previous to his death, the papers which he had signed to secure her a large jointure on the estate. I set off with my wardrobe and the purse of twenty guineas, which my father had given me, and, having a desire to see the world, I went on board of a merchant vessel. Six months afterwards, when we were at Liverpool, I went on board of a privateer. The remainder of my history you are already acquainted with.

"As soon as she had wreaked her vengeance upon me, my brother Philip was the next; but he was too young at that time to be turned adrift, so she put it off till the time should come, irritating and weaning my father from him by every means in her power. Three years afterwards she succeeded in having him dismissed, also, and you know how I found him out. All these circumstances were very well-known in the neighbourhood and to our own relations; and one only, my aunt, called upon my father, and, after a long conversation, my father consented that my sisters should go away, and remain under her charge. My step-mother's violent temper, her exactions, her imperious conduct, which was now shown even towards him, with what my aunt had advanced, had to a certain extent opened my father's eyes. He perceived that she had no other view but her own aggrandisement, and that she cared little for him. Her repeated attempts, however, to make him sign in her favour, in case of his death, were successful, and it was not till after her conduct had alienated him from her, and he deplored the loss of his children, that he committed the deed to the flames. About three years after I had quitted the house, my eldest brother, who had information of all that had passed, and who remained in the army because he declared that he never would go home till after his father's death, was killed by a cannon-ball; and my second brother died of a fever about a year ago, when resident at the court of a native prince. I had heard nothing of these deaths, or of my father's, until my arrival in London; of course, I was most anxious to go down to Cumberland, if it were only to undo the wickedness which this woman had done, and to make amends to those whom she had so cruelly treated. I do not feel any spirit of revenge, but I feel that justice demands it of me."

"And I shall go with you with pleasure, to help you in your good work," said Amy, "and also because I want to see how she will now behave to one whom she has so persecuted, and who has become the arbiter of her fate."

"Well, Amy, I will not trust myself on this question. You shall be the arbitress of her fate, and what you decide shall be irrevocable."

"I fully appreciate the compliment you pay me," said she, "but I prefer that it should be decided in council, and we will call in my father to our assistance."

A fortnight after our marriage, we set off for London, in a coach with six handsome black horses, and eight armed servants in liveries on horseback. We arrived safely on the seventh day, and there we reposed for a time previous to setting out for Cumberland. My aunt was in London and attending the court, which I was not aware of, and with her were my two sisters, Janet and Mabel, whom I had not seen for years, and who warmly embraced me, promising that they would soon come down and take up their abode at the hall. They expressed their admiration of Amy, but, in so doing, they only followed the general opinion, for it was impossible to see and not admire her elegance and beauty. My aunt showed us every attention, and we were presented to his Majesty, who was pleased to compliment Lady Musgrave in very flattering terms. We were joined in London by my brother Philip, who had paid off his ship, and the day after he joined us I said:

"Philip, there are only you and I left. Do you recollect when you inquired about the diamond, the day we met on board of your ship, what reply I made to you?"

"Yes; you said that you were afraid that you could not afford to make me a present of it."

"At that time I did not think so, Philip, but now I know that I can, and I have desired Mr Trevannion to put out to good security the 38,000 pounds that the diamond was sold for, in your name, and for your use. You'll not hesitate to accept it, Philip, for you know that I can afford it."

"I do not hesitate, my dear Alexander, because I would do the same to you, and you would not refuse me. At the same time, that is no reason that I should not thank you kindly for your generous behaviour."

Philip accompanied us on our journey to Cumberland. It was tedious, for the roads were anything but good, but the beauty of the scenery compensated for the ruggedness of the way. In six days we arrived at the Hall, where Mr Campbell, who had called upon me on my arrival in London, had preceded me to make preparations for our reception, which was enthusiastic to the highest degree. We were called upon and congratulated by all the county, who were delighted to find that such a personage as Amy was to be the future mistress.

As soon as all this bustle and excitement was over, I sat down with Mr Campbell to look over the state of affairs, and to set things to rights.

After having done justice to many claimants, engaged again the old servants that had been discharged, promised farms to the tenants who had been unfairly turned out, etcetera, we then proceeded to decide upon what was to be done to the Dowager Lady Musgrave. It appears that at my father's death, when she found that the deed had been destroyed by his own hands in presence of others, she became frantic with rage, and immediately hastened to secure the family jewels, and every article of value that she could lay her hands upon, but Mr Campbell, having due notice of what she was about, came in time to prevent her taking them away, and, putting seals upon everything and leaving careful guards in the Hall, my lady had gone to her father's house, where she still remained. She had, on my arrival, sent me a message, imploring my mercy, and reminding me that whatever might be her errors, she was still the lawful wife of my father, and she trusted that respect to his memory would induce me to allow her sufficient to maintain her as Lady Musgrave should be. We had the consultation that Amy proposed, and called in Mr Campbell as a fourth, and it was at last decided, that, on consideration that she removed with her family to a distance of fifty miles from Faristone, she should have an income of 300 pounds per annum, as long as she conducted herself with propriety and did not marry again. The last clause was the only one which she complained of. Mr Campbell had, at the request of my father, discharged Lady Musgrave's parent from the office of steward and called in the old steward to resume his situation, and before dismissal he had to refund certain sums of money not accounted for.

I have now told my eventful tale; I have only to add, that after all that I have passed through I have been rewarded by many years of unalloyed happiness. My two sisters are well married, and my three children are all that a father could wish. Such, my dear Madam, have been the vicissitudes of a "Privateersman" and I now subscribe myself,

Your most obedient,

*Alexander Musgrave.*

*The End.*

Milton Keynes UK
Ingram Content Group UK Ltd.
UKHW030718041024
449263UK00004B/402